SAMUEL PETER HEINTZELMAN

*and the
Sonora Exploring
and Mining
Company*

SAMUEL PETER HEINTZELMAN

Samuel
Peter
Heintzelman

and the
Sonora Exploring
and Mining
Company

DIANE M. T. NORTH

THE UNIVERSITY OF ARIZONA PRESS
Tucson, Arizona

About the Author...

DIANE M. T. NORTH, a student of the history of the American West, has served as a museum administrator and historic preservation specialist for a number of cultural agencies, including the National Portrait Gallery, the Advisory Council on Historic Preservation, and the North Carolina Division of Archives and History. Previous works include a study of Herman Ehrenberg, pioneer western cartographer.

THE UNIVERSITY OF ARIZONA PRESS

Copyright © 1980
The Arizona Board of Regents
All Rights Reserved
Manufactured in the U.S.A.

Library of Congress Cataloging in Publication Data

North, Diane M. T.
    Samuel Peter Heintzelman and the Sonora Exploring and Mining Company.

    Bibliography: p.
    Includes index.
    1. Heintzelman, Samuel Peter, 1805–1880.
2. Businessmen—United States—Biography. 3. Sonora Exploring and Mining Company—History. 4. Arizona—Industries—History. I. Title.
HD9506.U62N67   338.7'62'20924   [B]   79-15307
ISBN 0-8165-0679-5
ISBN 0-8165-0574-8 pbk.

Contents

Illustrations

Abbreviations

AC   Arizona Collection, Charles Trumbull Hayden
        Memorial Library, Arizona State University, Tempe

AHS   Arizona Historical Society, Tucson

CHS   Connecticut Historical Society, Hartford

HPF   Hayden Pioneer Files, AC

LC   Library of Congress, Manuscripts Division,
        Washington, D.C.

LJL   Louis Jefferson Long Library, Wells College,
        Aurora, N.Y.

NARS   National Archives and Records Service (RG stands
        for Record Group), Washington, D.C.

SCF   Benjamin Sacks Collection Files, Arizona Historical
        Foundation, Arizona State University, Tempe

SPH   Samuel Peter Heintzelman Papers, LC or USMA

USMA   United States Military Academy Library, West
       Point, N.Y. (AD: Archives Division; MD:
       Manuscripts Division)

YWA   The Western Americana Collection, Beinecke Rare
       Book and Manuscript Library, Yale University,
       New Haven

Preface

In the 1860s, during the disruption caused by the American Civil War, Indian uprisings, and frontier banditry, Arizona was called "a paradise of devils." Yet, for a brief period between the Gadsden Purchase in 1854 and the Civil War, a number of hardy, spirited pioneers and speculators tried to settle and develop the area of present-day southern Arizona. The efforts to obtain silver and gold, raise crops and livestock, establish communications and trading links with the rest of the United States and Mexico, promote the railroad, and institute political and judicial order by organizing a territorial government all intermeshed. During this formative period, a relatively small number of men assumed leading roles. Samuel Peter Heintzelman is an excellent example. Coming to the Southwest in 1850 as a career military officer, he soon became involved in all aspects of the settlement of the frontier. Heintzelman established Fort Yuma at the junction of the Gila and Colorado rivers and commanded the border post for four years. He maintained peace with the neighboring Indians, invested in real estate and ferry companies, advocated the use of steam navigation on the Colorado River, urged the adoption of a southern railroad route through Yuma to San Diego, and helped to found Colorado City, now Yuma, Arizona.

This book contains the edited portion of one of Heintzelman's journals—from August 3, 1858, through January 29, 1859—and documents his activities as president of the Sonora Exploring and Mining Company and director of its field operations south of Tucson, in Tubac, Cerro Colorado, and Arivaca, Arizona (or more properly, Doña Ana County, Territory of New Mexico). In 1856 Heintzelman, along with Thomas and William Wrightson, midwestern publishers of the *Railroad Record*, and Charles Debrille Poston, a Kentucky adventurer, organized the Sonora Exploring and Mining Company, one of the earliest and historically most significant U.S. companies formed to exploit Arizona's mineral riches. Eager to take advantage of the newly acquired territory, the mining company occupied the abandoned Mexican presidio at Tubac; purchased property in several locations, including the fertile Arivaca Ranch; hired engineers, geologists, and laborers; and began to search for silver. The company not only provided a source of employment but also encouraged the growth of companion functions necessary to sustain the growing population of miners and their families. In addition, it was this small band of entrepreneurs who lobbied for military protection and for the creation of a separate Territory of Arizona. The ventures of the Sonora Exploring and Mining Company and its subsidiary, the Santa Rita Silver Mining Company, extended into other areas. For example, when William Wrightson traveled overland from Cincinnati to Cerro Colorado in the fall and winter of 1858, along with mining supplies and equipment he carted a printing press that was used to print Arizona's first newspaper, the Tubac *Weekly Arizonian*.

The community that Heintzelman wrote about was

international—native American Indians, Mexicans, recent immigrants from Germany, Italy, France, England, Wales, Ireland, and the West Indies, and young men from all regions of the United States. Conditions were harsh, with food and supplies scarce and machinery inadequate. An awkward combination of German, Welsh, and Spanish mining techniques was used. Cultural differences became evident as conflicts arose between the expectations and demands of the U.S.- and German-born mine directors and the work habits of the Indian and Mexican laborers. Military protection was insufficient. Although the so-called Apache menace did not erupt until the American Civil War, there was a constant threat of robbery, destruction of property, and loss of life at the hands of lawless settlers, fugitive outlaws, filibusters, Mexicans, and Indians. Border relations between the United States and Mexico were in a state of flux, and political upheavals in Sonora affected the activities of its neighbors to the north. Indeed, in December 1858, President James Buchanan recommended assuming a temporary protectorate over the northern parts of Chihuahua and Sonora. Buchanan expressed concern about the inability of the Mexicans to decide their political future and preserve peace along the border.

Accounts differ widely as to the productivity of the Sonora company's mines, one of which—the Cerro Colorado or Heintzelman Mine was promoted as one of the richest silver mines in the world. In an effort to attract investment capital, Heintzelman, the first president of the Sonora Exploring and Mining Company, sought the financial backing of a major eastern industrialist, Samuel Colt. This Connecticut inventor and gun manufacturer invested heavily in the company and provided the capital necessary to operate the mines. In addition, he shipped thousands of dollars worth of his guns for sale in the West. As Heintzelman lacked the administrative talent, the time (his military duties took priority), and the money to manage the company successfully, Colt was able to outwit the midwestern directors and gain control of the Sonora Exploring and Mining Company by 1859.

The publication of Benjamin Sacks' *Be It Enacted: The Creation of the Territory of Arizona* marked the first time that extensive scholarly research credited to Heintzelman the importance he merits in the history of preterritorial Arizona, especially as a leading advocate for the establishment of the territory.[1] Previous historians had relied largely upon information supplied by Charles Debrille Poston, a pioneer who has borne the title of "Father of Arizona." Poston's Arizona career, in particular his association with Heintzelman and the Sonora Exploring and Mining Company, was notable. However, many of the reminiscences Poston compiled were written late in his life and, at times, tended to be self-aggrandizing. Heintzelman criticized Poston's business practices as haphazard, unwise, and costly. While the army officer wrote of sour flour and striking workers, Poston described gourmet feasts. The latter periodically submitted newspaper articles defending his right to land and mine claims, and he was involved in complex litigation. Since Poston outlived most of the early pioneers, he also wrote their obituaries. Those accounts, along with inflated stockholders' reports, have filled the pages of local and state histories and topical studies.[2] The following pages do not deny Poston his place in Arizona's history. However, with this edition of a portion of Heintzelman's journals and with the use of the Samuel Colt Papers and the correspondence of Colt's relatives and associates (the Jarvis, Alden, and Pierce families), students of southwestern history have the opportunity to reexamine and reassess this formative phase of Arizona's history.

Editorial Method

The Samuel Peter Heintzelman Papers were deposited in the Library of Congress in 1913 and 1914 by his daughter and grandson.[3] Heintzelman kept an almost continuous journal from 1825, during his days as a cadet at the U.S. Military Academy at West Point, until 1872, eight years before his death at the age of seventy-four. There are ten bound volumes for those forty-seven years. On January 17, 1874, Heintzelman, a retired major general, commenced to copy from the originals the first seven years of his papers. The remaining volumes are the originals.[4] It is remarkable that these papers survived the rigors of transcontinental travel through extremes of heat and cold, dirt, dust, and mildew, packed in saddlebags next to slabs of rotting pork, or in leather trunks that sometimes fell into rivers.

Few attempts have been made to change punctuation, capitalization, or word division of the journal segment that is edited for this book. The journal is written in standard English; its style is not archaic (except for the use of the plural form *don't* for both singular and plural references). Heintzelman's original usage has been retained; the vagaries of the text are his. Misspellings are corrected silently, but when the word intended is unclear, the original spelling is retained. When Heintzelman made a correction or insertion, it is noted in brackets, as are possible misreadings and occasional clarifications. Often Heintzelman abbreviated words, or his densely packed script was careless. As Heintzelman was unsystematic in the formation of paragraphs, I have broken the text into appropriate paragraphs after studying the change, or lack of change, in the progress of the entry. Notes identifying people, places, and events mentioned in the journals, defining technical terms, and translating Spanish are signaled by asterisks and daggers and are placed at the foot of the page; notes providing sources and suggestions for further reading are indicated by superscript numerals and located at the end of the book. Consult the map for the locations of places mentioned in the journal.

Heintzelman was a conscientious chronicler whose journal entries usually were written on the day of the events described. When he occasionally missed a day, or more, he wrote of those preceding events under the then current date. This immediacy may have restricted his sense of humor and perspective. Although the journals were seldom perfunctory, they were often concerned with external details that may seem petty and trifling to today's reader. Frequently the day's activities were chaotic, or so Heintzelman felt.

This military officer and southwestern pioneer spent an inestimable amount of time and energy recording his activities. The journals were not published during his lifetime; and we do not know whether he instructed his family in their future use, or whether he thought they would be useful. He did take care of them, as evidenced by their good condition and by occasional references such as this entry written while he was stationed in California on January 1, 1851:

I have spent most of the day in unpacking my books and arranging my journals. To show how unsettled I have been I find part of 1846 and on to this time unarranged. I will have plenty of leisure time here and be able to arrange all such matters.

It is difficult to ascertain his motives for keeping the journals. Did they provide an opportunity to unburden his mind, to express the constant worries and annoyances aggravated by others? Were the pages useful for weighing the advantages and disadvantages of a particular situation, to assist in forming a judgment, and for future reference? All of these aspects are revealed throughout the journals, which are a rich archive of historical, biographical, and geographical importance. The descriptions are invaluable, for as he formed impressions of his associates and activities, Samuel Peter Heintzelman also painted a self-portrait.

Acknowledgments

For assistance in my research I wish to thank the many helpful and generous individuals at those libraries and institutions across the country whose collections were used in this study. Special thanks go to the staffs of the Arizona Collection, Hayden Memorial Library, and the Arizona Historical Foundation, at Arizona State University. I am grateful for their aid and for the good cheer with which it was given. Thanks are also due to the University of Arizona Press for effecting publication. I owe a particular debt of gratitude —more than I can adequately express—to Bert M. Fireman, Curator, Arizona Collection, and Executive Vice-President, Arizona Historical Foundation. He introduced me to the study of Arizona history and suggested that I undertake this project. His aid, criticism, and encouragement guided and supported its completion. This work is dedicated to my parents, Arthur and Ruth Tarantino.

DIANE M. T. NORTH

Part I

Introduction

A
Southwestern
Pioneer

On Independence Day in 1850 Samuel Peter Heintzelman was directed to establish a U.S. Army post at the junction of the Gila and Colorado rivers, a barren, hot southwestern boundary, an emigrant route, and an Arizona-California-Sonora trade crossing. The military presence was needed to control the neighboring and sometimes hostile Indians, and to protect the newly acquired territory.[1] The spoils of the Mexican War had brought over 500,000 square miles of land to the United States. The Treaty of Guadalupe Hidalgo recognized the Rio Grande as the boundary of Texas, and for $15 million Mexico ceded New Mexico and Upper California, with the Gila River and an arbitrary line along the 32nd parallel as the southern boundary of these lands, the exact demarcation for a distance west of El Paso to be settled upon by a joint boundary commission. In addition, the United States agreed to protect Mexican citizens from Indians in the ceded territory and indemnify them for any injuries inflicted.[2]

When gold was discovered near Sutter's mill, argonauts rushed across and around the continent to the rich California mines. Military protection was needed. Army territorial commands were reorganized and a new Pacific Division was created that included California and the Oregon Territory. Within a few months of his return to New York from the Mexican War, Heintzelman, a West Point graduate, was ordered to report to the transport ship *Rome* for the ocean voyage around Cape Horn to the southern coast of California. As a forty-five-year-old captain and brevet major, he was assigned to command two companies of the Second Infantry at San Diego.[3] His activities during the next two decades were significant, not only for his own career, but also for the settlement and development of the American Southwest:

I have issued an order assuming command and marking the reservation and warning everybody off it. I called in the officers; read them the order and gave them a glass of champagne. I call our post Yuma.[4]

By the end of November 1850, after a four-week and two-hundred-mile desert crossing from San Diego, Heintzelman and three small companies of the Second Infantry had arrived at the junction. The post was located on the river bottom on the right bank of the Colorado (California side) opposite and about one-half mile below the mouth of the Gila. Four months later Heintzelman moved the post to an irregular rocky hill on the right bank of the Colorado directly opposite its junction with the Gila. The commander surmised, "I have no doubt my plan of encampment has given great offense as I do not allow each officer to pitch his tent where he pleases."[5] However, his choice of site was commended. On an inspection tour of western forts in 1853 and 1854, Colonel Joseph K. F. Mansfield reported: "Fort Yuma is beautifully situated. It is well selected and should be maintained."[6]

Because of the expense and difficulty of supplying the post, Heintzelman and his troops, with the exception of a guard of ten men under the command of Lieutenant Thomas Sweeny, were instructed to withdraw to a more comfortable and safe position at Santa Isabel, California, in June 1851. Reinforcements were sent out to the junction in November, but by December supplies were exhausted and Indian threats had heightened. Sweeny and his men abandoned the post; on February 29, 1852, Heintzelman and additional troops reoccupied it.[7]

Lt. Sweeny disliked and disrespected Heintzelman, and the former's journal entries are most revealing. Placed in the difficult and perhaps unfair position of being left behind with only ten men to guard the post, Sweeny exclaimed:

It is true I am still under the Major's command, but only in a general way; for I am as much the commanding officer here with my command, as he is elsewhere with his, and I think more so; nobody thinks of disputing my orders, while there is not one *he* issues that is not objected to by somebody under his command.[8]

The feeling was mutual. In his journal of March 21, 1851, Heintzelman noted sarcastically:

The officers of my command take quite a pleasant interest in their duties.... Sweeny has not been here at all, to see to his commissary store, or stores. I have attended to everything. There is no use of giving him any instructions; he is too ignorant of the plainest common sense matters to understand anything.

Sweeny also claimed that Heintzelman had instructed him, via the wagon master, to turn over the ammunition left in Sweeny's charge. The disgusted lieutenant replied, "A brilliant idea truly and worthy of the source from which it emanated!" Refusing to comply, Sweeny raged on about the danger from nearby Indians: "But what does H—— care, so that his scalp is out of danger!"[9]

However, the post commander managed to control the infrequent hostilities. While on a scouting patrol at the end of 1851 he and his troops successfully fought off an attacking party of Cahuilla Indians.[10] For this skirmish in Los Coyotes Canyon, Heintzelman was brevetted lieutenant colonel and received congratulations from the Pacific Division headquarters. Assistant Adjutant General Edward D. Townsend wrote: "No more important service has been rendered by the troops on the Pacific, than that just accomplished under your direction." Townsend thought "the peace of the Southern part of the State of California has been effectively secured by it."[11]

Another officer commented on Heintzelman's ability with the Yuma Indians:

They are all at peace now with us; though the Yumas, for three or four years, gave our troops great trouble. Major Heintzelman holds them in complete subjection and will so long as he is left to govern them without interference from agents less acquainted with their manners and customs, and perhaps less disposed to see justice done them.[12]

An excellent illustration of Heintzelman's understanding of the Colorado River tribes is contained in his report on Indian affairs at the junction. The report includes a history of the establishment of the post, its geographic position, and the historical and archaeological significance of the site. Detailed information is provided on the size, strength, location, physical nature, religious beliefs, habits, and interrelationships of the Colorado River tribes. Demonstrating a realistic comprehension of the Indians' future in the midst of the dominant white culture, the military officer suggested:

They will remain friendly so long as there is a sufficient garrison here to curb their robbing propensities. They will soon learn to respect our strength, if they have not already done so, and in time become accustomed to get from us things they now consider luxuries, but which will become necessaries. The vices of contact with whites will cause them to dwindle rapidly away, and another race soon occupy their places.[13]

Although the report was filled with valuable firsthand observations of Indian customs, Heintzelman decided to "wait for prolonged intercourse and more favorable circumstances" before providing additional information about the tribes. "They cannot comprehend the object of such inquiries," he wrote, "and their character, like that of all ignorant people, being suspicious, they give vague or contradictory answers."[14]

Throughout his life Samuel Peter Heintzelman demonstrated an eagerness to be informed about both practical and intellectual matters and a desire to learn new skills. Exemplifying the spirit of a burgeoning industrial society, he was fascinated by technological innovations. At Yuma he directed the installation of a system to pump water. He also obtained a patent for cavalry floats (a peculiar device to keep horses afloat while crossing rivers), provided instructions for waterproofing fabrics, and sketched ideas for laying a transcontinental telegraph, operating a water meter, raising weights, preserving crayon drawings, exhibiting maps, and fermenting oranges for brandy. He read books on philosophy, business, mining, history (especially military history), law, and contemporary literature.

Little is known about the influences that formed his character. Heintzelman's reminiscences of his boyhood and family life were few, but he did record what he had learned of his family history. He was born in the early morning hours of September 30, 1805, in his parents' brick house in Manheim, Lancaster County, Pennsylvania. His father, Peter Heintzelman, of Pennsylvania German ancestry, was a lifelong resident of Manheim, a merchant, and the village postmaster. One brother and three sisters survived infancy, but the brother, Henry, died at the age of twenty. Samuel was nearly seven when his mother, Ann Grubb, the daughter of a well-known ironmaster, died.[15] His family belonged to the Zion Evangelical Lutheran Church, and his parents and paternal grandparents are buried in the church's graveyard. As a youngster he may have attended classes at the church, for references throughout his journals indicate that he read and spoke German. By the time he was seventeen, in 1822, his academic training was sufficient to guarantee him entrance to the U.S. Military Academy at West Point. The appointment came from an enterprising young Lancaster congressman named James Buchanan, later to become fifteenth president of the United States.[16] Throughout his career, whenever the opportunity arose, Heintzelman would visit the influential Buchanan.

Of the forty-one cadets who were graduated in the class of 1826, Heintzelman stood seventeenth, a respectable but not outstanding position.[17] Upon graduation the young soldier received a brevet second lieutenant's commission in the Third Infantry. Sixteen months later he joined the Second Infantry and for six years served in the garrisons at Belle Fontaine and Jefferson Barracks, Missouri, and at Forts Mackinac and Gratiot in Michigan.[18] By 1831 Heintzelman was assigned to the Corps of Topographical Engineers to assist in surveying the southern and eastern shores of Lakes St. Clair, Huron, and Michigan.[19] After a brief tour at Fort Brady, Wisconsin, he was transferred to a staff assignment in the Quartermaster's Department and spent the next eight years (1835–1842) stationed in Florida and Georgia. While the United States waged a tragic and costly war against the unfortunate Seminole Indians, Heintzelman served as an assistant quartermaster and also investigated the Florida Militia claims. In 1838 he was promoted to captain.[20]

Yet he was dissatisfied with his situation. At the age of thirty-five he commented: "How rapidly time flies—here is another year gone and I still in Florida and poor as a church mouse in pecuniary matters, although someone has been so kind as to report in Washington that I have grown rich."[21] The promotion to captain had brought an increase in pay, but he still had no independent income. Besides, he was a bachelor and wished to change that stuatus: "All that is wanting is to get a wife."[22] In 1842, with circumstances unchanged, the captain expressed his discontent in this New Year's Day entry: "Still the struggle is for happiness and it is not to be found. The world will still jog on and I hope for better times, even should I die in despair."

Fortunately the military "jogged" him to duty in Buffalo, New York. It was here that, after many months of courting, he "had a gread load removed from my mind, ... I saw Miss Margaret Stuart and offered myself and after proper maidenly reflection was accepted."[23] They were married December 5, 1844. Within a year, while stationed in Detroit, Michigan, Heintzelman noted: "Yesterday at 20 minutes past 4 I was made a father. Margaret has a son. He is a fine hearty child and weighs 8½ pounds. Both are doing well."[24] This was Charles Stuart Heintzelman, who was appointed to West Point by Abraham Lincoln, was graduated in 1867, and rose to the rank of captain before his death at the age of thirty-five on February 17, 1881.[25]

Another child, a daughter named Mary Lathrop, was born on Feburary 27, 1848, while her father was encamped near Mexico City during the Mexican War.[26] Two other children were born to the Heintzelmans, but they died in infancy. Their father painfully recalled the death of one baby, a son:

The night before last I was reconciled to lose him, but yesterday I could not think of it. I felt relieved when he passed away so quietly and was glad he died in his mother's arms. I held one of his little hands. He will be buried Sunday at 12½ p.m.[27]

Although Heintzelman wanted a wife and family, his military career and business enterprises required long absences from home and repeated moves for himself and his family. Often he grieved about the situation. On a Sunday at Yuma he expressed his dissatisfaction: "I am getting quite tired of such a life."[28] Later he wrote, "It is *eight* years since I was married, nearly half the time we have been separated and how much longer no one knows. I am beginning to despair."[29]

Although the separations and transfers were troublesome and constant, Heintzelman chose to remain in the military. After the birth of Charles, Heintzelman was stationed in Louisville, Kentucky. He served on recruiting duty until the outbreak of the war with Mexico. Joining General Winfield Scott's command on its march to Mexico City, Heintzelman commanded a battalion, saw action in several battles, and was brevetted major for "gallant and meritorious conduct" in the Battle of Huamantla.[30]

The soldier and his contemporaries provide us with a description of his physical appearance. He was slender and slight of stature, and his bearing was proud. Throughout his adult life his weight fluctuated from 117½ to 144 pounds.[31] Photographs taken during the Civil War portray a tired man with sad eyes. His hair was dark and he tried to keep it so. As we shall see in the journal, he once used a preparation of beef marrow on it; and in New Orleans in 1861 he had his hair dyed.[32] As he grew older, his hair and the outer fringes of his full beard turned white. Generals William T. Sherman and Oliver Otis Howard noted that Heintzelman's voice had a nasal quality.[33]

The business ventures Heintzelman undertook while in command at San Diego and Fort Yuma document the kind of intense and varied support some members of the army gave to the newly acquired territory. He owned beach lots in San Diego and as late as 1872 was paying taxes on them.[34] In association with various early settlers at the junction, among them Louis Jaeger, William Ankrim, George Hooper, and George Johnson, Heintzelman's investments included interests in the entire operation of the Colorado Ferry Company, the major vehicle by which emigrants, wagons, and animals were transported across the river.[35]

This particular operation did not improve the commander's relationship with his officers, in particular, Lieutenant Sweeny. The latter, complaining about his duty to guard Yuma upon the withdrawal of the main force, decried, "As the ferry company would have to leave if I did 'Uncle Sam's' requirements have to yield to old H——'s private speculations, and the post must be kept up at all hazards."[36]

In 1857 Heintzelman sold half of his share in the Colorado Ferry Company to Louis Jaeger and also deeded to him half of his interest in the houses, boats, equipment, and livestock of the Pilot Knob Ferry, the competitor located about six miles down the river.[37] Other speculations included a grocery business and a ranch.[38] He advocated the use of steam navigation on the Colorado River both to supply the fort and to encourage settlement and increase commercial activity.[39] He also urged residents of Sonora to bring and plant fruit trees.[40]

Heintzelman's full profits from these schemes are unknown. He did earn additional money, but there is no reason to suspect that these enterprises made him rich or even that the occasional profits were continuous. For example, on May 20, 1853, he received his dividend from the ferry company. For the time from December 24, 1851, to May 15, 1853, Heintzelman earned $1,116.81, or about $68 per month. He commented in his journal that it was "a very fair business" and added:

We have due us and all will be probably be collected in all of Aug. $2,700 and our permanent property and stock is worth at least $3,000 more. I hope through this to make good my loss with the grocery and liquor business. The Ranch I intend shall redeem itself.

However, on January 3, 1854, he disclosed that he had collected $395.29 from the ranch but mentioned that an additional loss would amount to about $450.

Though Heintzelman was involved in business affairs, the official inspection reports indicated that he was fulfilling his military assignment most satisfactorily. Colonel Mansfield reported that the discipline of the post was good, and the arms and equipment of the troops were in serviceable order. He found the troops in "excellent condition and creditable to the service and to the officer in command," and noted that Heintzelman was entitled to "great credit for the improvments."[41] Heintzelman was less popular with some of his troops — a position familiar to many commanding officers.

Upon his arrival in California, Heintzelman received instructions to aid those emigrants traveling the Gila route who were destitute and suffering from lack of provisions by providing them with sufficient supplies to enable them to reach a settlement.[42] In February 1851, a family named Oatman, on their way west along the Gila, left the company of other emigrants at Tucson and the Pima Villages and decided to travel alone. According to Hubert H. Bancroft, Dr. John Le Conte, an entomologist, passed the family on February 15 and took a letter from Royse Oatman to be delivered to Heintzelman.[43] Sometime later (the date is uncertain) six members of the family were murdered by Indians about a hundred miles east of Fort Yuma, at a place now known as Oatman Flat. Two daughters were captured; one son, Lorenzo, survived the attack and later obtained the release of his sister, Olive, who had survived Indian captivity. The tragedy, known as the Oatman Massacre, was publicized and dramatized throughout the country.

In an official report Heintzelman described how he became aware of the killings: "I got a letter from the man asking aid and sent a small party to meet him; they reached the place after he was murdered."[44] The journal entries document that on February 21, Le Conte's Mexican companion, who arrived at the fort first, gave Heintzelman Oatman's letter. Heintzelman also learned that there were twelve American families at Tucson on their way to the post, but indicated that others in his command may have had more information. "Dr. Hewit is quite silent about what he has heard," the commander wrote. Dr. Henry S. Hewit, the assistant surgeon, had submitted his resignation prior to this incident.[45]

Le Conte arrived at the junction on February 24 and asked Heintzelman to send a party to aid the Oatmans. The next day Captain Delozier Davidson made a similar request, and Heintzelman sent "two men with *two* riding and *two* pack mules and a few provisions to go 100 or 120 miles up the river and give all the aid they can in getting them in." Heintzelman learned of the deaths on March 8. He planned to send men "to learn a little more about the emigrants dead on the road," but on March 10 he received word that some of his troops out on an expedition were in need of additional protection against the Indians. On March 27 he heard that the Indians had attacked the family on February 18.[46]

Hewit, Davidson, and Le Conte (whom Heintzelman referred to as "Bugs") blamed the commanding officer for not sending aid to the Oatmans soon enough. Conscious of international law and sensitive about U.S.-Mexican relations, Heintzelman reasoned that, because the killings took place on Mexican soil, he could not pursue the Indians. Heintzelman was convinced that he had done all that was humanly possible.[47]

Toward the end of Heintzelman's Yuma tour in 1854, two events occurred that were significant for his future. The Treaty of Guadalupe Hidalgo had not resolved a number of differences between the United States and Mexico, and disputes in the U.S. Congress over the results of the joint boundary commission survey heightened the dissatisfaction. Indian depredations in Mexico, the proposed transcontinental railroad, commercial and tariff controversies, and filibuster expeditions were among the issues that needed to be settled. Accordingly, James Gadsden, the minister to Mexico (and a South Carolina railroad man), negotiated the purchase from Mexico of approximately 30,000 square miles of land for which the United States paid $10 million. The land included the Mesilla Valley and the area south of the Gila River, the southern boundaries of which form the present boundaries of Arizona and New Mexico.[48] "Arizona" was legally a part of the Territory of New Mexico and was divided into a number of counties. The area referred to as the Gadsden Purchase was a part of Doña Ana County until 1860, when it became known as Arizona County. The Territory of Arizona was created on February 24, 1863.

With the Gadsden Purchase, land for a southern railroad route had been obtained, but neither a natural boundary nor a port on the Gulf of California was acquired. As early as January 7, 1854, because he owned lots in San Diego, Heintzelman hoped "to make a fortune if the railroad terminates in S. Diego. The engineers say the route from here [Fort Yuma] there is impracticable. I dont believe it. If they were told there must be a railroad they would find a practicable route."

Andrew Belcher Gray was completing a survey along the 32nd parallel for a railroad route for the Texas Western Railroad in connection with the line of the Southern Pacific.[49] Gray's party arrived at Fort Yuma at the end of May 1854 and was hospitably entertained by Heintzelman, whose acquaintance with Gray continued for a number of years. In 1855 at Newport Barracks, Kentucky, after a conversation

[14]

with Gray about the Texas Western Railroad, Heintzelman invested $1,000.[50] The next year Gray gave Heintzelman fifty-six shares of Texas Western Railroad stock worth $3.50 per share. "It is for my aid at various times," explained Heintzelman. "I would not decline it as they owed me justly more than that on the money I loaned them—the Railroad."[51] In the autumn of 1856 Heintzelman noted, "I think I can venture to take $30,000 more of 3 per cent stock, or $900 worth. This will give me $3,100."[52]

Heintzelman's support of a southern railroad route was tied directly to his other commercial investments—the development of the Sonora Exploring and Mining Company, and the growth of San Diego and Colorado City. In a letter published in *The Railroad Record,* the Cincinnati newspaper owned by his mining partners, the Wrightsons, Heintzelman urged the construction of a railroad from the mouth of the Gila River to San Diego, "for the benefit of this country, and the world at large."[53]

The Gadsden treaty also opened loopholes for U.S. speculators. On July 11, 1854, Heintzelman recorded:

Messrs. Poston and Ehrenberg arrived here. They went to Guaymas and Hermosillo and examined for a port on the Pacific or rather Gulf. They want to lay out a town here and are backed by capitalists in S. Francisco. They propose an arrangement with Ankrim and Jaeger for a town near the Ferry, or rather to include it.

The post commander had met Charles Debrille Poston, the politician and adventurer who became known as "Father of Arizona," and Herman Vollrath Ehrenberg, a mining engineer, explorer, and mapmaker. The meeting proved crucial to the location and development of Colorado City (present-day Yuma, Arizona), the organization of the Sonora Exploring and Mining Company, the exploration and exploitation of numerous mines in southern Arizona, and the establishment of the Territory of Arizona.[54]

An accurate account of the "founding" of the paper town of Colorado City remains to be written. Poston's often repeated story of its creation, related by the mining engineer Raphael Pumpelly in his *Reminiscences,* is legendary and questionable. Unable to pay the ferriage fee when they arrived at the junction of the two rivers, Poston said he and Ehrenberg bargained with the ferry owner, Louis Jaeger, to take them across in exchange for lots in the city they planned to survey.[55]

Heintzelman's journals record his role in the formation of Colorado City. On July 12, 1854, the day after Ehrenberg and Poston arrived, with the temperature hovering near 117° at the post, Heintzelman sent for Jaeger and "arranged to take up with the offer of these gentlemen about a town." Two days later Poston and Ehrenberg "called and took a sketch from my survey of the reservation and will stay a day or two to make a partial survey." By the end of July plans for Colorado City were being formed. On July 31, Heintzelman disclosed:

There are 20 proprietors and three Trustees. It commences at the Junction and runs down the river taking in all between the Boundary and river, some six or seven sections. The ferry gets part of two blocks where we now cross. Jaeger should have required the whole of the two blocks and equal shares for Ankrim and himself. The way he put down the names he and Ankrim got 1/20 together and each of the rest one. I have one share. This side of the river is ours, and I will object to any divisions of it into lots for others, or shares. I think it still the more valuable. I dont like the arrangement and would not have agreed to it. There are several persons on the river who have not the shadow of a claim [who] have [one] 20th [of a share].

A tract of approximately 936 acres was divided into seven sections, and the preemptionists filed their claims and incorporated the townsite in the name of the "Colorado Company" in San Francisco in August. Little mention of Colorado

City was made thereafter. In 1865 Heintzelman sent a power of attorney to the San Diego and Fort Yuma merchant, George Hooper, to sell his interest in it. The charter was forfeited December 13, 1905.[56]

On July 15, 1854, after more than four years in the Southwest, Heintzelman turned over the command of Fort Yuma. Returning to the East, he was reunited with his family in Buffalo, New York. In June 1855, he was sent to Newport Barracks, Kentucky, where he served as superintendent of the Western Recruiting Service. Promoted to major in the First Infantry, he remained at Newport Barracks, across the Ohio River from Cincinnati, until the summer of 1857. It was there that he and Poston organized the Sonora Exploring and Mining Company.

Charles Debrille Poston. Often referred to
as the "Father of Arizona," he organized
with Heintzelman the Sonora Exploring
and Mining Company.

The Sonora
Exploring and Mining
Company

When two weary travelers, Charles Debrille Poston and Herman Vollrath Ehrenberg, arrived at the junction of the Gila and Colorado Rivers, they had spent 112 arduous days crossing the southern Arizona desert from Sinaloa and Sonora. Often referred to as the "Father of Arizona," Poston was a quixotic character whose adventuresome and frequently troubled life was intertwined with the early history of the Territory of Arizona. Although Poston's own accounts of his long service to Arizona tend to be imprecise and exaggerated, his role as a pioneer should not be underestimated.

Poston was born in Elizabethtown, Kentucky, in 1825; at the age of twelve he was apprenticed to the clerk of Hardin County, Samuel Haycraft. The young man eventually became deputy clerk and in 1848 married Haycraft's daughter, Margaret. Poston left his family in 1851, moved to San Francisco, and worked in the surveyor's office of the Custom House, but by the end of 1853 his salary was reduced and he was replaced. In 1854 an opportunity arose for him to recruit men to undertake a reconnaissance in Sonora, Mexico, to locate silver mines and to obtain options on land grants in the newly acquired Gadsden Purchase area, but the party was forced to land at Macapule, in the Bay of Navachista, and the adventure failed.[1]

One of Poston's companions was the explorer and cartographer Herman Ehrenberg, and together they crossed the desert to Fort Yuma. Prior to this adventure, Ehrenberg had traveled extensively throughout California, Oregon, Latin America, and the Pacific islands. Born in Steuden, Germany, in 1816, he immigrated to the United States in 1834, joined the New Orleans Grays, fought in the war for Texas independence, and survived the massacre at Goliad. He went back to Germany, where he wrote a book about his Texas experiences. After studying mining and engineering, he returned to the United States in 1844. From then until 1854 he traveled, working as a surveyor, mapmaker, and possibly as a merchant. He aided the U.S. troops in Baja California during the Mexican War, joined the gold rush, and made a number of important maps of Honolulu, La Paz, Sacramento, San Francisco, and the Klamath gold region.[2]

After Poston and Ehrenberg had incorporated Colorado City, Heintzelman returned to the East, and in June 1855 was sent to Newport Barracks, Kentucky. Ehrenberg remained in the West, where he made the first private map of the Gadsden Purchase. He spent most of 1855 and 1856 in Sonora and southern Arizona exploring for mines. According to his own accounts, Poston left San Francisco and went east as the representative of California businessmen interested in promoting ventures in the Southwest. He sought financial assistance from eastern businessmen and lobbied to have Congress designate Colorado City as a port of entry, but was unsuccessful in both endeavors.[3]

Heintzelman was aware of Poston's efforts. In late February 1855, while Poston was in Washington, D.C., the soldier came into the city and, being unable to find lodging,

stayed with Poston for several days.[4] A year later Heintzelman invited Poston to visit him at Newport Barracks. Poston
arrived in Cincinnati on Friday, March 7, 1856, and registered
at the Broadway House. For the next twenty days Heintzelman arranged a series of appointments with midwestern
businessmen who would provide the capital necessary to
organize the Sonora Exploring and Mining Company.[5]

The day Poston arrived, Heintzelman introduced him to
Thomas and William Wrightson, brothers who edited the
Railroad Record, a publication that advocated western railroad
expansion, especially the development of a southern railroad route. "We had a long talk about forming a company
to explore for mines in the Gadsden Purchase, wrote
Heintzelman.[6] That evening he and Poston had dinner, and
together they drew up a plan for the company. On Saturday,
March 8, the two men met with Edgar Conkling, a brick-
maker, merchant, and the Mississippi River Valley agent
for the Southern Pacific Railroad Company. Nothing was decided. On the same day, Heintzelman also talked with two
Cincinnati doctors. "It was rather up hill work," he recorded.
One of the physicians "did not know who Gadsden was and
asked whether it was a private purchase."

Poston and Heintzelman met again with Edgar Conkling.
The major wanted the railroad agent to head the list of investors, but Conkling declined because of other business interests. They reached an agreement, however, for Heintzelman
disclosed that Conkling made" a proposition if I would give
$1,000 and put it in my name he would take half and give me
ten percent interest. I can raise the money and think I will do
it. They think my putting down $1,000 will give confidence
my having lived so long in the country."[7] The bargain was
completed on March 12. Heintzelman reported, "Things look
more favorable. I put down my name for 10 shares or $1,000.
Mr. Conkling will take half, but prefers that I should keep

the whole." At the same time, Conkling and Poston were negotiating. Heintzelman remarked that Conkling "has made some arrangement with Mr. Poston to take the same amount through the latter and pay in Pacific r.r. stock."

Heintzelman continued to discuss the proposal with other Cincinnati residents. He was optimistic. "We will no doubt succeed ultimately," he speculated.[8] On March 16 he invited William Wrightson and Poston to dinner. Plans were made for Poston to return to southern Arizona with men and equipment and begin reopening the legendary Spanish silver mines.[9] Later that evening Heinztelman wrote to George F. Hooper and enclosed a letter to Herman Ehrenberg, asking the latter to meet Poston in Arizona.

On Sunday, March 23, Heintzelman went to the Cincinnati offices of the *Railroad Record* and "got from Mr. Poston the form of agreement and corrected Mr. Wrightson's draft of articles of agreement for the company." The major and the editor asked Poston to write his instructions and submit them the next afternoon. On Monday, March 24, Heintzelman announced: "After dinner I went to town and we had a meeting and regular organization elected officers and adopted articles of association. I am President of the Sonora Mining and exploring company stock $100.000." William Wrightson was chosen secretary, and Edgar Conkling became the company's general agent. "Colonel" Poston (a title he thereafter retained) was listed as "Commandant and Managing Agent." The next day, "arms for the exploring party" were ordered. On the afternoon of March 27, Wrightson and Heintzelman bade good-bye to Poston, who left by river steamer for New Orleans and Texas. Heintzelman declared: "We are now fairly embarked in the enterprise."[10]

For the next few weeks the president of the newly organized venture spent time raising money to enable Poston to hire men and buy machinery in Texas. By April 10, the company had spent nearly $900 "for arms and other articles," including water bags, to send to Poston. On May 1, Heintzelman noted that the company had $1,200 for Poston to "draw on." This cash became available because one of the contractors for the Southern Pacific Railroad Company bought $1,000 worth of stock.[11] In addition, Heintzelman used the fifty-six shares of railroad stock that the surveyor, Andrew B. Gray, had given him.[12]

It is not known how extensively the officials of the Southern Pacific Railroad Company supported the Sonora Exploring and Mining Company. Poston's accounts diverge widely from what Heintzelman recorded. Years after any arrangements may have been made, Poston wrote that he negotiated with the railroad men. "They inquired how much it would cost to make the exploration," Poston declared. "I replied that I would start with a hundred thousand dollars if there was a million behind it."[13] On June 28, 1856, Heintzelman records that Thomas Butler King, a Georgia planter-politician, former collector of the Port of San Francisco, and promoter of the Southern Pacific Railroad, requested that his name be withdrawn as a stockholder. Six months later Heintzelman disclosed that he felt uneasy about King's relinquishing his stock and feared that Poston and King had made a "private arrangement" and that Poston "will play false" to the mining company. He warned Poston about dealing with King and the Southern Pacific, which was beset by difficulties. As noted earlier, Heintzelman had invested lightly in the railroad company. If the railroad officials did invest in the Sonora Exploring and Mining Company, the sum could not have been substantial, for Heintzelman and the Wrightsons had difficulty paying debts incurred by Poston.[14]

The largest investments mentioned by Heintzelman during this period were those made by John D. Park, a Cincinnati merchant, who bought $30,000 worth of stock, as did Brown

Brothers and Company of London.[15] How much each investor paid out initially, and whether installments were paid regularly, is unknown. The agreement with the Cincinnati printing firm of Middleton and Wallace that lithographed maps and drawings for the company demonstrates one method of transaction. On November 1, 1856, the printing firm invested $1,000 in the mining company by paying "half down and a note for the rest." The mining officials would then try to borrow as much money as they had received in cash and send the sum to Poston or deposit it with merchants with whom he was doing business. On December 2, 1856, Heintzelman "sold another share to Middleton, Wallace for 500—60 days and 500 in work." In addition, the company paid its staff in stock certificates. For example, Heintzelman wrote that Poston gave "5 shares of Sonora stock to Mr. Ehrenberg subject to our approval. This is not in accordance with our agreement and we disapprove but will agree to give Ehrenberg of our new stock $5,000."[16]

While Heintzelman continued to sell stock, Poston traveled to Texas, where he purchased equipment and hired mining engineers.[17] The "exploring party" journeyed overland during the summer months from San Antonio through El Paso and on to Mesilla in the Territory of New Mexico. There Poston was appointed deputy clerk of Doña Ana County, the jurisdiction of which included the western portion of the Gadsden Purchase. The adventurers arrived in Tucson about August 22, 1856, and were met by Herman Ehrenberg.[18] Several days later they participated in a meeting at which the residents of Tucson resolved to petition Congress to consider organizing Arizona as a separate territory.[19] By September Poston and Ehrenberg had moved forty-five miles south of Tucson to the village of Tubac on the Santa Cruz River, where they established the headquarters of the Sonora

Exploring and Mining Company in an abandoned Mexican presidio. The mining company eventually restored some of the buildings.[20]

Three months later the two men concluded negotiations with Tomas and Ignacio Ortiz, brothers and residents of Tubac who held title to a 17,000-acre site known as the Arivaca Ranch, about twelve miles southwest of the town.[21] On December 26, 1856, the company purchased the title to the ranch (including the rights to the mines and minerals), whose gently rolling terrain contained good grass for grazing, groves of cottonwood, walnut, and mesquite trees, a running stream, and about twenty mines. It is difficult to ascertain the exact sum paid for the Arivaca Ranch. The transfer documents record that the mining company paid $5,000 for the property,[22] but Tomas Ortiz later told Poston that the sum was $2,000. Stock certificates, which eventually became worthless, were included in the payment.[23] The mining company hired Thomas Corwin, an Ohio attorney and former U.S. senator, to examine the title papers. Corwin declared that the titles exhibited to him gave the company "a perfect fee simple in both the soil and minerals of that property."[24]

Ehrenberg and Poston purchased additional smaller parcels of land in and around Tubac.[25] Joined by two mining engineers, Frederick Brunckow and Charles Schuchard, they began to discover and open mines. On January 1, 1857, Poston announced the discovery of a vein of silver ore located in the Santa Rita Mountains to be known as Salero.[26] By February 1, Brunckow had reported the discovery of a "vein of Silver ore" located about one mile from the summit of the southeastern side of the Cerro Colorado. He named the vein the Heintzelman Mine. By 1858 Brunckow, whom Poston had hired for a share in the venture, was the administrator at Cerro Colorado.[27]

[25]

Heintzelman Mine on the Arivaca Ranch. The ranch and its mineral rights were purchased by the Sonora Exploring and Mining Company on December 26, 1856.

News of the purchase of the Arivaca Ranch and of the discovery of the Heintzelman Mine had not reached the Cincinnati officers in time for the publication of the first report to the stockholders. Nevertheless, the editors of the *Railroad Record* printed a handsome pamphlet, containing engravings of views of the Southwest, maps of the mineral regions, and a map of the Tubac headquarters. The report provided a brief history of the establishment of the company, an account of Poston's journey from Texas to Tubac, a discussion of the importance of Fort Yuma and of the potential significance of Colorado City as a center for trade, and descriptions of the mineral wealth of the territory: "No country in the world is richer than Mexico, in the value and immensity of its mineral products, and Sonora is conceded to be the richest of its provinces." The company officials promised that the results of their explorations would be "brilliant," "wonderful," "unexpected," and "startling."[28]

From the time of the publication of the first stockholders' report, accounts of the operations of the Sonora Exploring and Mining Company, including its financial status and the quality and quantity of the mineral production, were exaggerated. Early advertisements called the company "the most important Mining Company on this Continent" and noted that its lands were located on the line of the Southern Pacific Railroad "at the most favorable point for a seat of government for the proposed new Territory of Arizona, and of a branch railroad to the Gulf of Mexico."[29]

Hopeful of luring investors, desirous of enlisting the support of the federal government (to create a separate territory and provide military protection), and interested in encouraging the development of a southern railroad route through their properties, the Cincinnati officials relied on Poston's communications and did not supervise his transactions. Until the summer of 1858, the midwestern directors — soldiers, merchants, printers, and writers—had not visited the mines. Heintzelman was dissatisfied with Poston's messages and sought more information. He sent a copy of the company's first report to a fellow officer, Major William H. Emory (who had seen the Arivaca Ranch while engaged in boundary surveys), and asked Emory for his opinion "as to its value and the number of silver mines."[30]

Heintzelman applied for an extended leave of absence from his military duties to raise money for the company and to journey to Arizona to supervise its operations. He was granted leave from mid-summer 1857 until the spring of 1859. Although his wife's letters are not included in the public archives, Heintzelman describes how Margaret was bitterly provoked by his decision. She threatened to leave him. After efforts to appease her, the bewildered husband happily disclosed a change in her attitude: "This morning before we got up lying awake ... I threw my arms around Margaret and she could not resist the appeal. She said all was passed and we could commence anew."[31]

During the year before his June 1858 departure for Arizona, Heintzelman continued to promote and organize the mining company. By August 1857, the Sonora Exploring and Mining Company was incorporated under the laws of the state of Ohio as a joint-stock company with a capital stock listed at $2 million, divided into 20,000 shares of $100 each. In addition to Heintzelman, the original incorporators were Cincinnati businessmen—William Wrightson, John Kennett, E. C. Middleton, Samuel Flickinger, George Mendenhall, and John R. Wright.[32]

Within twelve days after the incorporation papers were filed Heintzelman recorded, "There is a report that some Ohio banks have broken. I am going over to see."[33] The next day he observed, "Still quite an excitement about the Life and Trust. No further news. It is no doubt a bad failure." By

September 5 he was able to assess what the failure of the New York branch of the Ohio Life Insurance and Trust Company would signify for the future of the Sonora Exploring and Mining Company.

Unfortunately, Heintzelman and his business colleagues were seeking capitalization of their mining enterprise just as the Panic of 1857 struck northern bankers, industrialists, and manufacturers. Money was scarce, and many banks failed. In a money market already glutted and overextended by speculations in land, mines, and railroads, the Sonora Exploring and Mining Company was hard-pressed to attract investors. William Wrightson tried and failed to sell stock to New York businessmen. He had gone east in the summer of 1857 and received promises of stock purchases upon the agreement that a corporation would be formed. With the onset of the financial crisis, Wrightson was unable to obtain any money from potential investors.[34] Heintzelman disclosed that the mining speculators must raise $15,000 to complete the purchase of the Arivaca Ranch, and he feared it would be difficult. The company officials decided "to sell the stock at less than 50 percent if we cant raise the money in any other way." Heintzelman confessed, "This Life and Trust failure has injured us very much."[35]

By the end of October the company's debts were increasing. The Ohio banking house was no longer able to lend money to the company. Drafts were protested for nonpayment. On December 9 Heintzelman wrote, "Drafts on Ohio Life and Trust co. to amt. of $2,250 are not paid. This is a ruinous thing for us. It absorbs all the money I placed at the Colorado." Later he added, "The prospect looks gloomy enough." Poston, who had been in San Francisco ostensibly to sell stock, and Ehrenberg, who had remained in Tubac to oversee the mining facilities, now were expected "to rely on their own resources."

Heintzelman moved to Washington, D.C., and began visiting congressmen, senators, judges, government officials, and military officers. He circulated reports and maps about the company and the territory and exhibited specimens of ore from the mines. On December 18, a fellow West Point graduate, Major William Chapman, introduced Heintzelman to the firearms inventor and manufacturer, Samuel Colt of Hartford, Connecticut, who had other financial interests in the Southwest. Heintzelman recorded the details of the first meeting: "After breakfast I met Major Chapman and he wished me to see Col. Colt., the Pistol man, about our mines. I went with him and had a talk. He has under consideration the propriety of furnishing $10,000 for our stock at 25 per cent. We are to see him again on the subject."[36] Heintzelman feared that Sylvester Mowry, a young promoter of similar ventures who was also meeting with Colt, would induce the latter to "go in with the Sopori mine and so he drop ours."[37]

The following day Heintzelman gave Colt a copy of the stockholders' report. The 1857 report listed title to 17,700 acres of land and eighty mines, twenty-five on the Arivaca property, twenty-four in the Santa Rita Mountains, twenty-nine surrounding Cerro Colorado, and two veins referred to as the San Coyetano tract, eight miles southwest of Tubac. It was estimated that the ore would yield an average of over $1,400 per ton of silver; and it was suggested that the mines could employ 5,000 workers for an indefinite period. However, the company acknowledged that little work had been done—one mine was cleaned out and opened to a depth of eighty feet and two others to depths of fifty and thirty feet.

Heintzelman, speaking of Colt, explained, "He is quite taken with our mining co. and I am to see him again after he has read the Report. I want him to read it carefully."[38] That evening Heintzelman and Colt conferred. Colt proposed "to furnish $10,000 by the steamer of Jan. 5th, and $10,000 of his

Samuel Colt, firearms inventor and
manufacturer. At a time when investors were hard to find, Colt bought
shares in Heintzelman's company
for $10,000 and a shipment of arms.

arms in two or three lots, for $100,000 stock. Or in other words for our stock at 20 cts on the dollar."[39] Heintzelman told Colt he would consider the offer. Chapman advised the major to accept, for as Heintzelman noted, "If we want more aid and means he will then be so much interested that he can and will give it, besides we can get from him machinery on credit."[40]

After spending most of Sunday, December 20, with Colt, Heintzelman concluded the bargain, subject to the approval of Conkling and Wrightson.[41] The major commented: "Lt. Mowry is very much disappointed at my success and fears he is cut out. He told me that he feared I would prevent him doing anything. I think on the contrary it will aid him. At all events the first overtures were made to me and I had a right to push on if he even was cut out. It was not my place to hold back."[42] In fact, Colt eventually became one of the directors of the Sopori Land and Mining Company and of the Arizona Land and Mining Company, companion corporations to which Mowry sold land.[43]

Heintzelman urged his Cincinnati colleagues to accept Colt's offer, especially since Poston and Ehrenberg were requesting supplies and equipment. On Wednesday, December 23, Wrightson and Conkling telegraphed their approval of the arrangement. Heintzelman speculated, "If I succeed in getting the money from Colt then our troubles are over."[44] Colt replied on December 27 suggesting that Heintzelman come to Hartford to select the arms. Heintzelman was relieved. "I am glad to get his letter as we have met with so many disappointments I could not help at times having doubts."[45]

On New Year's Day, 1858, Heintzelman arrived in Hartford. Samuel Colt gave him a check for $10,000 and the invoices for the shipment of arms. Heintzelman gave Colt the stock certificates and immediately began to pay some of the debts Poston had incurred.[46] When the major returned to Washington he received a letter from Ehrenberg. Heintzelman related, "The picture of affairs out there is gloomy enough. I fear they will discharge the men and quit work. They undertook to do too much, with our limited means."[47]

Although the financial circumstances of the Sonora Exploring and Mining Company looked brighter, in reality little work was being accomplished at the mines. In June 1857, Poston had left for San Francisco and did not return until the following year. Ehrenberg had been placed in charge of the company's operations. There was little cash for buying food and supplies or for hiring laborers. The work of opening, clearing, and draining the old mines was tedious and dangerous; machinery did not arrive, and work was delayed. Adobes had to be made before crude huts could be built to shelter the Mexican laborers. Buildings at Tubac needed to be repaired, wells had to be dug, and gardens had to be planted and irrigated. The smelting works at Arivaca awaited construction. Wagon roads connecting the silver mines had to be cleared. Supplies were scarce—they were sent out from New Mexico or shipped across the desert from the junction of the Gila and Colorado rivers. At times the Pima Indians provided the men with grain. When an American, Henry Crabb, led a disastrous filibuster expedition into Sonora in the spring of 1857, the miners were unable to travel freely into Mexico to trade.[48] The situation improved by the next year. Although Indian attacks were infrequent at this time, the pioneers worried about Apache raids. Except for the residents of Tucson and the soldiers at Fort Buchanan, there were few U.S. settlers in the Santa Cruz Valley. The company was eager to see "as good a class of citizens as it is possible to go there."[49]

There are no population figures for the year 1858. The 1860

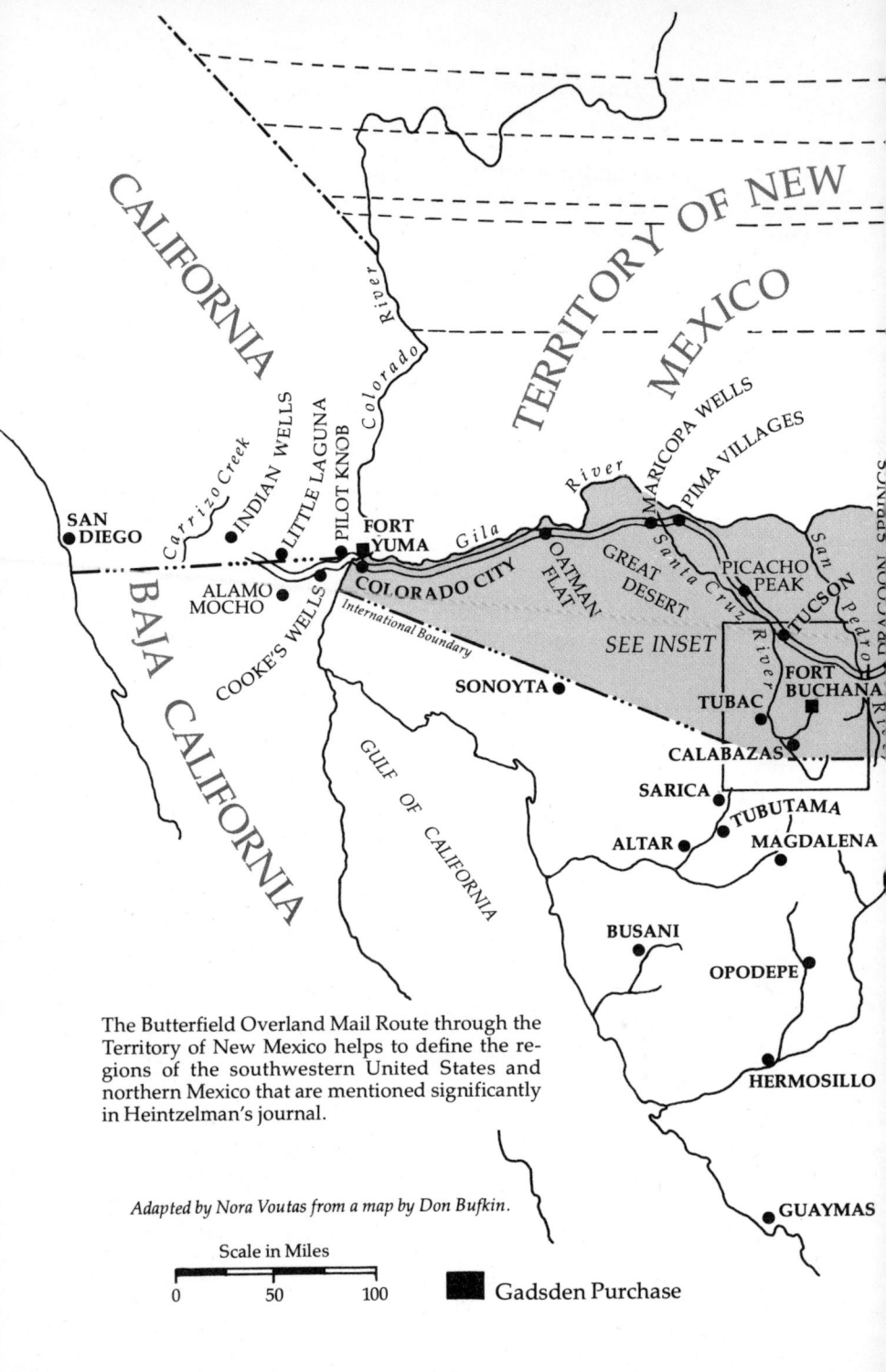

CALIFORNIA

TERRITORY OF NEW

MEXICO

BAJA CALIFORNIA

Colorado River

Carrizo Creek

INDIAN WELLS

LITTLE LAGUNA

PILOT KNOB

SAN DIEGO

ALAMO MOCHO

COOKE'S WELLS

FORT YUMA

COLORADO CITY

International Boundary

Gila River

OATMAN FLAT

GREAT DESERT

Santa Cruz

MARICOPA WELLS

PIMA VILLAGES

PICACHO PEAK

TUCSON

San Pedro River

DRAGOON SPRINGS

SEE INSET

SONOYTA

TUBAC

FORT BUCHANA

CALABAZAS

GULF OF CALIFORNIA

SARICA

ALTAR

TUBUTAMA

MAGDALENA

BUSANI

OPODEPE

HERMOSILLO

GUAYMAS

The Butterfield Overland Mail Route through the Territory of New Mexico helps to define the regions of the southwestern United States and northern Mexico that are mentioned significantly in Heintzelman's journal.

Adapted by Nora Voutas from a map by Don Bufkin.

Scale in Miles

0   50   100

Gadsden Purchase

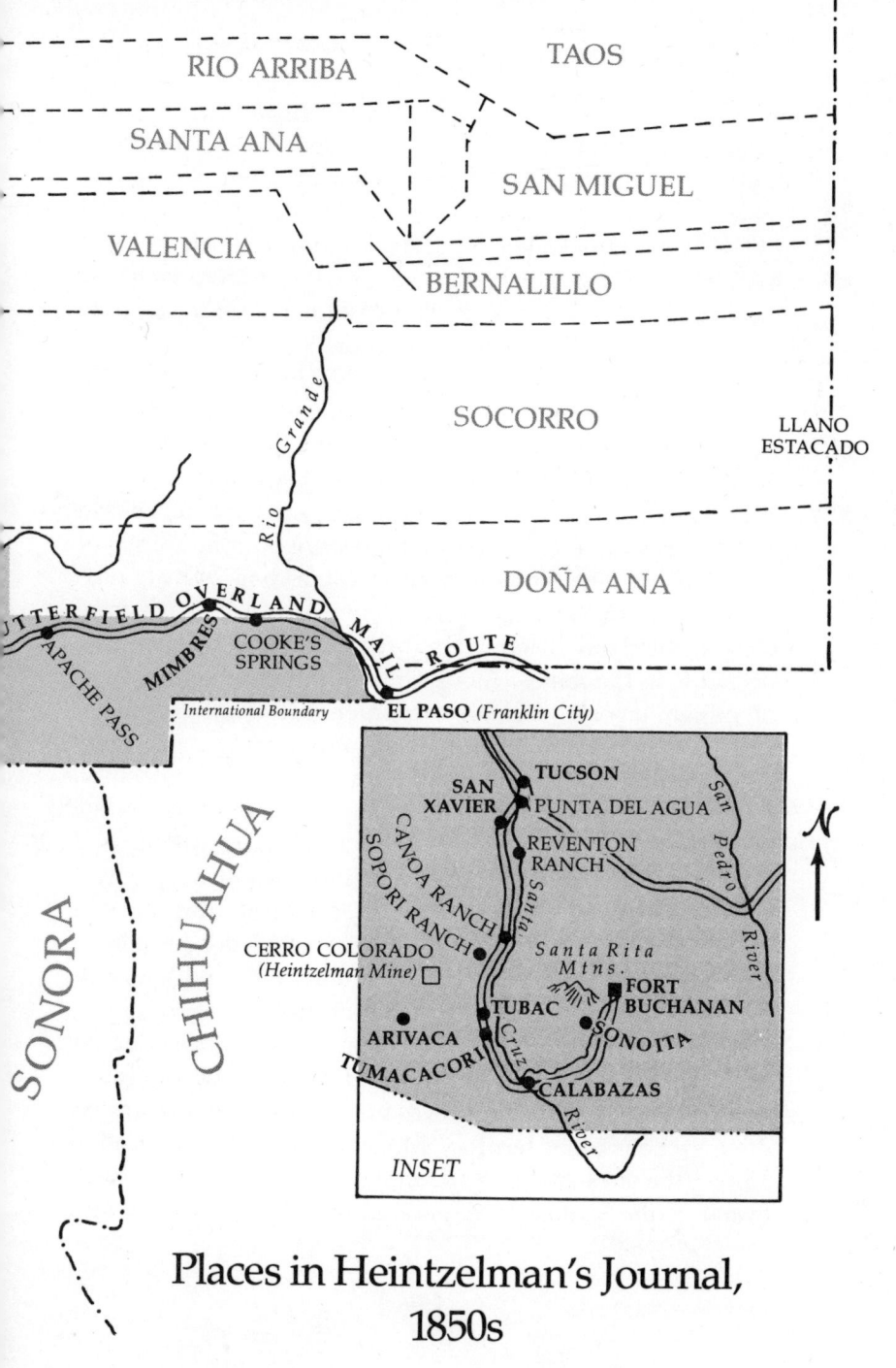

RIO ARRIBA

TAOS

SANTA ANA

SAN MIGUEL

VALENCIA

BERNALILLO

Rio Grande

SOCORRO

LLANO
ESTACADO

DOÑA ANA

BUTTERFIELD OVERLAND MAIL ROUTE

APACHE PASS

MIMBRES

COOKE'S
SPRINGS

International Boundary

EL PASO *(Franklin City)*

SONORA

CHIHUAHUA

INSET

TUCSON

SAN
XAVIER

PUNTA DEL AGUA

CANOA RANCH

SOPORI RANCH

REVENTON
RANCH

Santa Cruz

San Pedro River

CERRO COLORADO
(Heintzelman Mine)

*Santa Rita
Mtns.*

TUBAC

FORT
BUCHANAN

ARIVACA

SONOITA

TUMACACORI

Santa Cruz River

CALABAZAS

N

Places in Heintzelman's Journal,
1850s

federal census for the County of Arizona, Territory of New Mexico, lists an aggregate population of 6,493 people (Indians: 2,109 males and 1,934 females; whites: 1,687 males and 742 females; "free colored": 15 males and 6 females). More than 900 people resided in Tucson; in Tubac there were 231 males and 122 females, including 43 Indians. Of these, only 23 men were born outside Mexico or New Mexico. At the Arivaca Mines there were 61 people (40 white males, 12 white females, 2 black males, 4 mulatto males, and 3 mulatto females). Cerro ("Sierra") Colorado listed 33 white males and 11 white females. At Cerro Colorado and Arivaca there were 20 children under eighteen years of age. The white females in Tubac, Arivaca, and Cerro Colorado were born in Mexico or New Mexico. The Santa Rita Silver Mines had 20 male residents, 16 from Mexico, 2 from New York and 1 each from Ohio and Ireland. There were three multiracial families connected with the mines. Along with the expected occupations of miner, laborer, farmer, carpenter, merchant, teamster, bricklayer, blacksmith, seamstress, and washwoman, there were two Fandango musicians and two schoolmasters, all four with Spanish surnames. Generally, the non-native (non-Mexican, New Mexican, or Indian) residents had greater wealth and property, yet there were only a few occupations undertaken by them that differed from the services provided by the natives. These included hotelkeeper, smelter, machinist, civil engineer, millwright, and lawyer.[50]

Despite the vastness of the country and the rigors of settling in "Arizona," the area the company decided to inhabit—Tubac, Cerro Colorado, and Arivaca—was a usable, workable space. The terrain was not so rugged nor so arid as other sections of the territory. Movement and communication among the sites could be accomplished easily on horseback, even into the Santa Rita Mountains, eventually occupied by a subsidiary branch of the mining company that relied on the established presence of earlier settlements.

The German mining engineers — Herman Ehrenberg, Frederic Brunckow, and Charles Schuchard — received no direction. In the early stages of the operation they opened up a large number of mines, thus crippling their ability to develop a few and produce some ore. In addition, the engineers had to adapt their technological knowledge to the available equipment and to the skills of the Mexican laborers. By December 1857, the company employed twenty-eight laborers, but Ehrenberg wrote that he would have to discharge most of them.[51] When the company issued its second annual report to the stockholders on March 29, 1858, it admitted that "work has been done on other shafts to prove the value of the ores but none of them have been carrying to the paying point, owing to the want of furnaces to smelt the ore when raised."[52]

Limited quantities of ore were shipped to the East and to California in 1857 and early 1858, but accurate reports are unavailable. A case of ore specimens was exhibited at the Cincinnati Merchants' Exchange in July 1857, and again at the annual fair of the Ohio Mechanics Institute in September and October.[53] A San Diego shipper, William Conklin, was hired to transport about nine tons of ore from Cerro Colorado to San Diego, but he left about five and one-half tons at the junction of the Colorado and Gila. It was shipped by schooner to San Francisco.[54] By July 1858, the ore was being smelted by the San Francisco firm of Wass, Uznay, and Warwick, a few crude smelting furnaces were in operation at Arivaca, and ore had been shipped to Hermosillo, the capital of Sonora, 200 miles south of Tucson.[55]

Estimates of the character and value of the company's ores heightened the directors' expectations. During 1857, the first full year of operation, the company had the silver ores from the Heintzelman Mine assayed. The results of eight separate analyses for value per ton varied from $322.94 to $2,816; for value per pound (average) the estimates ranged from $0.16 to $1.4075; and for grains per pound (average) the estimates were 51.99 to 520. The averages for the eight assays were: value per ton, $1,424.45; value per pound, $0.7114; and grains per pound, 263.03.[56] In 1857 the company announced that one assayer found silver in the ratio of 237 ounces to the ton of 2,000 pounds and 33 percent of copper.[57] By 1858 the company declared that Louis A. Garnett, of the U.S. Branch Mint in San Francisco, found silver in the ratio of 7,040 ounces to the ton of 2,000 pounds.[58]

Heintzelman received conflicting reports about the value of the mine named for him. In September 1857, Poston claimed that "the Heintzelman mine is probably the richest in the world-known." After hearing from Edgar Conkling, Heintzelman admitted, "The ore dont yield as well as the assays."[59] On March 12, 1858, the major received word from Poston that "a space in the H. mine 150 ft. long 25 deep and 3 wide will yield two million and a quarter dollars and that 10 hands can get it out in one year." Heintzelman promptly circulated the news around the city of Washington: "I have read an extract from Mr. Poston's last report and have astonished all who hear it. The Heintzelman mine is in 'bonanza.'"[60] When Heintzelman received notice of Ehrenberg's sudden resignation, he disclosed that the engineer revealed new information. Ehrenberg wrote "of accounts from the mines being 'polished' and tells of assays of Küstel [Guido Küstel, a recently hired mining engineer] yielding only 600 and some dollars and not $6,000." Heintzelman feared that the communications from the mines "have been calculated to deceive."[61]

In March 1858, Heintzelman traveled to Cincinnati to attend a board of directors meeting. At the meeting a subsidiary company, the Santa Rita Silver Mining Company, was organized. On March 21, 1858, a memorandum was signed by Heintzelman and William Wrightson that allowed the latter to form a "Branch Company, to occupy and develop the Silver Mines in the Santa Rita Mountains." Heintzelman initially opposed the establishment of the company, but by the time he reached Cincinnati he had changed his mind. On March 28 he wrote, "We strongly recommend the Santa Rita Company." Incorporated under the laws of Ohio, its capital stock was listed at $1 million, half of which was to be given to the Sonora Exploring and Mining Company as the purchase price of ownership of the mines and for work already done. Dr. George Mendenhall was elected president and William Wrightson, secretary; other board members included Heintzelman, Thomas Wrightson, Thomas H. C. Allen, Truman Hillyer, and James Applegate. By May, two Cincinnati engravers, Horace C. Grosvenor and Phocion Way, were sent out to Arizona to establish headquarters and supervise the company's operations in the Santa Rita Mountains. By 1859, seven mines were being worked there.[62]

In addition to the creation of a subsidiary company, by-laws for the Sonora Exploring and Mining Company were adopted and a stockholders' report was issued. Heintzelman was reelected president, although Edgar Conkling, who was chosen vice-president, had hoped to obtain the presidency. Samuel Colt, Samuel Flickinger, and E. C. Middleton were elected directors. Heintzelman revealed that factions had formed among the directors. He was displeased that Middleton was elected, for he feared that when he (Heintzelman) and William Wrightson were absent, Conkling would be able to control the board.[63]

Returning to Washington, Heintzelman related that Colt was dissatisfied with the outcome of the meeting. On April 2 the major wrote that Colt "says he dont know anyone in the company but me. It is his own fault. He might have seen most of the stockholders had he visited Cincinnati." Colt made an additional proposal to provide the company with $5,000 to send out more men and to provide $5,000 worth of arms, each proposal in exchange for stock at 25 percent.[64]

As Heintzelman prepared to leave for the mines, Colt lent him $500 to help resettle his family in Newport Barracks.[65] Heintzelman thought that his chief purpose in going to Arizona was to "make our people economize and work the mines or rather reduction works."[66] Colt wanted Heintzelman to take with him "a full force of practical men" to aid "in developing that which under late management has been so long sleeping." Colt would select the men and pay for their transportation and supplies in exchange for stock at a reduced price. The arms manufacturer urged Heintzelman to assume control and reminded him that if he failed it would "reflect back upon us."[67] Unable to convince Heintzelman of the value of his plan, Colt sent his young brother-in-law, Richard W. H. Jarvis, to Arizona in July 1858 to look after his interests and provide an assessment of the operations.[68]

When Heintzelman arrived in Tubac on August 17, 1858, he found that the ore was not as rich as had been estimated. The company's debt totaled $10,000, and there was no cash to pay the workers. The amalgamation works at Arivaca were not built (and there was no money to build them); the furnace at the Arenia Mine was idle; the mining engineers were dissatisfied; and more laborers were needed. According to Heintzelman, Poston had incurred needless expenses, especially in the management of the Tubac headquarters. Heintzelman used personal funds and transferred some of his own stock certificates to pay the workers. According to

Raphael Pumpelly, a mining engineer, the Mexican laborers received $12 to $15 per month, the workmen at the furnace $1 per day (for a twelve-hour day), and the U.S. laborers $30 to $70 per month, including board. A flour ration was allotted each worker. Lacking cash, the company often paid in stock certificates (and later in redeemable scrip). [69]

During the six months that the company's president stayed in the Southwest, he and the workers were troubled by malaria, lead colic, lack of adequate food and supplies, and inclement weather. Although Heintzelman set an example of hardiness and self-sacrifice, he was unable to direct the men to be more efficient and hard-working. He could not even exert pressure on his own brother-in-law, Solon H. Lathrop, who was unwilling to part with familiar comforts.

One major difficulty, as perceived by Heintzelman, was the company's inability to organize and direct the Mexicans to work steadily and accomplish a task with thoroughness. Instead of training the Mexicans to do a specific job, the engineers would do it themselves. They could not rely on a constant number of workers. Fiestas, news of gold discoveries, civil strife in Mexico, Apache raids, lack of cash to pay salaries, and the unstable relations between the United States and Mexico due to American-led filibuster expeditions would cause the numbers of workers crossing the border to fluctuate. Some Mexicans stole from and murdered their U.S. employers. Heintzelman's journals indicate that he regarded the Mexican laborers (but not all Mexicans) as lazy and socially inferior; and he thought most of the workers were theives. He does not appear to have treated them harshly, however.

Heintzelman managed to build several new furnaces, reduce expenses, and nearly complete the amalgamation works. The company's engineers—Herman Ehrenberg, Frederick Brunckow, and Guido Küstel—were knowledgeable and used the experience they gained at Cerro Colorado and Arivaca to open other mines and to educate other miners, through their books, articles, and reports. The company's equipment consisted of dry stamp mills for crushing ore, mule-powered and later steam-powered arrastras (mills) for grinding ore, a retort (in which substances were distilled or decomposed by heat), a number of barrels, and several different furnaces for smelting and refining. Equipment was located at the various mines; later, more elaborate reduction works with steam-powered engines were set up at Arivaca.

Two different amalgamation processes were used. Patio amalgamation, a primitive method of separating silver from other metals, was a familiar Mexican process. Brunckow reported that, although the quicksilver loss was great, the method could be successful if poor and easily ground ores were used. The ores were crushed and ground into a fine powder in an arrastra, mixed with salt, moistened, and piled up on a stone bed. Quicksilver was added intermittently, and the mass was kneaded by driving mules over it. The animal waste added chemicals, mainly ammonia, which stimulated the collection of residual silver. Lime or magistral (sulphate of iron) was added, and after several weeks, depending on the weather, the amalgam was retorted.

The other method, the barrel amalgamation process, was initiated by Guido Küstel and referred to as the European or Freyburg process. The ore was crushed again, sifted twice, and put in the arrastra and ground with water into a fine powder. It was dried, crushed again, mixed with 8 percent salt, and roasted in a reverberatory furnace until the metal formed into chlorides (about five hours). Of this powder, 800 pounds were put into amalgamation barrels, together with a quantity of water and 75 pounds of copper balls. The barrels were set to revolve for several hours so that a stiff paste formed; 400 pounds of quicksilver were added and the barrels were set to revolve for twenty-two hours. More water was added to thin the paste, and the barrels were set in motion again. After two hours the barrels were opened, and the quicksilver and the amalgam were run out into troughs and put into canvas bags. The surplus quicksilver was pressed through the porous bags by its own weight, and the remaining stiff amalgam was retorted. The silver was melted in a refining furnace and cast into bars that were marked with the company's stamps and numbered with the assay yield. The value in dollars was marked also.

In the 1859 stockholders' report, and in mining magazine articles, Brunckow described the company's smelting process for separating the impurities in the ores. Because the ores contained a nominal quantity of quartz, the smelting process was difficult. The blast furnace used to smelt the ore had several sections: the lower part was built of a fireproof, fine-grained quartz sandstone; the upper part and the smelting "house" were built of adobe. The smelting chamber inside the furnace was twelve inches square. The blast was produced by a double bellows worked by one man. Three parts of lead ore were added to one part of silver ore and, after fusion, the molten lead that accumulated in the furnace's basin was run off into an exterior basin. As it cooled, a crust was formed that contained sulphides of copper, lead, and the impurities. This was taken off the top of the lead bath and kept separate. The lead was put into castings in the form of cakes, ten inches in diameter, weighing seventy-five pounds. Six of these lead cakes were put near one another on edge, on two closely spaced declining iron plates. Charcoal was put between and around the cakes and fired, but caution was taken to protect them from air drafts. As the cakes began to melt and sink, the lead ran from the furnace into a basin and from there was cast into oblong planchas. The resultant lead was free from copper and yielded, according to Brunckow, about forty pounds of silver to the ton.

Each cake that was put upon the declining plates left a "skeleton" rich in copper and some silver. To separate the silver, the skeleton was broken into fragments and placed in the furnace along with the crusts taken from the top of the lead bath. More lead was added. The lead that resulted was cast in the form of cakes that were again placed on the declining plates, and the process was repeated. The remaining skeletons (containing little silver) were smelted in a reverberatory furnace (also referred to as a Castilian furnace), refined, formed into copper balls, and used in the barrel amalgamation process. The argentiferous lead was put into a cupella furnace, and after oxidizing, the remaining silver was refined. The oxide of lead was added to the lead and silver ore and again put through the blast furnace. The process consumed enormous quantities of fuel.[70]

Although all the methods described by the engineers were not in use when Heintzelman was in charge at Cerro Colorado, the processes that were being planned and the equipment that was being built demonstrate how German, Welsh, and Spanish techniques were adapted to the American Southwest. Prior to the investment of great sums of money, the purchase of large-scale equipment, and the stabilization of the frontier, the Sonora Exploring and Mining Company tried to be innovative and resourceful.

Yet, although improved techniques for reducing the ores were introduced, especially after the arrival of more machinery in 1859, the financial problems of the company were not solved. Thomas Wrightson had sold $2,500 worth of stock (at 50 percent) in the Sonora Exploring and Mining Company, and the same amount in the Santa Rita Silver Mining Company (at $20 per share). The directors deposited $2,500 with

William T. Coleman and Company, shipping merchants. Heintzelman made another arrangement with Colt, through Jarvis, for the sale of $1,500 worth of stock at $40 per share. These transactions, although helpful, did not substantially reduce the company's debts. By December 1858, with debts amounting to $6,292.91, the Cincinnati executive committee sold Colt 500 shares of stock at 25 percent with a twelve-month privilege of buying 500 more. Again Colt saved the company from bankruptcy. Heintzelman disapproved of the agreement, but he lacked the financial resources and the ability to challenge Colt and control the company.

Part II

The Journal

Editor's Note

Samuel Peter Heintzelman's journey to Cerro Colorado, Doña Ana County, Territory of New Mexico, began in Cincinnati, Ohio, on the evening of June 1, 1858, when he bade farewell to his family and friends and boarded the train for Buffalo, New York. After visiting briefly with his wife's relatives he took the train, via Albany to New York City, arriving in the afternoon of June 3. He stayed at the Astor House and visited with business associates until Saturday, June 5. Having paid $300 for a ticket, he boarded a steamer and set sail for the Isthmus of Panama, arriving at Aspinwall on Sunday morning, June 13. After an overland journey to Panama City he boarded another steamer for an agreeable fifteen-day voyage to San Francisco on which he traveled first-class, played chess, studied Spanish, and enjoyed the food. Arriving in San Francisco on Monday evening, June 28, Heintzelman met with his mining and military colleagues. On July 2 he wrote his required monthly report to inform the adjutant general's office of his address and began what would become a monthly report to Thomas Wrightson, the editor of the *Railroad Record*, in which he described the business activities of the Sonora Exploring and Mining Company. On Saturday morning, July 3, Heintzelman and his brother-in-law, Solon Lathrop, boarded the steamer *Senator* and four days later docked in San Diego. Lathrop, a former newspaper publisher, had been elected treasurer of the Sonora Exploring and Mining Company earlier that year. After Heintzelman returned from Arizona in 1859, Lathrop became the superintendent of the company's operations.[1] Heintzelman visited with friends whom he had not seen in four years and arranged to have goods and machinery shipped to the mines. Although he thought the location and surroundings of San Diego were pleasant, he complained about its citizens: "What a town of loafers this is and drunkards." He wrote that the son of a fellow officer was breaking in a wild horse, "riding him about the streets and through the Plaza." It was not until the evening of July 22 that Heintzelman and Lathrop were able to leave San Diego and begin their mule-team wagon trip across the California desert. Their departure for the junction of the Gila and Colorado Rivers was delayed because their driver had been fined $25 in cash for flogging another man.

August
1858

Steamer Colorado, Colorado city Tuesday Aug. 3, 1858
Yesterday we arrived here and are pleasantly located on board this steamer.* We met Capt. Johnson at Pilot Knob on his way in to S. Diego and he pressed us to go on board and stay. We yesterday morning reached Jaegers and took breakfast, then crossed and came up here.[1]

Considering all things we had a good crossing of the desert. At Carrizo† there is an adobe house with hay and barley. We found it more pleasant than lying in the sun all day. The road we found very tiresome. To Indian Wells is tolerably fair. We did not get there until 3 a.m. and found but little water and no mesquite.‡ We did not stay long but drove to the Little Laguna and there stopped a few hours and got mesquite. We reached the Alamo Mucho about 11 P.M. where we found plenty of water. 3 miles from there we found a man located digging wells. He has not succeeded. We bought some barley from him at 25 cts per pound. At Carrizo we paid 12½ cts per pound for hay.

---

*The *Colorado,* owned and operated by George A. Johnson.
†Carrizo Creek; consult the map for the locations of the numerous water holes, stage stations, forts, and other places mentioned in the journal.
‡The pods from mesquite trees provided food for livestock and could be used for fuel and for the preparation of liquor.

We met Mr. Breed the Director of the San Xavier mines* on his way in sick and all his men—left sick at the mines. He gave us much valuable information of our mines.[2]

We left at 6 P.M. for Cooke's Wells and had quite a pleasant ride, with a cool breeze and not hot in temperature. In fact I never found it so pleasant at Alamo Mucho. We reached Cooke's Wells at about 3 a.m. and found but five pails of Water for our five mules. More persons soon came and at 12 n. we concluded to leave for the river. The day was the warmest we have had and the ride very hot. About half way Mr. Lathrop got dizzy although he carried an umbrella and got in the wagon. I rode the mule over to the river. I found it hot but did not suffer any. We had but little water left in our keg and supplied some travellers who had none. Our ten gallon keg was nearly empty at Alamo and we put in a pail full of water there.

We met the mail† at Pilot Knob and missed the opportunity to write. Jaeger gave us a nice breakfast yesterday and had a room for me, but I knew it would be more comfortable here, besides we could have our axle overhauled. A blacksmith we met at Cooke's Wells, on his way to look for a new location volunteered to do it for us. It is now done.

At Pilot Knob I met Dr. Hammond. I crossed the river with him and several others to a cattle Ranch, owned by Mr. Cotlett‡ to dinner I supposed, but it was only to drink, so that I did not have much to eat that day.[3]

---

*The San Xavier Silver Mining Company was organized in San Francisco in 1857, but by 1858 little work had been done at the mine near the mission.
†"The Jackass Mail," or San Antonio and San Diego Mail Line, operated in the region from August 1857 until 1859.
‡George Hammond was the assistant surgeon at Fort Yuma. "Mr. Cotlett" was probably C. Cotlett, who signed a petition recommending the appointment of Lanford W. Hastings to the Supreme Court for the Western District of the proposed territory.

Last evening Lt. Hamilton* and D. M. Stuart called on us. Near 106 yesterday. This has been a cool summer. I looked at Jaegers register for June and it is the coolest month I have seen here—for June.[4]

I went with Mr. Lathrop over to the Post. We called on Col. Nauman† in my old quarters. They are finished, but I doubt whether more comfortable. We saw Lt. Hamilton, his wife and child a girl two months old, born here. She is not pretty. We also called and saw Capt. Stuart and his wife. I thought it the one he had at Snelling Dr. Summers‡ spoke of, but it is a second wife. They look comfortable and as if the climate did not hurt them. The quarters are fine but rather scantily furnished. I visited the mens quarters. They are large and airy. Many things are just as when I left. Mer. was only about 84° when we went over but it is now 108½° with however a fine breeze.[5]

I wrote my reports (monthly today and a letter to Margaret). We will probably start tomorrow afternoon.

Last Camp on Gila river before taking the Great Desert to Tucson Thurs. Aug. 12. 1858.

We found it would be better to start in the morning so delayed until Thurs. Aug. 5. We left at 5½ a.m. Yesterday Lt. Hamilton and his wife spent the day on the Steamer with their infant—a girl. From the way they went on you would have supposed that it was the first child. We had a little dust storm in the afternoon, before they left. I added postscripts to my letters and closed them. Several persons called in the evening.

---

*John Hamilton (1823–1900), a West Pointer.
†George Nauman (1803–1863), a West Point graduate and commander of Fort Yuma.
‡Possibly John E. Summers, who was commissioned a first lieutenant, assistant surgeon in the army of 1847.

Our Sonoran backed out and the Blksmith, but Mr. Elder*
the Engineer is with us. We let him join our mess.[6]

We had a hot ride and in fact we may say all the way. We
start on the Great desert of 80 miles with water about half
way, this afternoon. It is now raining a little and I fear will
rain hard. We have got along pretty well as far as our team is
concerned. We have come 190 miles and without accident will
be in Tucson Sat. morning. We were passed whilst in camp
by the first emigrant wagon, whilst in camp this side Oatman
flat. We saw the hill where he and his family were murdered
and saw their grave below. Several persons have opened settlements at various points on the Gila and soon will be able to
obtain forage etc. at them. We got corn and melons at the
Maricopa wells this side the little desert of 40 miles and here.
The melons are quite poor. Taste of pumpkins.

We met a Mr. Eddy,† or rather he got in our camp last
night. He is from Tubac and gave us a little information about
our mines. Mr. Poston will probably meet us at Tucson. Jaegers wagons must have reached Tubac, only yesterday.

We have kept a guard at nights the last three.

What a miserable country, this is we have travelled
through. To the right of the road nothing but barren mountains and desert plains. In most places the road is what we
must call very bad and it is quite crooked, to reach the Gila for
water. The overland wagon road party has improved the road
very much at many places by cutting out trees and bushes, of
Mesquite, cutting down slopes, and picking out the stones on
the mesas.

It is commencing to rain pretty hard and I must put up my

---

*Anthony Elder, who worked for Johnson's steamboat company before
moving to Tucson in 1858.
†Possibly John F. Eddy, an officer of the Arizona Land and Mining
Company and one of the incorporators of the Sopori Land and Mining
Company.

writing materials and prepare for it. One side of our wagon is closed now.

Tucson Gad. Pur. Sat. Aug. 14. 1858
["Sat. Aug. 15" crossed out].

We left our last camp on the Gila at 2¼ on Thursday and arrived here before breakfast this morning. We had not gone far before it commenced to rain hard, but it did not continue long. We prepared ourselves and did not get wet. It cooled the air very much and made the drive much more pleasant. We rode 30 miles and stopped at 9 P.M. till day light. We had with us a keg of water and gave the mules some. At day light we started and drove 10 miles to the Picacho, about half way stopped with plenty of water and grass. We left again at 2 P.M. 14th and stopped at 10 P.M. 6 miles from here. It was so dark and our driver so evidently at fault I did not dare to go further. We intended to drive in last night. This morning I started all at day light and we drove through town and a couple of miles further and are encamped on running water. The 80 mile desert is the least of a desert of the same distance this side Yuma. On more than half of it there is plenty of grass and water at several places. At the Picacho, half way it is said water never fails.

We met a man as we drove into town and learned that Mr. Poston is not here, so drove out and encamped. As we got breakfast we learned that the Eastern mail is in and we were preparing to go to town, when our driver insisted that he must go. I told him someone must stay in camp and it soon came I discharged him. We had concluded to do so before we arrived here, but would have kept him until Mr. Poston arrived, or the mails were all in. If the other mail gets in today we will leave tomorrow. Mr. Lathrop rode to town to write and I have stayed here to take care of our camp and write to Margaret. I hope to get a letter when Mr. L. returns. We consider it a good riddance to be clear of our driver. He is about as worthless a fellow as I ever employed and considers himself much of a gentleman. We will probably drive the team from here ourselves. We can easily do it. The town is small and dilapidated Adobe. They appear to have considerable ground under cultivation.

Mr. Lathrop has returned with letters. One from Margaret dated 24 June and another from Wrightson 9 July. I have added a long postscript to M. written to W. and to Sister Maria. Poston wont be in. Have several long letters from Conkling.

Tucson Monday Aug. 16. 1858 [*"Tubac" incorrectly recorded*].

I walked to town Sat. with Mr. Elder and saw Mr. McKibbin, brother of a member of Congress from Texas and Col. Walker Ind. Agent.* What a dilapidated place. There are but few houses and a miserable church.[7]

Yesterday Mr. Lathrop and I rode to town and saw Col. Walker, the Post Master Aldrich† etc. The latter took us to his vineyard and gave us as many grapes as we could eat. He has a patch of about three acres in grapes and fruit trees. It is not half cultivated and all the other fruit was killed by the frost. Mr. Elder went to town when we returned and has got employment from the great overland mail compy‡ and has left us. We have now our mules to take care of ourselves. I am in favour of hiring someone to do it. It is a business I do not

---

*The congressman was Joseph Chambers McKibbin (1824–1896), who served in the 35th Congress as a Democrat from Downieville, California. John Walker (1800–1873) was appointed by President Buchanan as Indian agent for the short-lived Tucson agency that included the Pima, Maricopa, and Papago Indians.

†Mark Aldrich (1801–1873), a Tucson merchant who later held a variety of local and territorial political offices.

‡John Butterfield's Overland Mail Company, which operated in the region from September 1858 to April 1861. See the map for its route from Tipton to San Francisco.

fancy. We can leave here in the afternoon and be at Tubac the next morning. Col. Walker says he will go with us. The duty of keeping guard over our mules all night is rather unpleasant when reduced down to two persons to do it.[8]

We had a heavy rain Sat. afternoon and a little yesterday. It is said to rain now nearly every afternoon. The grass looks luxuriant and does not appear to be that salt grass the Dragoons* met with.[9]

I am getting tired waiting for the Western mail and want to go this afternoon. Mr. Lathrop has gone to town to see.

Tubac. G. Pur. Tues. Aug. 17. 1858.

We left Monday afternoon at 6 O'Clock [inserted: "and got here at 1¼ P.M."]. We hired a man to drive us, but he backed out. We then were aided by Col. Walkers's interpreter Mr. Carson's† coming out. We soon got the mules in and started. I changed with the Col. and rode his horse and Mr. Lathrop drove. The road was fine and we reached the Punta del Agua at 9½—3 miles beyond San Xavier where we stopped the night. Here is where the furnaces of the San Xavier mining co. were erected. I saw a pile of adobes, the only trace left of them, and one man in charge—all the rest sick and gone.[10]

The road to here was very good. Near the Punta del Agua we passed a beautiful grove of the largest Mesquite I ever saw. I rode the horse of Col. Walker about 10 miles and the balance of the way in the wagon.

The distance yesterday was 9 m. to San Xavier, where is a large church‡ and 3 m. to Punta etc. to here 35 m. We reached

---

*In November 1856, Major Enoch Steen arrived at Tucson with four companies of the First Regiment of U.S. Dragoons. Unable to find suitable quarters and complaining of the grass, he moved the troops south.

†Moses Bradley Carson, described by Phocion Way as a "large, full chested, robust and stout looking man."

‡La Paloma Blanca del Desierto, the White Dove of the Desert, on the Papago Indian Reservation nine miles south of Tucson.

here, the end of our journey at 1¼ PM, a pretty good ride. We had a view of the Sta Rita, Mts, Cerro Colorado peak, the road to Sopori etc.[11]

We found Mr. Poston ready to receive us. The mail soon after got in and I got a letter from Margaret dated 2 July, with several others.

Tubac. Sat. Aug. 21. 1858.

We got an early breakfast and Mr. Poston, Lathrop and I started in a four mule wagon for Cerro Colorado, Wednesday morning. The distance is about 22 miles. A little over half way is Sopori. The road is fine and country beautiful. We stopped there and were introduced to Col. Douglass* the proprietor of the Ranch and mine and treated to water melons. They have a fine patch, with corn and sorghum, or Chinese sugar cane. The road from there is still good but not equal to this side. We there saw the first walnut trees. They are quite stunted, but sufficient for ordinary kinds of furniture. The mine we did not visit. It is a mile or two from the house. I understand Mr. Sayles† the agent of the Sopori Land & mining co. exhibited his papers, but that they did not make much impression on Douglass. He is in possession. I understand he has not given any power of attorney to any one to dispose of his mine. I dont know how Lt. Mowry will settle the matter.[12]

The Cerro Colorado District is a beautiful place. The country is rolling and covered with grass. We went and visited the mine. The diggings extend near 1.000 feet. and average 25 ft. in depth. The main shaft is 50 ft. deep and has to go to 60

---

*James Douglass (c. 1800–1859), owner of the Sopori Ranch, which he built about 1856, and an owner of the Sopori Land and Mining Company.
†Welcome B. Sayles (1813–1862), a confidential agent for the Post Office Department and also an agent for Sylvester Mowry's Sopori Land and Mining Company. The dispute between Douglass and Sayles was apparently one of the many challenges to the company's titles.

when a drift will be made to strike the vein, supposed to be 20 to 25 feet off. The rock is hard and the shaft sinks 1½ to 2 ft. a week. The ore is not so rich as at first. They have opened a new shaft across the ravine promises well. I visited the next day a number of prospecting shafts. Few have been carried sufficiently deep to decide their richness.

The furnace was put in blast and stopped just before we left. They run out 15 planchas* of lead and silver and were weighing them when we left. There is up a Mexican furnace will be put in blast next week. There are a number of buildings and some very good ones. A great deal of work has been done when the limited means are considered. The prospecting shafts, some to the depth of 30 feet involved no small labour. There are from 100 to 150 tons of ore on the surface. But little of this is however fit for smelting. Its character has changed. Yesterday we rode to Arabac† 8 miles and then 1½ to Los Alamos.‡ It is a beautiful valley. We found but few men employed at Arabac and the walls of the Amalgamation works but 4 feet high. With the means at command it will take a month to be ready for the machinery, although Mr. Poston wrote me long ago that they would be ready. We next drove to Los Alamos, where Mr. Schuchard is in charge. He is busied in getting out lead ore from the Arenia, or as it is now called the Providencia mine.§ The great difficulty is to supply our furnaces with lead ore. He has cut a tunnel some 40 feet long and intersected an old shaft.

He has also commenced a shaft further on, on the vein. He hopes soon to have sufficient ore to supply all the furnaces. He has a furnace with a Mexican bellows constructed on the

*Oblong castings of metal poured from the smelting furnace.
†Arivaca, also referred to as Aravaca, site of a former Pima Indian village on Aravaipa Creek, between the San Luis and Las Guijas Mountains.
‡A mine.
§Also referred to as Aranea or Arenias Mine, about one-half mile north of Arivaca.

place. It worked well and they got out the first trial 20 pounds of silver. The furnace now stands idle for the want of lead ore, as all is sent to the mine.* When I look at this furnace I dont see why it was not built a year ago or at least 6 mos. ago. The leather of the bellows, the principal material did not cost $10. Had it been done it would have saved us much embarrassment.

We have now from this furnace 20 lbs. the first smelting at Cerro Col. 14 lbs, the second 40 lbs and the last not known — in all 74 pounds of silver and all in one or two weeks, worth some $1,500. The production of the last few days of this week will be about $350. It will be readily seen that if these three furnaces were pushed vigorously we would soon more than pay expenses.

We had a little rain as we drove back. We stopped a moment at Aravaca and the Spaniard in charge treated us to some of the finest grapes I ever tasted, he just received from Tubutama or Altar. The houses at Arabac are more the old buildings repaired. At Los Alamos they have a few poor houses. At Cerro Colorado they are very good. What we want now is more laborers and miners. We have decided to try and buy the boiler and engine at the Colorado, that are in Lt. Ives's boat the Explorer and sold to the Steamboat co. for $1,000.† It will be economy if we can get them at a reasonable price. [13]

After breakfast the furnace went out of blast‡ and we soon started for Tubac. We stopped at the Sopori and got some melons. As we left it commenced raining and we had a succession of heavy showers. The rain did not extend to here.

---

*The Heintzelman Mine.
†Lieutenant Joseph Christmas Ives (1828–1868) commanded an expedition that explored the Colorado River in 1857 and 1858. An iron steamer, the *Explorer*, was built to specifications in Philadelphia and shipped in sections to the junction. It was reported that the steamer was sold at auction in July 1858 to Captain Johnson for $1,000.
‡ That is, the fire died.

Tubac Sun. Aug. 22. 1858.

The nights are delightful. We do not require any cover, only perhaps towards morning. I had the luxury of a bath last night in the Acequia,* where the water is not six inches deep, but still it was a luxury in this country where water is so scarce. I understand there is a bathing place where the water is breast deep.

I have been busy at little odds and ends neglected on our long journey. I also showed Poston the correspondence with Dunbar and set him right on that subject. Dunbars letters had put him all astray.† Poston talks the most discouragingly one moment and the most encouragingly the next. I do not see where the means will come from to put the Amalgamation works into operation, but will trust to his resources. If the ore was smelting as we were led to believe and the lead ore as abundant we could run three furnaces day and night and even put up more and soon make ample means. But unfortunately the character and quality of the ore have changed and it is even doubtful whether we can process lead ore sufficient to run one. I have commenced on our correspondence and wrote a letter to Ehrenberg. His letter is dated 5 June and directed to me at Washington. Had I received it there I would have been saved much trouble and have had sufficient means to put the machinery in operation at once. [14]

Mon. Aug. 23. 1858.

We this morning went with Mr. Poston over his accounts and I approved them. We have also arranged with some Sonorans some financial matters. We have besides the salaries due some $10,000 of debts pressing on us. This has disposed of near $3,000 and we have cancelled $1,000 more. I

---

*A canal or irrigation ditch.

†Edward Ely Dunbar, organizer of the Arizona Mining and Trading Company and owner of a number of trading posts. The correspondence mentioned has not been located.

Tubac G.P. Ter. Aug. 24. 1858.

I yesterday wrote to Mr. Oliver & this morning to Col. Scott. We are busy preparing for the mail & Mr. Poston is evidently turning over the business to Mr. Lathrop, expecting him to relieve him. I think it is decidedly the best we can do. Mr. Poston has done very well in many things, but is not the man to manage this business now — after it has assumed this shape. He has that Southern & Kentucky shiftless way of doing business. I would in 48 hours here change the arrangements & add to the comfort of every one here, & without adding to the expense.

Be prepared this morning to go to Arivaca & remain there till the Amalgamation works are in operation & then to go to Tubutama to see a rich Mexican there & get laborers. The only now is the want of laborers, where some time ago any number could be obtained, that they were flocking in to these rich mines. We can go, as I know we can conduct the business here. The only trouble we will have will be to deal with Lathrop when his train arrives.

Mrs. Wray from the Sta. Rita is here. He is very much pleased with their location.

I have been all the morning, or forenoon making up my accounts for expenses. To the time we left S. Francisco they amounted to $422.00. I started with $1,025. & drew three months pay bring it up to $1,718.60. $655.10 of this I still hold in my hands but expect to disburse for the company.

A Mex. woman at Sopie was last night bit by some reptile on the foot supposed to be a tarantula. They sent here for medicine & Mr. Lathrop sent ammonia, Chloroform & Brandy. It relieved her at once.

236

have to pay out some of my private funds. Mr. Poston has made a protest against the payment of Conkling his stock, but he is too late, as he has already received it and sold some, besides he has paid what he agreed to, if not in the time. I enclosed the Protest to W. Wrightson Sec.

Tubac G.P. Tues. Aug. 24, 1858.

I yesterday wrote to Mr. Cheever* and this morning to Col. Colt. We are busy preparing for the mail and Mr. Poston is evidently turning over the business to Mr. Lathrop, expecting him to relieve him. I think it is decidedly the best we can do. Mr. Poston has done very well in many things, but is not the man to manage this business now after it has assumed this shape. He has that Southern or Kentucky slovenliness of doing business. I would in 48 hours here change the arrangements and add to the comfort of every one here, and without adding to the expenses. [15]

He proposed this morning to go to Arivaca and remain there till the Amalgamation works are in operation and also to go to Tubutama to see a rich Mexican there and get laborers. The cry now is the want of laborers, when some time ago any number could be obtained, that they were flocking in to these rich mines. He can go, as I know we can conduct the business here. The only trouble we will have will be to deal with Conklin,† when his train arrives. [16]

Mr. Way‡ from the Sta Rita is here. He is very much pleased with their location.

---

*Benjamin Harrison Cheever, a director of the Sonora Exploring and Mining Company, the Sopori Land and Mining Company, and the Arizona Land and Mining Company, who kept Heintzelman informed about Sylvester Mowry's dealings.

†William Conklin, a San Diego freighter, who was contracted to haul machinery and goods to the Cerro Colorado Mine and ores from Tubac to the Colorado River. There was some disagreement over how much he should be paid for his services.

‡Phocion Way.

I have been all the morning, or forenoon making up my accounts for expenses. To the time we left S. Francisco they amounted to $422.05. I started with $1,025. and drew three months pay bring it up to $1.718.60 — $655.10 of that I still hold in my hands but expect to disburse for the company.

A Mex. woman at Sopori was last night bit by some reptile on the foot supposed to be a tarantula. They sent here for medicine and Mr. Lathrop sent ammonia, Chloroform and Brandy. It relieved her at once.

Tubac Wed. Aug. 25. 1858.

I got a table to-day and it is a great convenience to me for writing. I have continued my letter to Margaret and am near the bottom of the twelfth page. I also wrote to Dr. Summers at Ft. Kearny.

Mr. Poston is throwing the business all into Mr. Lathrop's hands. He has been writing letters in every direction preparing for the mail. Col. Walker returned from Ft. Buchanan. Major Fitizgerald has gone to the States and Capt. Ewell* is out on a scout. [17] We have a visit from Col. Douglass. I tried to learn from him something about the Sopori mining co. and Mr. Sayles, but cant learn any thing definite. There was evidently more done here when Sayles was here than Poston led me to believe. I have learned to distrust some of his statements. They are sometimes colored.

Tubac Thurs. Aug. 26. 1858.

We were quite overrun last night with persons going to Tucson to the Fiesta. It is the Saint day of St. Augustine the patron saint of Tucson and commences Saturday. Americans and Mexicans are flocking there.

---

*Edward H. Fitzgerald, who served in the West throughout the 1850s; Richard Stoddert Ewell (1817–1872), stationed at Fort Buchanan as captain, Company G, First Dragoons, and for a while an owner of the Patagonia Mine.

I wrote my report to Cincinnati and a letter to Dr. Tripler and to Mr. Conkling. We leave in the morning for Tucson and will have a stage full—a sick Mexican woman and a sick Mexican of the party. One of the Ainsa's is here sick and has been with us some time. He has a brother in jail in Sonora, suspected of being engaged with the filibusters.* They are brother in laws of Crabb. [18] It has been rather warmer to-day, but is cool again and raining in the distance. A man is in from Cerro Colorado and brought in the silver that has been refined amounting to 59 marks.† This is from about half the planchas—there is so much copper in them it is more difficult to separate than was supposed. Mr. Poston picked up a very pretty little piece weighing about half a pound saying it was the first yield and presented it to me. It is not by any means the first, as he handed Prof. Pierce‡ a fine specimen and also sent one to Kentucky to a friend. [19]

Below is an account of the smelting taken from the books.

From Los Alamos
    July 1st 1858— 5 marks   0 oz silver $ 40.00

From Los Alamos
    July 13 1858—19 marks   0 oz silver   152.00

From Cerro Colorado
    July 31 1858—27 marks   2 oz silver   218.00

From Los Alamos
    Aug. 20 1858—<u>39 marks</u>   <u>4 oz silver</u>   <u>316.00</u>
                90 marks   6 oz silver $726.00

From Cerro Colorado
    Aug. 26 1858—59 marks   6 oz silver   <u>472.00</u>
                                        $1,198.
             add estimated yield not refined—   <u>472</u>
                                          $1,670

---

*Augustin and Jesus M. Ainsa.

†From the Spanish *marco,* a unit of weight for gold or silver equal to about eight ounces.

‡A marine engineer and geologist who accompanied W. B. Sayles to Arizona. He was an employee of the Lopez Land and Mining Company.

This is not much of a yield for near two months, but then it is a commencement and in that lies all the difficulty. It must now be our business to increase this yield. I added postscripts to most of my letters.

Tucson Sat . Aug. 28. 1858

Left about sunrise [inserted: "yesterday"] for this place, in our old carriage, with six persons, having put in a new seat, one half sick—Col. Walker, Mr. Ainsa and a Mexican woman. We reached "Punta del Agua" at 11 and stayed till 3, and took a little girl, daughter of Mrs. Ortiz the widow of the man from whom we bought Arivaca. It made our wagon a complete hospital. The wagon (express) that brought Küstel and his family out was filled up with four mules and brought out four more, one a Mex. woman. Besides we had in our party six horsemen, making quite a formidable show. At Punta del Agua we met Capt. Ewell of the Drgs encamped. We had a lunch and some melons and whiskey and he joined us with some Ale and we had quite a lunch. The day was warm.

The evening we had an abundance of ringing of bells and firing of cannon, with beating of drums and hideous singing. We got a place to sleep on the mud floor in a building temporarily occupied by the O.L. mail co. The room is two with an archway and has been used for a ballroom. It is dusty enough. We made out to sleep, but not so comfortable as it would have been on the desert, or out of doors. It was in the first place very warm and had the new smell of a house just built and kept shut up. We do pretty well for eating. We have our meals at Phillips's Hotel, the Astor House of the place. The tea and Mex. sugar, without milk, last night were horrible, but the "chicken fixins" redeemed them. Our coffee this morning was bad but we had milk—with fried mutton we did pretty well.

I went this morning to see an anvil, made of the meteoric

stone found in the mountains in sight of this place and close to the road to Tubac. It is described and figured in Bartletts book.* I took some dimensions. It is 9 in to a foot thick of an irregular shape, 4 feet long and 4 feet high, allowing as they say one half to be in the ground. There is a circular hole leaving it only 3 or 4 in. thick below, as it stands and six or eight above and more on one side. On one side where it has been hammered and rubbed it looks like copper and above on the edge whitish like soft and malleable. It is sufficiently hard to answer for an anvil, without [torn, illegible] much. The general appearance of it is like dull silver or pewter. It has the appearance of having been moderately soft like clay kneaded in the hand and dropped on the stones. [20]

Mr. Ainsa was quite exhausted when we arrived last night but this morning is quite smart again. About midnight the widow Ortiz came to our room with her hat on ready for the journey and enquired of Mr. Poston for medicines. One of her *parientes*† at Tubac is sick and she is on her way back, although she arrived here only a few minutes before us.

The great fiesta commences today, of St. Augustine the patron Saint of Tucson. The mail is expected to-day from the East. We yesterday met on the road what the Mexicans call an Escopion or spittex.‡ They have wonderful tales of its poison. This specimen was about 18 inches long, with legs and tail resembling a lizard but the ugliest reptile I ever saw. It is covered with what appears to be bead work, in yellow and black figures. I killed it, put a noose around its neck and brought it in.

---

*The meteorite that both John Bartlett and Heintzelman saw is referred to as the "signet" or "Irwin-Ainsa Iron," a rare, ring-shaped meteorite weighing about 1,400 pounds with an external diameter of 49 inches. It is now in the Smithsonian Institution.
†Relatives.
‡A Gila monster (*Heloderma suspectum*), one of the two venomous lizards found in the southwestern United States and Mexico.

The great Fiesta is coming off. I suppose there are two or three hundred people about and they are dancing under a bower in front of Warner and Aldrich's store to a bass and small drum and a violin or two. All sorts of people are found there, except white women. There is not one. There are one or two good looking women, but generally the women are quite ordinary. The male part of the dancing is generally monopolized by the Americans. I found our old driver on the ground floor with his revolver and butcher knife under his coat. By the by he is now engaged in butchering. Most of the other gentlemen were in their shirt sleeves. As to the women, all made pretensions to dress in their best. Amongst married women, who had the reputation of being virtuous, were the mistresses of gamblers and murderers and women whose reputation was still worse. This morning an American named Stevens was admitted into the mother church to marry the daughter of a woman who is the mistress of a notorious gambler.* The church† is a small affair. Over the door is a bell and near by two others, one from its primitive appearance cast here, the other inscribed to our lady of Guadalupe‡ dated 1807.[21]

The town is much larger than at first sight appears and I am told contains 600 inhabitants. I doubt whether it contains the half.

I was introduced to an eccentric individual, of the Ky Marshalls, who has been a soldier and announces himself a

---

*Hiram Sanford Stevens (1832–1893), a Tucson merchant and cattle rancher, married Petra Santa Cruz (c. 1841–1916). Stevens later held a variety of political offices and served four years in the U.S. Congress.

†San Augustín del Tucson, probably at the east of Plaza de las Armas.

‡Our Lady of Guadalupe came to be regarded as a symbol of divine care for the Indians of Mexico. According to tradition, the Blessed Virgin Mary appeared before an Indian peasant on a hill outside Mexico City and instructed him to ask the bishop to build a church on the site. By the eighteenth century, the Most Holy Mary of Guadalupe had been chosen as the patroness of many Mexican cities.

candidate for Delegate.* If sustained by the proper persons he will be a formidable opponent to Lt. Mowry.[22] We had a little rain this afternoon cooled the air much. It was quite hot before. It stopped the dancing only a few minutes.

Tucson Sun. Aug. 29. 1858.

The dancing went on last night and we went early to bed. I have no idea when it stopped.

This morning the priest† did a wholesale business in the way of marriages. Most of them had been married before by Brevoort.‡ Out of eleven there were only two couples about whom any doubts were expressed and one was an American. One of the men had some negro in his veins. The women as a lot were about as ugly and unattractive, as I ever saw as brides. After the ceremony the Priest gave an address. I was surprised I understood as much as I did. The music escorted some home.[23]

The dancing commenced again and is at this moment interrupted by a little rain. I saw a very pretty dance and an amusing one. Stockings are not fashionable with the belles.

It is now after 3 P.M. and no mail. We are all very tired.

Last evening about an hour by sun the grand procession came off. St. Augustine in wood was carried on a platform, surrounded by a motley crowd, with music and singing and firing of guns. They took a short circuit, stopping several times to make a flourish.

Tucson Monday Aug. 30. 1858.

We had a little rain in the afternoon and cooler at night. Mr.

---

*Justus I. McCarty, also referred to as Major General Jeemis Ignatius McCarty, James McCarty, McCartney. He lost the election to Sylvester Mowry.

†Father J. M. Pinero.

‡Elias Brevoort, the sutler for Fort Buchanan and owner of the Patagonia Mine and the Reventon Ranch.

Lathrop was sick again from the cookery here I suppose. This morning it is getting warm. No mail now—after 10. O Clock. We propose leaving afternoon whether the mail gets in or not. I will close my letters ready for the P. office.

The music is still beating, but not much dancing.

Tubac Tues. Aug. 31. 1858.

We left Tucson at 3 P.M. yesterday and arrived here this morning between 7 and 8. We stopped last night about 9 O'Clock. We had a heavy rain and thunder storm and it became so dark that we had to lay by and stopped on the plain about 5 miles from the Canoa, until about 3 this morning, when although cloudy the moon gave sufficient light to see the road. The other wagon stopped before they reached the rain an hour or so and passed us whilst we lay by. We overtook them again before we got in. They had more of a load and not so good a team.

Soon after 10 yesterday I was entering the Plaza near where the dancing was when I saw two men rush out of a grog shop close by with their pistols in hand. Van Alstine was following Cotten.* When near the middle of the street Cotten nearly halted and looked back over his left shoulder and at the same time appeared to be raising his pistol, then lowered it. As he was raising it the other man fired and I supposed missed, but he shot Cotten through the back, the ball making its exit near the left nipple. Cotten then ran on and Van Alstine turned back. I afterwards saw Cottens pistol and the ball after passing through him, must have struck the upper cap and recess where the cock strikes. He says he did not map the pistol, but he must have had it cocked. Van A. says he did not shoot the man in the back and that Cotten had his pistol drawn on him.

---

*Nelson Van Alstine (c. 1815–1898) owned a ranch in the Santa Cruz Valley about two miles north of Tubac, where he served as constable. Cotten's identity is uncertain.

Cotten's pistol was not pointed at him whilst I saw them.
Cotten ran near 100 yards and took refuge in a Mexican woman's house. When we left he was in a very critical situation
and the general opinion was that he cant live. He was drunk
at the time and had been quite abusive to several persons. He
was a moment before quite abusive to this man for which he
struck him, when C. drew his pistol. The other rushed at him
drawing his own, when the affray took place as I have
described.

Another cause of the difficulty was that V. A. the evening
before (he lives here at Tubac) left with his Mex. wife and her
sister a young girl. That night a Mex. from Sonora ran away
with her and slept with her. V. A. found it out and wanted
to make this man live with her, or he would kill him. How it
was settled I dont know. This man Cotten rather took the
Mexicans part.[24]

It rained very hard here and it ran into the store, in several
places. Our house stood it well.

Mr. Lathrop is still rather sick. I must give him some good
advice. There is another revolution preparing in Sonora*
and laborers are running away—we will soon have plenty of
miners here. Mr. Poston goes to-day down to Arivaca to remain there till the Amalgamation works are ready. I am in
hopes that we will have them in operation sooner than we
anticipated.

Mr. Küstel has been here, with the balance of the silver. It is

*In 1856 the Mexican government, engaged in a reform movement,
selected a successor to replace the conservative governor of Sonora,
Manuel María Gándara, but he refused to allow the appointee to rule.
The inspector of the National Guard and leader of the liberal forces,
Colonel Ignacio Pesqueira, ousted Gándara, but the fighting continued.
Pesqueira took office, but Gándara sought the aid of the clergy and the
Yaqui Indians. Pesqueira confiscated Gándara's estates and forced him
to seek refuge in the United States. Fighting continued, the French ar-
rived, and Gándara returned briefly. By 1867 Pesqueira was again serv-
ing as governor.

16½ marks. I read his letter. He says his last smelting had yielded 49 cts per pound, but in this includes the silver in the lead ore from Arenia mine. The selected ore from C. C. has only yielded 40 cts per pound. This is less than the average as there was selected ore sent away to Sonora and S. F. The ore left for Amalgamation will only yield, he thinks, 200 dollars per ton. This is quite a falling off from $1.000, as he has estimated. They are getting better ore from across the ravine and I am in hopes that with the new labor soon to arrive that we will be able to get out enough rich ore to keep our amalgamation works in operation if not our furnaces. He dont expect to resume smelting until to-day or tomorrow. I fear the yield will fall below my estimate of one fourth of his estimate or 25 cents per pound.

It is cloudy and cool and looks like rain.

When we left to go to Tucson, we had not had meat for several days. There is none here now and the beef brought to kill did not come in, last night. This is the way things go on here.

Afternoon. The people from the Fiesta drop in on their way home. Mr. Poston has left for Arivaca. It has been cloudy all day and a few drops of rain. The mail was not in at 7 P.M. when these people left. A man is in from Sta. Rita, to get spouts* for their houses. How fortunate to have such a place to go to for anything they want. They will never realize the difficulties we had.

---

*Drain pipes.

September
1858

Tubac. Sept. 1st. 1858. Wednesday.

I was in hopes last night that I would have a room to myself to sleep in, for the first time since I left San Francisco, but Mr. Lathrop is sick and chose to occupy Mr. Poston's bed and vacate his room. He has been pretty sick but is better this afternoon. He will have to be more prudent till he gets acclimated. We had a sprinkle of rain this morning, but it did not amount to much. I tried various ways to pass the time, but did not succeed well, until about the middle of the afternoon when the mail arrived. I got three letters from Margaret, dated 9, 16 and 24 July. Mary is doing quite well, but I have the sad news of the death of Dr. Triplers little son, as suddenly as little Willie Whistler's was.* It is a sad blow to both. He had particularly set his heart upon him. They took the body to Detroit.[1]

I got no letters from Cin. I got a letter from Jno. Bull.† He wishes to know about some mines to lease.[2]

---

*Charles S. Tripler, a surgeon in the U.S. Army; William Whistler, a colonel in the Fourth Infantry.
†John Bull, a New Yorker interested in investing in silver mines.

I got several orders—Major Dashiel is dismissed for not sending his accounts—Promotions to 3 July and A system of Target practice for troops.[3] Elizabeth* is no better. Matilda and her mother had not got to Newport. Lt. Hendershott had left and Lt. Mc'Lean† was there.[4] They heard from Dr. Summers‡—all well. He thinks the Mormon war ended.[5]

Tubac Sept. 2. 1858. Thurs.

A beautiful day. I sat up till near eleven reading the papers. The Mormon war is ended—another revolution in Mexico—Zuloaga expelled—a great earthquake in the city.§ 50 persons killed and damage 5 or 6 millions.[6]

We sent the mail in to Arivaca to Mr. Poston. I wrote my monthly report and wrote a note to Major Townsend.// We killed a beef to-day and have meat again. There has been none here for a week. Our fare at dinner has been Bean soup, Frijoles, Calabazas# and cucumbers with bread. Other meals pancakes, bread, and tea and coffee, without sugar and sometimes without milk—occasionally butter.[7]

It is a great nuisance here to carry on business without money. If two months were passed we might get on well.

---

*Elizabeth Stuart Lathrop, Margaret Heintzelman's sister and Solon H. Lathrop's wife.

†Henry Bascon Hendershott (1824–1906) and Nathaniel Henry McLean (1827–1884), both West Point graduates.

‡John E. Summers, who was married to Margaret Heintzelman's sister Caroline.

§The Mormon War (1857–1859) was a dispute between the Mormons and federal officials about jurisdiction over the Utah Territory.

Mexico's attempts at constitutional reform heightened the controversy between the conservatives, led by General Felix Zuloaga, and the liberals, led by Benito Juárez. By 1861 the liberal forces were victorious.

On June 19, 1858, a severe earthquake near Mexico City killed about fifty people and caused approximately $6 million in damages.

//Edward Davis Townsend (1817–1893), an assistant adjutant general on the Pacific Coast.

Frijoles are beans; calabazas are pumpkins, gourds, or squash.

Dunbar writes that Coleman & co.* proposed to put in $5.000 for S. Ex & M. co. stock at 50 per cent. If it is the case I dont see why it was not accepted. From letters they had in their possession they knew the money was wanted here.[8] There is no excuse for someone not writing this mail. Mr. Lathrop is still quite sick, though perhaps a little better. It is hard to tell as he is constantly groaning and grunting.

Our Mex. cook wanted to leave to-day. He had a quarrel afterwards with our driver or man in charge of the yard and animals. One drew a knife and the other a pistol and I had to interfere.

Mr. Poston's brother† with 10½ pounds of silver came in this evening and brought Reports and letters. The letters give a gloomy account of affairs. I am going with Mr. Fuller to-morrow to Sta Rita and Fort Buchanan to try and make arrangements with Capt. Ewell and Mr. Doss‡ to get of their lead ores to keep our furnaces in operation. Something must be done. Mr. Poston writes of going into Sonora for laborers and supplies.[9]

Tubac Tues. Sept. 7. 1858.

I left with Mr. Fuller on Friday morning for Sta. Rita 10 miles. We rode mules and got there in two hours. The road is by no means bad and without much labor can be made a wagon road, although we were told it would be very expensive. Mr. Grosvenor§ has selected a very beautiful place. His houses are comfortable and he has established system in

---

*The California and New York shipping and commission merchant company owned by William Tell Coleman (1824–1893).

†John Lee Poston (1835–1861), storekeeper at the Cerro Colorado Mine.

‡George W. Fuller, a claimant to the Salero Mine, worked at the Santa Rita Mines. Richard M. Doss (1827–1869), an early owner of the Patagonia Mine, also owned the Cross Roads Tavern at the Canoa Ranch and sold and delivered lumber.

§ Horace Chipman Grosvenor, the Cincinnati engraver who had gone to the mines earlier in the year.

everything. I soon saw all that was to be seen, but the mines and concluded as soon as we got dinner to ride on to Ft. Buchanan. We got there at dusk, 18 miles over a pretty rough trail. A few miles before we got to the Sonoita valley we saw the tracks of three Indians where they had stopped for water.

We found Capt. Ewell at home and stayed at his house. Then Dr. Irwin called and Lt. Lord.* Lt. Lord was stationed with me at Newport. The next morning before day light Capt. Ewell and I started for the Patagonia mine,† owned by him and some others. He let me have a horse to ride. It had rained hard during the night and the road was slippery. We rode fast and by 8½ A.M. were at the mine, 22 miles. Part of the road is very bad. I went down into the mine, near 50 feet deep in a bucket. The vein is near three feet wide and plenty of metal. It is a lead ore and said to contain near $100 per ton of silver. [10]

We then went to the Houses. I had a long talk trying to get them to send us some of their ore to smelt with ours and we return them the silver. I had [at?] last made an agreement with them for 9 tons, we to pay ½ cent per pound of the freight. One of the men was to see about wagons, but he has not let me know. We took a cup of coffee before we started and at this house got some bread and butter and a cup of milk. The place is high up in the mountains. We got a glimpse into the Sta Cruz valley. Here is pine timber and we got some lumber from them. We took another road with a better trail, but 24 miles long. We left at 10½ a.m. and reached the fort at 2½ P.M. It was a pretty hard ride. I stayed the next day

---

*Bernard John Dowling Irwin (1830–1917), assistant surgeon at Fort Buchanan and a partner in the Union Silver Mining Company; Richard S. C. Lord (1835–1866), who served with the First Dragoons and was an owner of the Patagonia Mine.

†The Patagonia Mine, in the mountains near the Mexican border about twenty miles south of Fort Buchanan, was owned by Captain Ewell, James Douglass, Doss, Lord, and Isaiah Moore. It was subsequently sold to Elias Brevoort, to Henry Titus, and in 1860 to Sylvester Mowry.

Sunday, because I was tired, partly to hear whether they got the wagons and because Mr. Brevoort would ride with us Monday, yesterday. I went down to the store. He has a comfortable place and a fair stock of goods.

Capt. Ewell lives rather comfortably and it is the first civilized place I have lived at since my arrival in the country. He has a slave woman for cook and sets a neat table and in a civilized manner. I also for the first time since I left S. Francisco have had a room to myself, a luxury I appreciate. The Post has only the three officers I have mentioned and is rather a straggling affair. Major Steen and Lt. Hastings* do not bear a good reputation—in fact both are a disgrace to the army. [11]

I tried to sell some stock to Capt. Ewell and have his proposition. I also have an offer from Mr. Brevoort. I have written to Mr. Poston and we will then decide. We breakfasted with Mr. Brevoort and left at 7½ A.M. We reached Sta Rita at 12½. Mr. B. rode on and we stayed to dinner. I then went with Mr. Grosvenor to see the Salero mine,† a mile and a half from the House, on the mountain side. A road is easily made to the mouth of the mine. I intended to go down into the mine, but there is too much rubbish. [12]

We left at 2 P.M. Mr. Grosvenor along, to locate a road and got in at Sundown.

I found letters from Mr. Poston and a note from T. Wrightson. His brother was in N.Y. Dont know whether he sold my stock or has done anything. The note is very unsatisfactory. The wagons left on the 15 July—this note is the 22.

I saw a man at the Fort can make the apparatus and dies to coin money in a few days. I wrote to P. about it and sent the letter by express this morning. I am in favour of accepting all these propositions. We want money badly.

---

*Enoch Steen, of the First Dragoons; David H. Hastings.
†One of the mines owned and operated by the Santa Rita Silver Mining Company.

Mr. Küstel has been here and has enlarged his furnace and is much pleased with it. He expects to get out $100 a day. We hope soon to be out of our difficulties.

It was very cold the night before last at the Fort. We had a very heavy rain. A Mex. came in and reported a trail of 30 or 40 Indians about 20 miles east of the Fort going to St. Cruz. Another party levied a contribution on one of the stations of the mail party. It is much cooler here.

Ft. Buchanan is about 5.500 feet above the sea and this 2000 ft. lower. The Agua Caliente is several springs of tepid water. The valley of the Sonoita* is not well supplied with water. Not near enough to irrigate all the land. The hills are covered with fine grass and plenty of water in many places.

I have just seen a man from the Fort. The wagons have gone for the ore and it will be here in three or four days. Mr. Lathrop has another chill and is vomiting. He makes a great to do over it. I think he will have to go to Cerro Colorado or to Sta. Rita. Mr. Grosvenor has gone home.

Tubac. Wed. Sept. 8. 1858.

The mornings are sensibly cooler. The mer. this morn. was 66°. I wrote to Mr. Cheever that Mr. Wrightson† would pay him the $500 and to return my note, the collateral and all the other stock unsold. I wrote also to Mr. Wrightson to sell enough of my stock to pay the note and write for and pay the note. I fear Cheever is a little slippery. We sent out to Cerro Colorado this morning some paper for cigarritos and pinole‡ and I wrote to Mr. Küstel about the coinage of money. I have been writing on my letter to Margaret.

Our messenger returned from Arivaca. Mr. Poston says he cant do anything but must go to Sonora for men and

---

*An early settlement site known for its agricultural resources.
†Thomas Wrightson.
‡A cereal of corn ground with sugar into a powdery substance.

supplies. He is very bitter about Conklings* not paying him the money and very unreasonable. His letters to me are a full justification to me for what I did.

Conklin arrived from Arivaca with his train. He called and we had a long discussion with him about his pay. He brought a letter from Poston detailing his contract which C. partly admits. His delay at S. Diego has been a very heavy damage to us and Poston claims it against his last contract with us at S. Diego. In a court of Law Conklin would stand no chance, as our damages are more than the worth of his train. I dont know how we will settle it. We cannot do anything without Poston. He writes he will leave tomorrow for Tubutama and Altar perhaps for labor and supplies. He has discharged all at Arivaca, as worthless. We are very much embarrassed for the want of money and I dont see how we are to get it. I do hope Wrightson† has done something in New York with the Coleman's or will bring some funds along.

Tubac. Thurs. Sept. 9. 1858.

The weather is getting decidedly cooler, but still quite pleasant. We got another note from Poston. A small order was not paid and he wants money for his expenses. He knows the company has not a cent here. I sent him a little. He can lay all our difficulties to his own letters.

Conklin takes his meals with us. He has not said a word about his contract to-day. Mr. Lathrop kept his bed to-day. It is his day for a chill and there is a prospect of his escaping it.

Our stores we left on the road have got along. Mr. Poston kept most of them and opened the champagne to celebrate the arrival of the machinery. He had better waited till it went in operation. The order he wrote about that had not been

---

*Edgar Conkling, one of the company's Cincinnati directors.
†William Wrightson, who was en route to the mines.

Tubac and the Santa Rita Mountains, where the Santa Rita Silver Mining Company had its operations. Arizona's first newspaper, the *Weekly Arizonan*, was published in Tubac.

paid was for fruit—$12. We paid one for fruit for the same place only a few days amounting to $18. It is folly to buy luxuries when we want necessaries. There is an utter want of management about such things here. No one attends to our kitchen. It is left to a Peruvian cook. When he thinks we dont want meat we do without. I answered Jno. Bull's letter about leasing silver mines.

Friday Sept. 10. 1858.

Conklin was here and we had a talk. We told him decidedly we could not settle without Poston's presence. That will be after the mail arrives and we will then probably have Wrightson here and will know better what to do.

We have been looking into matters and find our expenses throwing out salaries are a little over $2.000 a month. This is only a rough estimate, as there are no data, without great labor to arrive at them. Our furnace is expected to yield $100 a day or at 25 working days $2.500 a month. We must increase the yield or look elsewhere for resources to put up our works. Some of our men returned from the mines. The lead ore is more abundant and better quality and things are getting along pretty well. They sent in 26 marks 4 oz. of silver. Mr. Poston left yesterday morning, before my letter with the money arrived.

Tubac. Sat. Sept. 11. 1858.

Thompson* from Sonoita near Altar is here, or was with the notice of the protest of a $1.200 draft. We told him what Ehrenberg wrote and that the draft had not come back, but would be paid. If that vessel with our ore is lost† we will be in a bad situation, even with the negotiation of the sale of stock to Coleman & co. of $5.000. [13]

---

*Possibly Thomas A. Thompson.

†The schooner *Elizabeth Owens,* which was carrying ore from the Heintzelman Mine to San Francisco.

A man, german, from near Altar left this afternoon. He talked about putting up the adobes for our Amalgamation works and Mr. Poston was to see his partner.

Mr. Grosvenor and one of his men are here to get animals shod. They came by Calabazas and saw our lumber and ore on the road. Mr. Lathrop is up and much better. Mrs. Klein* is sick. We discharged our worthless cook and have had a better dinner prepared with the aid of her daughter. Wrote to Dr. Sloan† at Sta Fé. [14]

Mr. Lathrop had a fine desk made and we had it put in the room we usually sit in.

Tubac Sun. Sept. 12. 1858.

Warmer this morning. Mer 70° at 6 a.m. After breakfast we took our Concord wagon‡ and drove 3 miles to the Tumacacori Mission.§ It is on the Sta Cruz river and has plenty of water for gardens and a few acres of land. They had a pretty little church, now without roof. It is occupied by two Germans who are there by authority of the old Governor of Sonora and have been for the last six years under every disadvantage. The robberies of the Apaches have kept them poor. They have a good garden and a few grape vines. They showed us the slag of old furnaces where the Padres smelted silver ore. There are no doubt rich silver mines near at hand. They gave us some grapes. [15]

When we got home we found Mr. Brunckow and the Mexi-

---

*Mrs. Klein and her daughter were Küstel's sister and niece.

†William James Sloan, medical director of the Department of New Mexico.

‡The Concord Coach was manufactured by the Abbot-Downing Company of Concord, New Hampshire. The model owned by the mining company was specially designed for mountain travel.

§Now a U.S. national monument, in 1858 the mission was in ruins and the surrounding lands were held by Don Francisco Aquila for his brother-in-law, Manuel María Gándara.

can store keeper from Cerro Colorado here. We had a long conversation with Mr. Brunckow about our mines. A number of miners are here with our checks asking pay. I handed over $50 to pay the most pressing. There are more than $200 of them here. The vast amount $1.000.000 of ore* in sight is all out on the ground and now amounts to about 100 tons of ore and 70 tons of it will not yield over 200$ per ton. Of the ore now coming out not more than 1/20 is smelting. The shaft progresses finely and in two weeks will probably be deep enough for the commencement of the Fronton.† If Wrightson only comes this mail and his wagons this month we will do well. I go down to the C. C. mines in the morning.

At 4 P.M. our lumber and lead ore passed through town. I have finished and closed all my letters and we are making up the mail. I want to drive down to C. C. tomorrow in the Ambulance‡ and take a bellows, scales, flour and the carpenter§ to set to work on the mule power. I send off eleven letters.[16]

Tubac Monday Sept. 13, 1858.

Poston has allowed a carpenter to keep a barrel of whiskey on tap in his shop and yesterday we had an unusual amount of drunkenness. I wanted to go to C. Colorado and take the carpenter along, but he is now still too drunk to go. There is no use of my going without him. Mr. Brunckow was to start at the earliest dawn and now he will not be off until after breakfast. This will be the last of the grog shop, on our premises.

---

*This figure is unclear. If $1 million, it would be a figure of grand delusion. Heintzelman may have hoped that the 100 tons were worth $1,000 each.
†Part of the wall of the seam.
‡Another name for a version of the Concord Coach.
§John Streit, or Estreet, was head carpenter for the Sonora Exploring and Mining Company.

Some Mexicans arrived last night with Peaches, dried figs and onions. The peaches are fine looking but were pulled too early.

We got out a pair of scales. I was weighed and only weigh 132 pounds. Mr. Lathrop when he left Buffalo weighed 196 — now he has lost 40. It is 4 P.M. and the mer. 90°, though out of the sun it is pleasant.

We had last night a fire, alarmed Miss Klein. We were in bed. It was nothing but a Jacal* in rear of our quarters and soon went out.

Tubac. Sept. 16. Thurs.

I left Tuesday morning in the Ambulance with a bellows, scales etc. for Cerro Colorado. There was no room for Streit the carpenter so we left him to ride a mule. A few miles this side Sopori we overtook the wagons with the lumber and ore. They kept on and reached Cerro Colorado after night. I only stopped a moment at Sopori.

We reached C. C. between 12 and one P.M. I went around with Mr. Brunckow and saw how things got along. In the old shaft there are two tons of ore that will yield $1580 per ton and 10 tons more not yet assayed, but readily got out. Across the ravine are pockets of ore that yield $1.500 per ton, but small. There is some smelting ore. We will at once put up another furnace and a mule power to work them.

Next morning I went over to Arivaca and saw young Poston. Some adobes are made, but none laid. One arrastra† is done and three more under way. We have but few men there. I then drove over to Los Alamos. Schuchard is at a new vein, but neither it or the old yield much ore. He changes his

---

*An Indian hut.

†A crude mill for grinding ore. Heavy rocks were dragged over ore that was placed in a circular stone bed. Power was supplied by animals harnessed to an extension of the rotating center post.

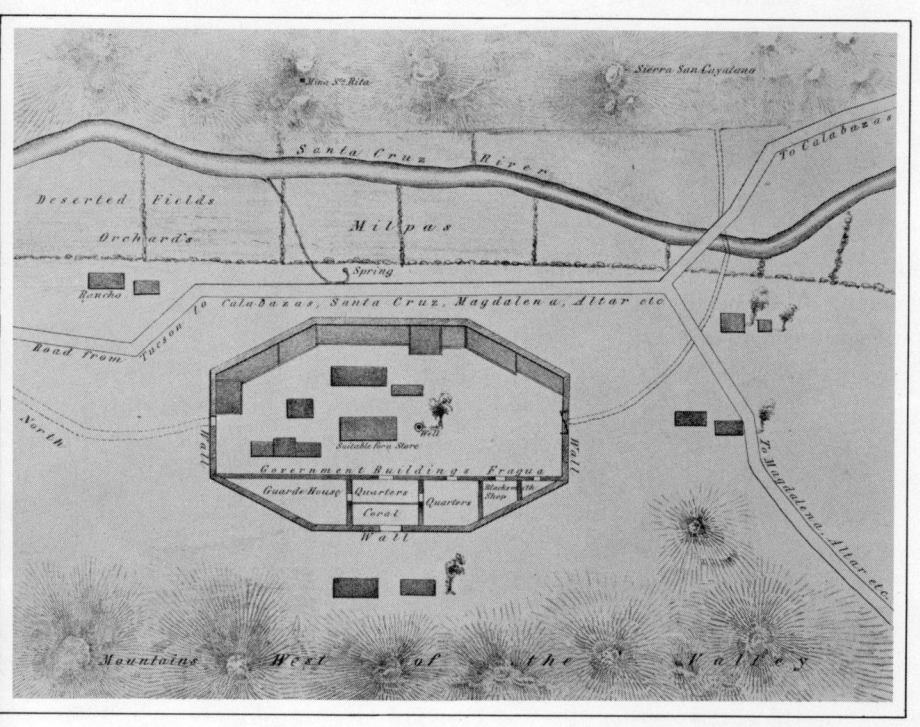

Headquarters for the Sonora Exploring
and Mining Company were established
in an abandoned Mexican presidio at the
village of Tubac on the Santa Cruz River.

workmen to new places too often. We cant rely upon much ore for a month to come. We intend taking over our mining Engineers and deciding what to do and then he must stick to it. I am decided in my mind to break up Los Alamos and only keep there an overseer and miners. We have too many establishments and too great a staff for so few laborers. There has been a great expense there and little really valuable work done. If the corral there was at C. C. around our piles of ore it would be worth thousands of dollars to us.

At Arivaca I tried to get back some of our stores, but they are pretty well disposed of. I got back to C. C. as they finished din.

The ore was unloaded at 2½ P.M. yesterday the furnace was lit. They have 600$ H. ore prepared. This morning they had three planchas out and on assay it will yield $1.000 the ton. The Patagonia lead ore yields but 39 oz the ton. It is a great disappointment to the owners. Col. Douglass was there to learn the result. Some of the ore they sent is not worth much.

I left at 8 a.m. and stopped a moment at Sopori. This side where the road from Tucson meets our road I met the Stage with Lt. Mowry, Mr. Jarvis and Mr. Mc'Kibbin, on their way to Sopori. We stopped a moment. They will be here tomorrow. They know nothing of Wrightson. Some Mexicans killed two Americans and wounded another at Dragoon springs, for plunder.

Our overland mail is in and I have not a letter from any one. Mr. Lathrop got one from Dr. Summers—all well and reinforcements stopped. He got a letter from his father, but not of a late date.

Mr. Lathrop has gone up to Sta Rita. There is a letter to Grosvenor from Wrightson and may contain some news. There is no excuse for his conduct in not writing regularly. There is now no telling when he will be here. With Mr.

Jarvis's aid I am in hopes to do something. The Atlantic Telegraph cable is finally laid. That first message between Queen Victoria and Prsd. Buchanan has not passed yet. I got the Harper's Mag. Margaret sent the mail before.

This afternoon I went and took a bath in the famous Sta Cruz river. When the water runs a mule could drink it dry, but I found a hole with water a little over knee deep and that but little over my length. There is however an Acequia draws off considerable. A few miles above or below there is no water running.

I have for once since leaving San Francisco had a room to myself, except the three nights I was at Ft. Buchanan, and took advantage of it to open the preparation Margaret gave me for my hair. It is beef's marrow and I gave my head a good rubbing. I promised to use it and must now try and do so regularly. Mr. Lathrop has a room to himself but prefers to sleep in mine since Poston left. He appears to have no idea that anyone wants privacy sometimes. If the bed was wide enough he would not object to a male bedfellow!

We saw a comet yesterday morning at Cerro Colorado, a little East of north.* Mr. Brunckow discovered it a few mornings before. It is larger than a star of the first magnitude and its tail about 5 degrees. [17]

Tubac. Fri. Sept. 17. 1858.

A pleasant day. I had a nice time of it with a room to myself to sleep in. I got up at day light to take a look at the comet, but it was too late. Mr. Lathrop returned about 10 and saw it last night at Sta Rita.

I got off the wagons to C. Colorado this morning with a full load. About eleven a.m. Lt. Mowry and Mr. Mc'Kibbin rode up on horses. Last night at Sopori the Indians stole their

---

*The Great Comet of 1858, or 1858 VI, discovered on June 7, 1858, by Giovanni Donati.

mules and nearly all at the place. This is the first stock lost there in two years. They stayed till afternoon and go on to Calabazas and the Fort. We had a long talk about politics etc. He says my Regt. came near being ordered to this Territory. I am glad it was not done. I would rather go to Texas. He also said it was in contemplation to put me on the duty of selecting sites for military posts in the Territory.

Gen. Garland* has gone home sick with dropsy—not expected to live.[18] I got a note from Mr. Poston. He was as far as Altar. He has hired labour to be here in 8 or 10 days. Dont say a word about supplies.

Tubac Sat. Sept. 18. 1858.

Lt. Mowry left yesterday about 3 P.M. and scarcely an hour after I was surprised to learn his stage was coming in. After all the cry the Apaches did not steal the mules. All were found and Mr. Jarvis drove in with them. I doubted from the beginning, but all the old inhabitants here said it was so and I gave in. I presume some wild animal stampeded them.

Mr. Hülseman† our store keeper is sick. He is better this morning.[19] We had Mr. Lathrop grunting and groaning again. He went to Sta. Rita and there they had venison cooked in manteca‡ and he eat of although he knows it always makes him sick. He professes to be well again this morning.

I had a long talk with Mr. Jarvis last evening about our company affairs. I was surprised to find him so well posted as to Poston's operations. I let him into some of our plans and he approves. I cannot learn from his conversation whether he has any funds to aid us. I think Col. Colt has authorized him

---

*John Garland (1792–1861), commander of the Department of New Mexico.
†Frederick Hülseman, principal storekeeper for the Sonora Exploring and Mining Company, was in charge of the company's office at Tubac.
‡Lard or cooking fat.

to draw for a certain amount if he thinks advisable. The Col. wants to make an investment, but I dont know any to advise. The best thing he can do is to loan us a few thousand dollars on good interest.

The mail got in at 3½ P.M. We got letters from Ehrenberg. The schooner with our ore stopped at Guaymas and San Diego and was expected momentarily. I also got a letter from Wrightson. Has sold $2.500 of stock at 50 per cent in Sonora and $2.500 in St. Rita at $20. Amount $2.500 at Coleman & co. in San Francisco. It relieves us very much. Not a line from Margaret. We leave in the morning for the Fort. Mr. Küstel is in and our wagon has returned. I dropped a line to Mr. Poston.

Ft. Buchanan Monday Sept. 20. 1858.

Mr. Lathrop was sick again Sat. night & took to bed. He was better next morning and he and Mr. Jarvis and I rode up here in our Concord stage. We left about 8 and got here at 5 P.M. We stopped a moment at Calabazas. I cant see the great value of the place. The road is pretty good. The distance to here is estimated at 46 miles. We found Mowry and Mc'Kibbin at Capt. Ewells. We stopped there, but the Doctor took Mr. Lathrop and I was provided for by Lt. Lord and had the luxury of a room to myself.

Ft. Buchanan Tues. Sept. 21. 1858.

Warm yesterday. The Election came off yesterday.* I would not sign the Election returns, if I was one of the Judges. Everybody voted, even when they could not attend the polls, or even some were not here. Mexicans and all, soldiers as well voted. I drew pay for Aug. of Brevoort the sutler—$232⁶⁰

---

*The election for a delegate to Congress in which Sylvester Mowry defeated Justus I. McCarty, 3,100 votes to 11.

and this morning made out my pay for Sept. $229, and leave it with Lathrop. He had a chill yesterday and will stay here till after Saturday. We saw Mr. Miles.* He lets us have $1.000 till Dec. and has some property he wishes us to take and pay in six months. Capt. Ewell I think will take some stock.[20] We bought a few things from the Sutler. The prices are extravagant. We leave this morning, Jarvis and I as soon as we get breakfast. Capt. Ewell had a fever last night.

Tubac Wed. 22 Sept. 1858.

We left yesterday at 8½ a.m. and got 9 miles when I discovered that we had left our purchases at the Sutler's store. We at once turned back. As we were going up we met Mowry and Mc'Kibbin on their way down. We got here before them. We got to Calabazas about dusk and encamped outside the walls. This morning before day we started and were here by breakfast. We found Mr. Poston here and the house full of people. I also got letters from Schuchard and Brunckow. The former is sick and the latter writes the furnaces stopped and the men wont work, without their pay. We will now pay off all here and in the morning there — at C. Colorado.

Mr. Poston has been talking in the most unreasonable manner about our affairs. I think however that now we have the management we will be able to carry the work on.

It was very cold last night. We saw the comet last night a little S. of W. and this morning another a little E. of N.

We have been overrun with people all day. I handed Mr. Poston $150 to pay some miners and others. We had near a thousand dollars more presented, but could not pay.

Conklin was here and we had a long discussion. He saw Poston and finally agreed to accept his proposition to pay 20 instead of 25 cts per pound. He goes to Ft. Buchanan to

---

*Edward Miles (1818–1863), a Tucson merchant.

see about buying some mules and I will give him a note to Lathrop. I have already written him two and sent Fuller with the first. Mowry and Mc'Kibbin are here and Brevoort and Mercer have been. Mowry tells me that he learns from Poston that he holds Ronstadt's* title to the Sopori mine and not the compy.[21] I had a warm discussion with Poston about affairs here and Conkling. He is rather unreasonable. We go out to C. Colorado in the morning.

Cerro Colorado Fri. Sept. 24. 1858.

We were up early yesterday and after breakfast started for this place. Lt. Mowry in his stage started for Sopori with an American (Hall) who has mined in Sonora. On the way we met Brevoort and pressed him to visit our mine. He partly promised but did not come. We wanted to visit the Sopori mine, but they were not going before afternoon so we only stopped a moment. [marginal note: "The oz. of silver is worth $20. 64/100."]

We found the furnace almost ready and it now is in blast and does well. We went into the mine and whilst there struck off some rich ore. It assayed 28½ per cent. A piece I picked up on pile outside yielded 53 per cent or $21.878.40.† The richest yet found. There is considerable rich ore out and in sight. A ton of this would relieve us from embarrassment. We went this morning to Arivaca and Alamos and got back at sundown. Nothing doing at Arivaca or Alamos. No hands. I went with Jarvis to see the lead mine. Poston too *tired*. His brother is sick, but well enough to go with us to relieve

---

*Frederick Ronstadt, who in 1854 reportedly acquired papers to the Sopori Ranch. In 1856 Poston claimed that Ronstadt left the papers with him, and the Sonora Exploring and Mining Company seems to have bought the title. There was some dispute as to whether Mowry also claimed these rights, but it was resolved in favor of the Sonora company.
†Yield refers to the weight of valuable metal obtained per ton of ore.

Schuchard who is sick. I got very tired staying there, but could not get Poston away until towards evening. At Arivaca we met Ortiz's daughter with some people from Altar and she gave us some peaches. They were pulled too early, but are good. We saw the comet, morning, and evening. I thought at first that I saw two, but this is so far North it is seen morning and evening. Quite warm to-day. We saw some Antelope on the Arivaca.

Tubac. Sat. Sept. 25. 1858.

A warm day. We left after breakfast and reached here to dinner. Mr. Poston is in bed with fever. I got a note from Mr. Lathrop. He is better, but fears he cannot sell the stock to Capt. Ewell. Lt. Mowry left this morning and borrowed Mr. Jarvis's repeating rifle with out *your leave,* much to his disgust and has also taken a pair of his blankets and lost on the way Mr. J's great coat. Save me from my friends.

We find several persons in possession of our quarters. I found my things overhauled and cant find some of them. I fear from Lathrop's letter we will want the money Miles loans us some days before we get it and that Ewell wont take the stock. I wish Brevoort had called and seen our rich ore.

I wrote to both Wrightsons, Hooper and Jaeger and commenced a letter to Margaret. I then learned that our mail does not leave till Monday.

Ehrenberg told me in San Francisco that everything was provided for the Amalgamation works but Quicksilver and Mr. Poston has repeatedly said the same. Mr. Küstel wants nails and glass. No nails (20 oz.) or glass can be found in Sonora, probably short of Hermosillo if there. It is merely possible they may be procured at the Fort. The Sutler has no 20 oz. nails. Such neglects are unpardonable. There was no glass at the Colorado and probably we will have to send to S. Francisco or make nails. I wish Wrightson was here and we would at once relieve Poston.

I heard Jarvis this evening tell one of the men that he would probably stay here till next fall. Mr. Poston says he has with him $10.000 in money.

We had a warm ride to-day, but at the house the mer. was 87°. We brought in 15 lbs. 2 oz silver or 30 marks 2 oz = $242 the produce of one weeks work. This falls considerably below Brunckows estimate of $700 per week. This was not refined the week it was smelted.

Tubac. Sun. Sept. 26. 1858.

Mr. Küstel has discovered a new mineral substance like chloride of silver. Its chemical composition is 75 p.c. silver and 25 chlorine. Under the blowpipe it gives a green color in vapor and stains the coal same color. Amalgamates with mercury, and under blowpipe gives on charcoal the green color again. Mr. Schuchard thinks the green color is occasioned by the metal osmium. The mineral he thinks is Osmium Chloren.

I wrote a letter to Mr. E. W. Eddy San Francisco.

Tubac Monday Sept. 27. 1858.

Warm to-day—mer. 91°. Our mail left this morning. Conklin is back. Mr. Lathrop got back at one P.M. He is well but weak. He bought a few tents and made a good contact for some "vigas and tabletas"* for the Amalgamation works, all to be delivered in 30 days.

A man accused a man named Miles of Tucson of keeping $1.600 he lent him and they had an arbitration. Miles could only say he had no recollection of the transaction. The man swore positively and it was decided in his favour. This cut us out of the $1.000 we expected to get from Miles. We pay for the vigas after our works are in operation. The payment for the lumber we have will be put off a while.

---

*Beams or girders, and split or sawed timber.

Poston was sicker last night and has been light headed to-day. He has talked again about Conkling and his not paying that money.

Tubac Tuesday Sept. 28. 1858.

Mer. at sun rise 63°. I wrote to Capt. Ewell and sent it this morning by our wagon gone after Miles enquiring about some articles we want for our works. After breakfast we discussed Conklin's affairs about the freight. Mr. Poston dragged in Conkling's about stock and money loaned the latter and we had quite a warm discussion. He soon found us all against him and became more reasonable. Mr. Jarvis took me aside and proposed taking stock for Col. Colt to relieve us. I finally concluded the arrangement and we took three drafts for 500$ each in N.Y. for stock at $40 a share. He afterwards paid us $100 and took 40 shares. I returned Mr. Lathrop the three certificates of 10 shares each I got of him when I went to Ft. Buchanan the time before last. We settled with Conklin at 20 cts the pound, giving him a draft for some 800$, the balance after deducting what he got from us in goods and supplies and debts we assume. I am quite relieved having this matter settled.

Mr. Schuchard is in. The furnace at C. Colorado has stopped — Saturday and they are fixing the refining furnace. Most of the men have left. We will not have out as much silver as we expected. As soon as our mail gets in I will go down and see what can be done.

Mr. Poston is better. He, Hülseman and Henry our driver* and José our servant all leave on the 1st. of Oct. for Magdalena† to attend the "fiesta," like a pack of children and

---

*Possibly Henry Effling or Alfeng, the major-domo at Tubac.
†In October, pilgrims journeyed to Magdalena to honor the Jesuit missionary St. Francis Xavier.

take the Ambulance, I suppose. They will go and all our operations are suspended.[22] I wish Wrightson was here. We would soon relieve Poston. He is no longer of any service to us, but a decided injury. He only serves to make persons dissatisfied and himself raises objections to everything we propose.

Tubac Wed. Sept. 29. 1858.

Troubles never end. This morning two Americans employed at Cerro Colorado came in with a note from Brunckow, but not a word said about affairs there. The men have left and say there is not a Mexican employed there — that all have left for the "Fiesta." One would have supposed this intelligence of sufficient importance to have been communicated.

We have had another negotiations talk with Fuller and also I have had a long one with Schuchard. He commenced as unreasonable as the rest. I at length convinced him and he remains and waits for his money. I blame Poston for all this. He has led them to believe that all they had to do was to ask for their pay and that we would pay them. When we would not they seemed to think we did not wish to.

Miss Klein and her mother want to go to C. Colorado tomorrow — and for me to go with them. I presume we shall go, although the Ambulance is wanted by Poston and crew for the "fiesta" Friday morning.

Conklin's wagons I believe have left.

P.M. He has also left. We have settled with Fuller and he leaves tonight. We gave him a note for $100 — the bal. due him and an order for the stock he has not yet. The mail rider for the Fort passed, but our man is still back. As far as we can learn his mule is sick. Always something goes wrong.

The mail came in just before dusk. I got letters from Margaret dated 9 and 24 Aug. The first postmarked 11 Aug.

Newport and of course too late for the preceding mail. I got a letter from Wrightson dated 8 Sept. at S. Antonio. He expects to start in a week. Not a word of other news. Cheever has written that he will take my stock and send on to Margaret $500, but has not yet done it. It is strange he has not written to me. He had no right to take the stock on our agreement. Mr. Lathrop has had a time settling with one of our men who leaves. All this difficulty occasioned by Mr. Poston letting them believe that we can pay them if we choose. Margaret writes that she has just seen young Wrightson with a letter from Poston in which he says they were taking out $500 a day. The impression conveyed is smelting, but he means taking out of the mine and no doubt intentionally made ambiguous. What is the use of resorting to such shifts when the plain truth is rich enough.

It is a great relief to us to be rid of Conklin, Fuller and Moohrmann* in one day.[23] I leave in the morning with Mrs. Klein and her daughter for C. Colorado and expect to return immediately. Mer. 91° to-day.

*Theodore Moohrmann, an associate of the Sonora Exploring and Mining Company.

October
1858

Tubac. Fri. Oct. 1st. 1858.

I was up early yesterday, in hopes to get off, but Fuller and Moohrmann had to be waited upon and then did not leave till near ten. We at last got a late breakfast and it then consisted of only coffee and dry bread. When I supposed all ready then the women had something more to put into the wagon. It must have been 8 a.m. when we left. Our driver Henry was too sick to go, so we took the cook—former blacksmith, and a man who had been to the mines, to assist. We got out then about one P.M. Both Mrs. Klein and her daughter then began to complain. The weather was warm, the water warm, the room small etc. etc. They were in a fever to go and when they got there would have been glad to have been back, I am satisfied.

On our way out we met Mr. Meyers* coming in with the last silver refined. 23 lbs 6 oz. It was much more than I expected.[1]

I find all the Mexicans have not left. There are six barreteros

---

*Possibly Charles Hermann Meyer (1829–1903), an assistant to Küstel.

and 2 Tenateros* in the mines and a few other men. Louis the Blksmith† banded the forward wheels of the Ambulance, but we had to wait for the mules to change them, ours are tender footed till near 8 P.M. and did not get back here before 2 A.M. this morning. It will be some time before I will again take such a ride for such a purpose.[2]

This morning before day they were up and just as the sun rose Poston, Hülseman, Henry the driver, José the servant and the Herdsman left for the fiesta at Magdalena. I am glad they are gone, but still we are not alone. Schuchard is still here—two men discharged at C. C. and Miles from the Fort. How many more I cant tell and Meyers the assistant to Küstel, who is disgusted and quits. He and Brunckow cant agree. I have heard a good deal of complaint lately about various persons and matters in Mr. Poston's happy family. I see also the absolute necessity for the Director to live at the mines and not here. This establishment I will reduce very much and that in a short time. I will put up a tent at C. Colorado and live there. I will put up the other furnace, horse power and finish a house commenced for a Blk smith shop and now not needed. It has one large and two small rooms.

Yesterday was my birthday. That was an agreeable way I spent it! Made my monthly reports. Wrote to Margaret, Wrightson-Sec. and T. W. We have an opportunity to send our mail in tomorrow. We had a nice shower of rain this afternoon—laid the dust cooled air. A messenger arrived late in the evening from C. C. for medicines. Louis our blacksmith and cook has the fever. Mr. Lathrop made our tea and bread.

Tubac Sat. Oct. 2. 1858.

It has been raining around the country and a few drops

---

*Barreteros are miners who work with picks, wedges, or crowbars; tenateros carry ore from the depths of the mine to the surface.
†Possibly Louis Quesse (1823–1877).

here. A man came in for C. C. for medicine last night. Brunckow and Streit the carpenter are sick. A team came in to-day. We have already got three more hands. We had a long discussion last night about Dunbar. I to-day showed Mr. Jarvis the correspondence with him, has I hope put matters in a different light. I also read him some of Poston's letters.

I got up at day light and wrote to Conkling. Mr. Schuchard went to Sta Rita this morning and the two men left for Tucson and took our letters. Our table is quite reduced. We appear to get along as well without a cook as with one. Louis is better and will I believe get us supper.

Tubac Sun. Oct. 3rd. 1858.

Our wagon came in from C. Colorado. Three men have arrived. We have the weekly reports. They expect to start the furnace tomorrow. We feel quite rejoiced at the prospect. There is no doubt we will have plenty of hands in a few days. Our carpenter is in sick, but hopes to escape the fever and will return tomorrow. The black Smith is not well yet. We want him to iron the Horse power. I dont see how we can do without him. A little rain in the neighborhood. Our wagon has started back. There is no use of my going out until the mechanics can go to work. If I had one of the tents we bought the other day I would put it up and locate there. We expect them this week. The building I proposed to finish those two women occupy, having taken the carpenter off his work to fit up for them. I will do almost anything to keep them away from here. If we can we will get a man into this house to keep a boarding house and shut up our free hotel. Our expenses are not half what they were and at all our establishments not one-fourth. Answered Major R. Allen's* letter asking us to smelt some ore of the San Xavier Min. co.[3]

---

*Robert Allen (1812–1886), one of the incorporators and the president of the Arizona Mining and Trading Company.

Tubac Mon. Oct. 4. 1858.

Meyers and Streit the carp. left for C. C. this morning. I will go tomorrow in our small express wagon and get Miles man to drive me. Grosvenor came in this morning and brought me a small deer. The morning was cool. Grosvenor left after dinner. Mr. Jarvis rode to the Reventon* to get eggs and matches. The store was locked. I wrote to sister Maria. Louis has gone out with Kirkland† to the "Canoa"‡ to sleep. I am the only person sleeps in the house tonight and I suppose it is the first time it has been so since reoccupied by the Sonora Exploring & Mining co. I was going to C. C. in the morning, but if I wait another day the Bk. Smith will go with me. His services are so important that I will wait. The rain a few afternoons made quite a flood in the Sta Cruz river, but it only lasted a very short time. The Acequia was carried away. It is already repaired, but I do not know by whom. I took a bath in the river, but it is getting cool. The pond is about 10 feet long and knee deep.[4]

Tuesday Tubac Oct. 5. 1858.

Nights are cool. I would have gone to C. C. this afternoon, but Louis is not so disposed. The notorious Capt. Titus§ passed through town this afternoon with some half dozen of his men, all that are left on his way to the Fort. Moses Carson, the Interpreter of the Pimas is with them. Titus is disgusted with the country and goes home. The people, I suppose, are too poor to rob. They did not stop, but passed straight through. Brunckow took off a man from his work and sent

---

*A beef cattle ranch south of Tucson on the Santa Cruz River.

†William Hudson Kirkland (1832–1910), a trader in the Santa Cruz Valley.

‡The Canoa Ranch was one of the oldest productive ranches in the valley, located thirty-five miles south of Tucson. A hotel of sorts was established there.

§Henry Titus, owner of the Patagonia Mine, manager of the Union Silver Mining Company, and a former filibuster.

him in for a bag of flour. We sent some out they did not like. The furnace was started yesterday and they have 400 pounds of silver and lead out. I wrote to Capt. Ewell again about a carpenter. There are 9 of those filibusters besides Titus.[5]

Cerro Colorado. Wed. Oct. 6. 1858.

We got a late breakfast and started for here. I brought Louis. A man came as far as Sopori to get Miles's horse, we want to buy and Kirkland came all the way to go to Arivaca to get some yoke oxen. We had a mean team and did not get here before 2 P.M. The furnace is in blast. But few (3) men in the mine. I saw the ladies. Their situation is forlorn enough. If I had been here I would have done more for them than Brunckow did. We brought some vegetables from the garden. They have no idea of returning to Tubac. Not so warm as usual.

Cerro Colorado Thurs. Oct. 7. 1858.

We had a little rain pass to the West of us. The weather warm. I was afraid our Blksmith would go back to town with Meyers, but he at last went to work. I have written to hire a new one. I see we must get rid of most of our people and start with new ones. The furnace still continues to do well. We are getting out excellent ore. Mr. Küstel suggested starting one or two barrels. He says that it can be done with very little labor. I approve of the plan heartily and will aid him all in my power. It is difficult to understand exactly what can be done. The simplest things are at first impossible and in a few days they fall in with it. When I proposed the mule power, it was too expensive. After losing several weeks they thought it best.

A great many of our tools have been lost through the most culpable neglect. A Mexican (Espinosa) at Arivaca carried the tools and table and kitchen furniture as well as the richest ore. Mr. Poston himself discharged him and allowed him to take off every thing. There has been no system and no care of any thing. It is difficult, without money to get order out of chaos. With two barrels we will soon have money.

C. Colorado Fri. Oct. 8. 1858.

I was up this morning as soon as light. After breakfast I attended to the mechanics. Work goes on slowly. We want to get an entirely new set. A Mexican came and we bought some flour and peaches. We sell them at a bit a dozen and pretty good peaches. They are from Tubutama. It is cloudy and raining around us. About dinner a man came in and brought our letters from Tubac. I got one from Margaret dated 2 Aug. Some news though not so late as two received by the overland mail. Mr. Lathrop sent me one from Bill Peck* dated Buffalo Sept. 13. It came by the overland and should have been here a day or two earlier. There is nothing special in our letters. I wrote two to Lathrop. He and Jarvis are both sick.[6]

C. C. Sat. Oct. 9. 1858.

We had a few drops of rain last night. To-day has been cool and cloudy. Rain around us. Our furnace got clogged by not having an expert asst. smelter and stopped before day, leaving some ore prepared. We are now at work preparing the refining furnace.

The blacksmith is going to Tubac. If he dont return tomorrow I will discharge him and try wooden spindles. All his work this week could have been done in a day. 5 men arrived to-day from the fiesta.

Yesterday Mr. Küstel and I worked one hour opening a window in the furnace wall to let out the smoke and fumes. The antimony lime and lead make fumes rather deletizous. Yesterday we worked at the furnace.

---

*William Peck, a book and stationery merchant in Buffalo, New York.

We are like the Esquimoux—we eat candles, or at least its equivalent tallow. Everything is cooked in it and it does not make the most palatable dishes. Our cook cant bake bread. The cry was the flour and when I came the bread was miserable and so hard you could scarcely break it. He has good flour now and if possible the bread is worse.

C. C. Sun. Oct. 10. 1858.

The comet is progressing rapidly to the West. Its change of position is very perceptible, each night to the naked eye. I got a line from Mr. Lathrop last evening. He has had another chill and fever and is quite sick.

This morning a fellow I hired as mason took French leave. He went into the store and helped himself to two mats to sleep on. They were taken away and he commenced to make a fuss with Brunckow. I told him the mats were for sale and asked him who let him have them. He took his horse and left. We think it a good riddance. I was only sorry I could not send a note to Tubac, not to let him stop at our house there.

We had great delay in getting animals and did not catch them till 11 O'Clock. We had an early dinner, Mr. Küstel, Brunckow, Methner* and I rode to Los Alamos, on the trail and examined the Arenia lead mine and another vein Schuchard thought much of. The latter has very little ore and that full of quartz. The other is not much more promising, but we have determined to work it as soon as laborers arrive. When we got here we found 13 [15?] had arrived and 5 yesterday. More are coming from Tubac tonight. So we will soon have plenty of hands, without sending as Poston did to Sonora and buying them and then have them all run away. We stopped at Arivaca and looked at a site for the dwelling house. There is nothing doing at either of these places, Jno.

*Theodore Methner, an assistant to Brunckow, was in charge of smelting operations for the Sonora Exploring and Mining Company.

Poston was up to-day sick and so is Anton.* We have three gentlemen from Sonora to look at our mine.[7]

C. Colorado Mon. Oct. 11. 1858.

We have now 40 men—yesterday came 16. We have a full complement in the main shaft, men at the vaso† and furnace and preparing the ground for the mule power. I am in hopes the iron work will be done tomorrow. Louis did not get down till late, but then he had to wait for the barreteros to finish sharpening their bars. I went down into the shaft. 3 or 2 feet will bring it to where we commence a fronton. The wagon got back late last night and brought the man who went to Sonora for his woman. He goes to work tomorrow. The arrastras are done and we will commence grinding ore. I got a letter from Mr. Lathrop. He and Mr. Jarvis are both quite sick. I would have gone up this morning, but I cant leave here. The dilly dallying and delay is quite disheartening. It is from the highest to the lowest. The fire is lit in the vaso and I hope to start the furnace again tomorrow.

After dark the little wagon arrived with Mr. Brown,‡ Mr. Küstels brother in law—as an assistant. There also came along a carpenter. An excellent one. We hired another who commences tomorrow. Our second furnace is to be commenced tomorrow. The fire was lighted in the refining furnace about 2 P.M. and at 8 P.M. the first planchas were put in. Lathrop and Jarvis are both better. The Ambulance is back and the report of its being broken fake. Mr. Poston left at Magdalena sick—no great loss to us. The vessel with our goods had not arrived in the river when they passed. To-day has been hot.[8]

---

*Anton Elsner, an employee of the company.
†A receptacle or container in which the ore is heated in a reverbatory furnace.
‡William M. Brown.

[102]

Tubac Tues. Oct. 12. 1858 [*"Tucson" incorrectly recorded*].

I started this morning another furnace before I left. The foundation was laid. I also had men at work preparing to put up the mule power. Mr. Brown, Mr. Küstel's brother in law and an excellent carpenter arrived last night. I could not get the mules till late in the day and so waited and brought another plancha of silver, in all 23 marks. I saw for the first time the process of refining. Mr. Küstel came up with me in the little wagon and drove most of the way. We did not get off until about 11 a.m. and reached here about 4 P.M. We found Mr. Jarvis in bed but Mr. Lathrop up. Both have been quite sick.

Cerro Colorado Wed. Oct. 13, 1858.

We had a nice supper and also breakfast. Mr. Küstel cooked the meal well and made excellent hot bread. We looked at the machinery in the store house and decided what we want and left about 9 a.m. Henry the driver has fever and is of no use to us. We harnessed our mules ourselves and Mr. Küstel drove. We stopped at Sopori and got butter milk and a bag of green corn and some squashes. In fact overloaded our wagon so that we did not get here until 4 P.M. I partly engaged butter for this place at 75 cts the pound. Our ride was hot and disagreeable. The smelting furnace went in blast last evening. One plancha out. The refining furnace finished just as we arrived.

Jno. Streit has the fever again. The big wheel of the mule power is up. The blk smith has done next to nothing.

Before I left this morning, or rather before breakfast I wrote to Margaret. We got this time 61 marks of silver or $488. Not so much as Brunckow estimated and more than Küstel.

I this moment got a note from Arivaca. The German* has

---

*Identity uncertain.

been sick, but has arrived without hands. He is anxious to go on if we will let him have ten hands. He shall have all we have. Haberman* goes up to Tubac in the morning with the silver.

Cerro Colorado Thurs. Oct. 14. 1858.

We got breakfast very late. We soon after got our mules up and Mr. Küstel, Brown and I rode to Arivaca and Los Alamos. We stopped some time at the former place and decided what to do. We will send some men to commence the Roasting furnaces. The man who was engaged by Poston to build the houses is at Los Alamos and has been sick. He is without hands. We have a mason and will go in without him. I am in hopes now the work will go on in earnest. Mr. Brown will I presume stay at Arivaca and superintend. One of our men there has the fever.

Cerro Colorado Fri. Oct. 15. 1858.

The furnace stopped last night, on account of the fire proof adobes giving out. When I spoke about using stone, Mr. Küstel said that the adobes is better, but that it must be made sometime before. What folly to commence before he was ready. We only got out $150 for this week. They are now at work putting up the mule power. We have two carpenters and two men and Küstel to measure and such measuring. They measure from no definite point and measure again and again, until I got so disgusted I go away. All the forenoon is gone and not two hours work is done. Work that should have been made in the shop and could have been done better than is now done at every disadvantage and half a dozen men stand idle to look on at one man working. Our breakfast as usual we did not have till after 8 a.m.

---

* C. G. Haberman, a mining engineer in charge of the reduction works at Cerro Colorado.

Mr. Küstel has just told me they smelted *three* days in July, altered the furnace and commenced again the *ninth* of Aug. Total time they have only smelted 25 days and nights. Most of the detention has been the want of lead ore.

Haberman got in soon after dinner and brought a note. They are better. We want $1.000 in silver by the 18th and the furnace not running. It is a great loss our furnace stopping. It appears we have overdrawn on Gonzales, as $400 is for him, $600 is due—next mo. in S. Francisco.

A fine breeze all day has tempered the heat. Brunckow is sick.

C. C. Sat. Oct. 16. 1858.

Very windy to-day. I sent the wagon to town. It is very windy. I fear the mule power will not be finished. J. L. Poston got in this afternoon with the mail. No letters from home. Two from Conkling and a copy of P.s letter to the co. in abusive style. I got a letter from Hooper. Jaeger will not bring the goods unless he gets 14 cts. and 6.000. He is a scamp. He begged me to let him haul for us. I got a letter from Cheever in which he says he sold my stock but has been sick. Will put the money in N.Y.

The day before yesterday I felt badly, well yesterday and to-day had a slight chill and as slight a fever. I have been busy day and night and much in the sun.

I had a sharp talk with Küstel. His niece told him I promised the light wagon to go to-day to Tubac and return Monday. I did say they could have it if any man but the Blk S. would drive and return tomorrow. This is the second mistake—I will have an interpreter next time. Brown drives them and we lose another day, though Küstel says they will go to Arivaca Monday. We got $100 [read $1,000] from Miles from Tucson. The draft cant be cashed although but $250.

Cerro Colorado Sun. Oct. 17. 1858.

I did not sleep well last night and perspired freely. I was unusually cold. All day has been a haze on the mountains like Indian summer. The first I have seen. I spent the forenoon reading the papers and writing a report to the Sec. of the compy and also a long letter to Conkling. I read an excellent report on the S.P.R.R. made at a meeting in Cin. and have authorized Mr. Conkling to act as my agent in the matter. The amount due by me is only about $255. I dont feel particularly well to-day and took two blue pills this morning.

I have just measured the main shaft and it is 58 feet deep. This week will get it down to the place to commence the fronton.

C. C. Tues. Oct. 19. 1858 ["*Mon. Oct. 18*" *crossed out*].

The wagon got in late Sunday night and the women also. Most of the things sent for came. The ojo* came in the exp. wag. and the *ladies* had it in their room although they have one. I sent Mr. Brown in to get it. They have ours. They are disposed to grab everything. They even wanted to take down the shelves at Tubac and here take all the eggs etc.

Yesterday Mr. Küstel and Mr. Brown rode to Arivaca and have commenced work on the Amal Works under Mr. B's direction. Methner went to Los Alamos and started the miner on the lead mine. The carpenter worked all day on the mule power and it proved a total failure. They are now disposed to try my plan. The furnace started last evening, also the refining furnace. We got out only $144 — about. It has nearly all been paid out already.

I sent an express to Tubac yesterday with my report to the Sect. and a demand for coin to be sent by the overland mail.

---

*Perhaps a corruption of *olla*. Heintzelman may be referring to a wash basin or chamber pot.

Mr. L. I presume left last evening for Tucson, on horseback. I fear he will not stand it.

I have commenced regulating things here. We have our breakfast early and this moment 11½ a.m. the dinner bell rung. I stopped it and ordered dinner back till 12. There is no use losing half an hour work, when you get so little out of the mechanics.

I had a chill and vomiting yesterday and had to lay abed. It commenced at 10½ a.m. I feel much better to-day, but I have to be about too much. The sky is a little overcast, makes it more pleasant. Things have gone on tolerably well to-day. The furnace dont work very well, although they have had near a week to repair it. Jno. Streit the carpenter, told me the bellows worked one half easier. Now I find he has reduced the stroke and the velocity has to be increased, being a decided disadvantage. I tried half the day to get a shade over the man at the bellows and at last had to call a man and assist him to do it. It was not five minutes work. They were wasting the liquor and I wanted a faucet in it and at last had to go to work at it myself. This is the way things go on.

C. C. Thurs. 21. Oct. 1858.

I wrote a letter to T. Wrightson urging in the strongest manner the sending that money. I went more in detail than I could in the Report. I had scarcely finished my letter when I had a chill and kept my bed the balance of the day. I sleep in the corner of the Carpenter's shop, on a broken cot, with a keg of powder under the side. Whilst I lay there a saw was filed, planing and mortising all at the same time. I cant be very nervous.

The furnace stopped last night after running 48 hours. I had given orders to have one of these rooms plastered to kill the bugs, so the *ladies* could occupy it should it rain. Without a word to me Mr. Küstel took them and put up a chimney in the room his sister lives. It took all day. We will not finish both the furnaces, or at least so far that the new one can be finished whilst the other is running and there will be no more of these delays. Mr. Brunckow goes this morning for fire stone.* They have to do at last as I wished. Every adobe has failed lately. The furnace runs badly—not $100. The main shaft is 60 ft. and fronton commenced.

C. Colorado Sat. Oct. 23. 1858.

Some change took place in the mode of working in the fronton—in the tasks and the Mexicans refused to work. So it is stopped for the present till they come to terms. But little work was done yesterday, I being sick abed and a very heavy wind blowing all day making it difficult to work in the open air. The old furnace will not be ready till Mon. noon and nothing yet done to the new one. Perhaps something will be done to-day. The mule power is not done yet. Little was done there. Too windy to do much at the Blacksmith shop. My chill commenced before 10 yesterday and I kept my bed. I lay on the floor till afternoon near the fire and then had the cot I fixed with rawhide, brought in and put in the backroom. I find it much more comfortable and slept some in the afternoon and better at night, notwithstanding the bedbugs they made such a hiss about. I was not near so much bitten on the floor of the carpenter shop. I made myself a half tin cup of lemonade and found it most refreshing. It was cold and very uncomfortable all day yesterday and at night a few drops of rain. To-day is quite pleasant.

I wrote to Dr. Irwin for a prescription and medicines. Finished my letter to T. Wrightson and also to Jarvis or Lathrop. I wrote to Mr. Lathrop again in the evening.

---

*Stone capable of withstanding a considerable amount of heat, perhaps to be used as a means for striking fire or to cover part of the front of the furnace.

C. Colorado. Sat. Oct. 23 1858.

Some change took place in the mode of working in the furnace — in Mr. Parker & the Mexicans refused to work. So it is stopped for the present till they come to terms. But little work was done yesterday, I being sick abed & a very heavy wind blowing all day making it difficult to work in the open air. The old furnace will not be ready till Mon. morn & nothing yet done to the new one. Perhaps something will be done to day. The mule power is not done yet. Little was done there. No weather to do much at the Black smith shop.

My chill commenced before 10 yesterday & I kept my bed. Lay on the floor till afternoon near the fire & then had the cot I had fixed with raw hides, boring hit in & put in the back room — I find it much more comfortable & slept some in the afternoon & better at night, notwithstanding the bed bugs they made such a fuss about. I am no near so much better as on the floor of the carpenter shop. I made myself a half tea cup of lemonade & found it most refreshing.

It was cold & very uncomfortable all day yesterday & at night a few drops of rain. To day is quite pleasant.

I wrote to Dr. Irvin for a prescription & medicines. Finished my letter to Z. Wright sine & also to Jarvis or Lathrop. I wrote to Mr. Lathrop again in the evening.

C. C. Mon. Oct. 25. 1858.

Yesterday was my sick day. I did not have quite so hard a chill. I took a very slight breakfast & kept my bed. I think it came on a little earlier than usual. Mr. Kuster went out in the forenoon & killed two horn. I was quite surprised at an invitation to help him eat them.

The wagon got in at sun down, with a letter from Mr. Jarvis. Mr. Lathrop has not returned & our peons who went to Tubac for money are still waiting for him. I fear he has been taken sick again. Mr. Jarvis is better. The tents we have been so long looking for have arrived.

Kirkland who is getting out timber for us was met by a party of about 30 Indians near the Quinery & relieved of some of his oxen & blankets. He will however get out our timber. Mowry passed through Tubac for Meson

254

Entries from Heintzelman's journal for
October 23 and 24, 1858.

C. C. Mon. Oct. 25. 1858.

Yesterday was my sick day. I did not have quite so hard a chill. I took a very slight breakfast and kept my bed. I think it came on a little earlier than usual. Mr. Küstel went out in the forenoon and killed two horses. I was quite surprised at an invitation to help him eat them.

The wagon got in at sun down, with a letter from Mr. Jarvis. Mr. Lathrop has not returned and our peons who went to Tubac for money are still waiting for him. I fear he has been taken sick again. Mr. Jarvis is better. The tents we have been so long looking for have arrived.

Kirkland who is getting out timber for us was met by a party of about 30 Indians near the pinery* and relieved of some of his oxen and blankets. He will however get out our timber.[9] Mowry passed through Tubac for Tucson Saturday. Reports having settled the Sopori titles, including arrangement with Poston. Jarvis gives no particulars.

Two of Gándara's sons† were in Tubac, but everybody there is sick and no cook so they left for Tumacacori. I am sorry we could not show them more hospitality. Mr. Jarvis sends me some castor oil, a small pattern of an emetic and some quinine. It will be difficult to send my letter to the Doctors. Schuchard, who came to stay whilst Mr. L. went to Tucson has left again for Sta. Rita. He might have stayed and taken care of Jarvis and the house till L. returned.[10]

I got a letter from Poston dated Magdalena Oct. 18. He is recovering, but wants the Ambulance the end of the month to return. The weather is getting colder and no blankets for the Peons.

Got a letter from Dr. Summers dated 23 Aug. Caroline will go to Newport to stay this winter with Margaret—to get her

---

*A source of lumber, in the Santa Rita Mountains.
†Gándara had four sons: Juan, Jesús, José, and Francisco.

teeth fixed. I also have a letter from T. Wrightson dated 6 Sept. enclosing an address from Committee of Stockholders S.P. R.R. He offers to attend to my stock. I wrote to Conkling about it a few days authorizing him to attend to it.

C. C. Tues. Oct. 26. 1858.

I spent all afternoon at the mule power and thought we had it fixed, but the mule was not steady and we had at dusk to put on the man power. This is my chill day. I took 2 grs quinine an hour before the time and lay down. I had but cold fingers.

Whilst I was lying down Lathrop drove up in the Ambulance. He was sick at Tucson and also last night at Sopori. He got back Sunday and paid the men all off out of $75 he got for a crate of panoche.* The draft he could not get cashed. The stage co. lost a stage and passenger in a dust storm near Alamo Mocho. Jarvis is better and has gone to Sta. Rita. Mr. Buckley† rode through a camp on the Mimbres 200 miles from here and called out who they were. The answer was a mining co. for Tubac. He counted 10 wagons. They must be Wrightson. He may be here any day. Mr. Küstel returned late last evening. Things are going on well at Arivaca. I hope tomorrow to commence on our Amalgamation tubs. Wrote to Poston at Magdalena.[11]

C. Colorado Wed. Oct. 27. 1858.

Mr. Lathrop and I have had long talks about company matters and arranged them for the future as well as possible. He left immediately after dinner. I wrote letters to Margaret and T. Wrightson.

We got a cart ready and were loading it with ore for Arivaca to be crushed and ground, when the tongue broke. At the

---

*Native refined sugar.
†William M. Buckley, a superintendent for the Butterfield Overland Mail Company.

same moment the lever to the bellows at the furnace broke. We were preparing another and no delay occurred. A carpenter of the name of H. J. Olds* who came here sick died at 11½ A.m. We bury him at sundown. The first death at this place. [12]

I got my trunk into my room and have put sheets on my bed and otherwise added to my comfort. I feel pretty well to-day. Suarez came to-day with a little flour, cheese, beans and peaches. We brought all and he has started back. He reports a revolution at Hermosillo. Weather pleasant to-day.

C. C. Thurs. Oct. 28. 1858.

Everything has been going on very well to-day. All we want is more laborers. The carpenters have commenced in earnest on the Amalgamation machinery. The Wheel and belt for the fan are now ready and will I presume be tried tomorrow. Mr. Küstel, took his sister and niece with him on his visit to Arivaca. He is back and brings the good news with a very fine specimen of lead ore from Los Alamos. We are now sure of a supply for at least the few weeks till our amalgamation works are in operation.

This was my day for a chill. I took two gains of quinine and have not felt the least symptom. I was weighed to-day and weigh only 125 pounds. I have not weighed so little since I grew up. I feel pretty well but weak. The weather has been warmer to-day.

We buried Olds at sun down. He died of consumption and the first death at this place since its permanent occupation 25 Jan. 1857.

C. C. Fri. Oct. 29. 1858.

I ventured to-day for the first time since I was taken sick to

---

*The company published a notice of Olds's death but was apparently unable to locate his relatives.

eat some meat at dinner. We killed to-day, but it was badly fried with chili.

I wrote a long letter to Cheever and explained fully our progress here at the mines. I again urged him to return my unsold stock that I would not sell any more at par. We put on the belt and tried our fan. It works very well. We have too few men and nothing is doing on the new furnace. The carpenters are back at work on the wood part of the Amal. machinery. Mr. Brunckow and I examined Olds's effects, but cannot find where he is from.

C. Colorado Sat. Oct. 30. 1858.

The weather is turning warmer. I had the best sleep I have had since I have been at C. C. I put sheets on the other day and have been able to add a pillow and another blanket. I have felt well but weak to-day. I lay awake a great deal at night.

Our furnace has worked well, but had to stop at 3 P.M. from the want of ore for smelting. The refining furnace is in operation and we expect as this weeks work to get out a little over $400. Next week we will smelt the litharge* to separate the copper and we will get some silver. Before the end of the week we hope to have smelting ore again. A Mexican carpenter has just arrived. Mr. Brunckow is at work on the new furnace.

This afternoon I got a package of letters. One from Margaret dated 9 Sept. All well, but Mary's leg not yet healed. I fear all the diseased bone was not removed. I got a letter from Cheever 13 Sept. Has sent the note to Margaret and the $500 deducting the interest. He says he has sold some of my stock on time. My letters will spur him up to sell all or return what is not sold. Sayles was expected home in a few days. I got a

---

*Lead monoxides, a reddish yellow crystalline solid used as an oxidizing agent and made by heating lead in a current of air.

letter from E. W. Eddy dated 11 Oct. Nothing of importance. Always overhead and care in business. Two Depts on the Pacific Gen Hearn commands the Northern.[13]

C. C. Sun. Oct. 31. 1858.

I was up early and we soon had the mules and started for Arivaca. Methner and Miller the carpenter went along. The tire was coming off and we had to turn back and fix it. On our way over we met Mr. Brown and young Poston coming over. We stopped a moment and drove on. We visited the lead mine Arenia and found some excellent ore. They have out over a ton and as much good ore in sight. We will have enough to keep the furnace in blast at least till the Amalgamation works are ready. We stopped at Arivaca. The roasting furnace is nearly ready. No ore has been ground yet, on account of want of men. The work goes on pretty well. On our way over we saw four Antelope or deer, at the distance we could not distinguish. The waters have risen. The Acequia at Los Alamos is now full. I finished my letter to Lathrop and sent it with two planchas of silver to Tubac by Louis the Blk smith.

Mr. Brunckow is now suffering very much from lead colic.* He is exceedingly imprudent. The weather is quite pleasant.

---

*Severe abdominal pain associated with lead poisoning.

November
1858

Cerro Colorado Monday Nov. 1st. 1858.

A pretty cold night and cool all day. We got *five* more hands and have not *six* men in the mine. We are collecting smelting ore. Mr. Brunckow is still quite sick with lead colic and nothing done to the furnace. We are putting up a wall to try and cut off the fumes from the bellows men.

I wrote a long letter to Margaret and also one to Dr. Summers. I expected Mr. Lathrop, but it is now so late in the afternoon I dont think he will be here. The yield of the furnace last week from Monday eve. to Sat. at 3 P.M. was $440. We smelted some of last weeks silver and some picked from the bottom of a vaso makes in all $482. This week will be much less.

There is a Mexican here with *five* peons going to work a vein of silver he has discovered near San Xavier. It yields 4 marks the cargo, or about $212 the ton. I dont think it will pay unless very abundant in ore. The ore we have smelted thus far has yielded $920 a ton and we dont get along well. It dont pay our expenses, though some are unnecessary for the furnace and should be charged to the Amalgamation account.

I wrote to Jno. Bull that I cant yet recommend to a compy any mine. Mr. Brunckow is so sick we have to send to Tubac for medicine, after sending to Arivaca. I wrote a line to Lathrop.

C. C. Tuesday. Nov. 2. 1858.

Louis the BlkS. took a miff and was leaving. He will stay out his month. We got some five more men to-day and are getting smelting ore. Brunckow is still sick and our only smelter, so nothing is doing at the furnace, but preparing the material to smelt. The Ambulance got here at 1½ P.M. One wheel will be set at once and all on the express wagon. The ox cart arrived from Los Alamos with lead ore. 8 cattle have strayed. We sent after them.

Tubac Wed. Nov. 3. 1858.

I left in the Ambulance at 8½ A.M., stopped a moment at Sopori and was at Tubac a little before 2 P.M. I found our house full. Col. Douglass was here on his way to the Fort, Gándara's eldest son and several Mexicans and Mr. Schuchard. The cook was sick, so Lathrop and I cooked a little dinner. He brought from the Fort for me from the Commissary, Bacon, rice, sugar, coffee. I was introduced to young Gándara and had a few words conversation with him. He is still at the Mission of Tumacacori with some Mexican friends. He dont speak English. Grosvenor of Sta. Rita was also there.

I went at business at once. Capt. Ewell has tried, or rather his man Doss and smelted down two [ferreas?], without results. He (Capt. E.) is very anxious to have us smelt 300 pounds of his ore for him. We will do it if possible. He and Doss have quarrelled.

Fernandez* a Mex. with goods at Tucson, has agreed to take the plancha of silver (156 oz.) I took up and give us gold

---

*Possibly Juan Fernandez, a merchant who was born in Spain.

for it and as much more as he has gold. We sent Schuchard to Tucson on horseback this morning for the coin. This will at once enable us to pay our hands for several weeks I hope. As soon as Mr. Buckley the stage agent who has gone to S. Francisco returns with coin to pay his debts, Mr. L. goes to Tucson to try and get our $250 draft cashed. The two together I hope will enable us to pay our hands till we can amalgamate.[1]

I also arranged and send one of our wagons to the Canoa tomorrow to go after timber. A Mr. Pachen and his family who stopped at our house on their way to Tucson, will be back Sat. and we will then complete an arrangement for flour etc. etc. and Quicksilver to pay in drafts in S. Francisco at 4 mos. This will help us.

C. Colorado Thur. Nov. 4. 1858 [*"Oct." incorrectly recorded*].

I left at 8½, stopped a few moments at Sopori and got some butter, the first here for a long while, at 75 cts per lb. We got here in the Ambulance at 3 P.M. Our furnace is running. It did not do well last night, from neglect of Mexicans, but is doing well now. At Tubac this morning it was quite cold and in fact I was cold on the road for several hours.

Yesterday Mr. L. showed me the Reports he has written and the business letters and the answers of such as required it. He also showed me a letter from Matilda as late as 24 Sept. All well she says—but nothing definite about Mary's leg. Mr. L. and I had a long talk about the family. He dont like some of it. He did not spare Mrs. Norton.* I think he has just cause for complaint. I think some of them are very unreasonable.

It is getting quite cool this evening.

C. C. Fri. Nov. 5. 1858.

Last night was cold, but pleasant to-day. The Ambulance

---

*Possibly a relative of Heintzelman's wife.

did not get away till late. The wagon left for the timber. We had our corral repaired, sent more ore to Arivaca—from the other side of the Arroyo. It is said to be quite rich. The furnace does well and will probably run till midnight. Got the wheels rent of the Exp. Wag. Our well gets along. We have water, but will carry it to the bed rock and then deepen the others. Brunckow is much better.

I have been trying for some time to reduce expenses at Tubac, in fact break it up, leaving only the store with one man and a porter, or semi assistant. Mr. Lathrop is now there, with a Concord coach and four mules, a $200 horse (American) and a good riding mule, driver at $50 a month, cook at $35 and boy at $4.—all this for one man and whose duties are at this place and I am here, and without a servant attending to them. We have a cook at $12 cooks for some 15 and he has a boy at $10 to assist him. Mr. L. has extras daily, wine etc. We have had a few pounds of butter, the only extra. The establishment must be broken up and he must come here. He is now waiting for Kirkland to come and take the house. If he dont come soon I will shut it up and let a person take care of it. The expense of looking to it will be much less than now. All the animals there are fed on corn—all ours here, that work daily, get what grass they pick. The whole arrangement is a bad one. No excuses will continue it.

C. C. Sat. Nov. 6. 1858.

Quite cold last night and ice this morning. If the furnace had run till about midnight we would have smelted all the ore prepared, but about 10 P.M. the [unreadable] was burned out* and the furnace so much injured they had to stop. It requires much care to smelt this refuse from the vaso furnace; but this accident is to be attributed to nothing but neglect.

---

*Heintzelman tried to use a French word for the refuse.

Half the work done on another furnace (liquitative)* yesterday, was done so badly that it dried and cracked and has
fallen down. A day was spent on the old vaso in getting out
the deposit. I proposed removing a few adobes to get at it
easily and do it with half the time or labor, but it could not be
done. Now to prepare it, they take them down. These are but
specimens of the manner in which business is done here. We
have reduced ore to the amount of some $3.000 the last three
months. I think it very little if anything exceeds the cost of the
quarrying the ore and smelting it. All this is enough to disgust one with the whole concern. If I could get a few good
American families with the business I would make a clean
sweep.

The Ecrevin is burned up and I dont know now whether I
will be able to start another furnace until I get another. Had I
been told before I went to Tubac, that they are so easily destroyed I might have sent to Magdalena and had another in
ten days or so. Now I dont know when an opportunity will
offer. I have been waiting for some time for the tents and then
for some men to prepare the ground to pitch it. With my
assistance it was done in a manner today. A trifle of work was
done on the new furnace. Part was taken down and about as
much put up, so that nothing is gained. The vaso is nearly
finished and the Liquitative furnace was lit at 3½ P.M. Mr.
Küstel worked at it when the mason could have done it better
in less time.

We had musty flour at dinner. I sent a note to Mr. Lathrop
to send down tomorrow 700 pounds in the Ambulance. The
store keeper dont know flour is wanted until he sells the last
pound. Many others are just like him. Yesterday the mason

---

*Probably a reference to liquation, a method of extracting metals from
their ores by heating the material and "melting out" the desired metal,
which collects in the lowest point in the furnace. Heintzelman also refers to this as the "liquative process."

was at his work with the trowel in one hand and a cigarrito in the other.

Cerro Colorado Sun. Nov. 7. 1858.

To-day is warmer than it has been for several days. The liquitative and sweating process stopped at 8 P.M. having run out 4½ planchas. It will be continued tomorrow and then the refining process. The silver obtained is scarcely worth the expense, but it is necessary to separate the copper from the lead, the latter being wanted for future operations.

We caught one of our men to-day going off with 36 pounds of our richest ore. The man I sent to Tubac last evening will also bring back some ore stopped from another. We let these off, but promised the next 50 lashes.

Mr. Küstel and his family have gone to Arivaca and I understand to Los Alamos, to see whether they will like it. There is plenty of house room there and I hope it will suit them. Any where to be rid of them.

We had an auction last evening and sold the effects of Olds. They brought some $40 odd dollars, including a horse and saddle. I wrote to Eddy and send it up to Mr. Lathrop to put in a draft for $35 14/100 to pay the Doctors (Tripler's) indebtedness to Mr. Alex. G. Abell.

The Ambulance came at 3½ P.M. and much to my surprise Mr. Lathrop was not along and worse than all he sent but $65 to pay what he knew would be over $100. He wrote a long letter but quite unsatisfactory. Pedros and family have passed through on their way to Sonora. Buckley has not returned — sick at the Colorado. Jaegers teams are on the way. Wrightson must have been at the Rio Grande about the 3rd or 4th and may be here about the 20th to the 31st.

I got a letter from Cheever. As usual so badly written I will have to read it several times before I can make it all out. He has sold but 20 to 25 shares and on 6 mos. time. I am glad he has sold no more and when he gets my letters he will return the unsold. He (Mr. L.) also sent me a letter from his cousin Jed about the mail arrangements to Tubac and private matters. One from Ehrenberg—not very satisfactory. I also got one from Dunbar full of complaints. I wrote a long reply to Mr. Lathrop and gave him my views, which I dont think he will like.

C. C. Monday Nov. 8. 1858.

A warm day. Work goes on slowly. I have a man trying to prepare to pitch my tent. A woman is repairing it. When it will be done no one knows. All work goes on very slowly. Mr. Methner is at work laying the inside of the new furnace, instead of the mason we have, who if he can do it at all, slow as Mexicans are could do it in half the time. He laid in two hours *three* stones. I believe there were three. He spent a day last week in pulling out a few stones Brunckow put in and putting them back. The fault I find is that all our principal men, instead of showing the Mexicans how to do things undertake to do it themselves and thus take double the time. The carpenters will all be called off to do what any Mexican can do just as well.

The wagon from the Pinery has arrived and brought two sticks 14 feet long in place of two 25 feet long and the teamster has broken his hounds.* I have two or three notes from young Mr. Poston, not in the most respectful tone. He had better look out, or he will find we can dispense with his services. Our men have had no meat for three days and we none to-day, from the neglect of our worthless storekeeper. He let the flour get out without saying a word.

The old woman (Mrs. Klein) came to me and insisted I should sell her three pounds of butter. I told her I had not so

---

*Side bars of a wagon used to increase the rigidity of the parts connected.

much to spare, but that I intended to give her some. She insisted she knew better and must have it. I told her I did not have so much and that I had sent part of it to Tubac and Arivaca and that she could not have it. She is an old hag and every body is heartily tired of her. We will all be delighted when next week comes, as it is understood they then go to Los Alamos. Mr. Küstel and they I believe will stay there. There are the best houses out of Tubac.

C. C. Tues. Nov. 9. 1858.

We sent the wagon to Arivaca with the timber and it is back. The liquative process is over and the refining which commenced at sun down yesterday is going on. The prospect now is that the stone work of the furnace, the new one, will be done to-day. Tomorrow I hope the chimney will be carried up. Mr. Lathrop rode down on our American horse and got here before dinner. We go to Arivaca in the morning. I got my tent up. A miserable affair it is. I will move in, in a day or two. Kirkland will probably take our house next week. It is like drawing teeth to get Lathrop away from there.

Wed. Nov. 10. 1858.

This has been a warm day. After breakfast I set one man to repairing a broken wagon to go after timber and another to prepare the roof for the chimney of the new furnace to pass out and then got on a mule and Lathrop on a horse and we rode to Los Alamos and Arivaca. There are 7 cargos of lead ore ready. At Arivaca we found a fire lighted in the roasting furnace to-day it and the work going on well on the Amalgamation building. The arrastras have commenced grinding but do not do much, as the stones are too small. Mr. Brown gave us a very good dinner, mostly cooked by himself. We were home by 2½ P.M. We looked out a new and shorter road as we went over.

I found but little done at the furnace. The difficulty is water, although there was plenty to make mortar for a new house. I have ordered young Poston over here to take charge of the store and intend to discharge the Mexican we have, as he is not honest. I this morning drew the draft of a letter to Dunbar, in answer to his.

Thurs. Nov. 11. 1858.

I called Mr. Lathrop as day dawned. He got ready, threw the Riata* around a post and came in the house. When he went out his horse had started for Sopori and he lost half an hour. I was mistaken about the water. There was a scarcity for the house but plenty for mortar. Mr. Methner was at work in the interior of the furnace and laid 18 Adobes. The carpenters were at work on the roof, preparing it to let the chimney through. It might and should have been done in an hour, but allowing them three, and the aid of four carpenters he would still have the balance of the day to lay 18 Adobes. There was no art in laying them. Two on two sides, three behind and three on end on the back. I dont think Job ever undertook to erect a smelting furnace. It was a month this morning since I made them commence this furnace. At home a mason would be discharged who would not build one in less than a week. This is a specimen of the manner in which work is done here.

Mr. Brown discharged 4 men yesterday because they would not take damaged flour. It is not very bad as we had it several days at our table. He also discharged the Arrastra maker for the same reason. This is not much loss as he is rather worthless, only we have not the money to pay him.

Yancey† passed through here, on his way home, having taking his new sick wife to her friends in Sonora. He had not been married a week, until he hung around our house to get

---

*A lariat, often of braided rawhide.
†Possibly Joseph Yancey, a rancher.

breakfast. Mr. Methner was on the roof most of the afternoon and I the last hour or more and we nearly got the chimney finished. The men worked till after sund. Mr. Küstel sent back the Arrastra man and goes down him self tomorrow.

C. C. Fri. Nov 12. 1858.

It has been warm the last two days and cloudy this morning. Mr. Küstel and Mrs. Klein rode in the Exp. Wag to Los Alamos this morning, with a load of their traps. I believe she stays and he returns for her daughter's and the rest of their things. He this morning insisted on taking the window out of the house they live in, and to Los Alamos. I was strongly insisted it should not go and finally had to ask him whose opinion, as to what was best and proper to be done should govern — his or mine. I told him the glass was expected every day and when it came a window, to fit should be made for them. He was not satisfied.

The chimney was finished this morning and preparations are making to start the old furnace with the remainder of the slag etc. from the vaso, not before the smelted and then go on with the H. ore. Work will also be done on the new furnace. Four old hands and excellent ones returned to-day.

The Ambulance got in about 3 P.M. with flour, some goods, a little manta.* The wagons with the "Tabletas" will not be in for a day or two. The Pima and Maricopa Indians some 40 on their way to the Fort to try and get arms. They lost a chief and two warriors in a fight near the mouth of the San Pedro and say they killed 7 Apaches. Two of the Apaches have been near Tubac — drove off Kitchens† cows, but he got them back

---

*Coarse cotton cloth.
†Peter Kitchen (1822–1895), who owned a ranch near Calabazas, was known for his ability to fight off Indian attacks. His house provided a refuge for travelers.

and tried to drive off Carother's* — did not succeed. No news from Wrightson or Jaeger's wagons.[2]

C. C. Sat. Nov. 13. 1858.

Henry gave away most of his corn and turned out his mules. This morning he could not find one — since found. We gave him one and he left at 12 n. Our carpenters and blkS. have gone to Tubac on a frolic. The slag is all smelted — at 10½ — now on the H. ore. Furnace does well. I fear we will suffer from the scarcity of water. We have commenced digging the third well — to have one to drink — one for the mules and one for the washer-woman. Mr. Poston went back to Arivaca this morning. Mrs. Klein sent her cots etc. by a wagon to Los Alamos. Quite warm to-day.

Sun. Nov. 14. 1858. C. Colorado.

The furnace appears to work well, but turns out the planchas slowly. Mr. Brunckow has gone to Los Alamos and will see about lead ore. I fear we will have difficulty in keeping up a supply of good. He will look at the mina Blanca. He says the vein is thin, but metal good. I sent the wagon over to Arivaca with the three long sticks of timber. Mr. Küstel came over and at precisely *two* minutes past one P.M. I had the pleasure of seeing him drive off with his sister and her daughter. They detained the wagon this morning one hour and he had to wait some time for them. They carried off everything they could lay their hands on. They came in the little Exp. Wag. and I am sure they have now three loads. Several other persons with baggage also came with them.

At dusk Louis and Haberman returned and Hülseman arrived and the latter brought me $150. No letters from Margaret. I got a letter from T. Wrightson dated 19 Oct. with

---

*James H. Carothers.

correspondence with Dunbar of the old character. Also letters from Ehrenberg to Lathrop—not very satisfactory the last. Ore has not yielded much silver. It is possible to get from scoria* enough to pay balance of drafts still due, or soon to become due. There is also a letter from Dunbar to Poston, Director of the Mines, L. opened. It is business and also full of complaints.

Mr. Brunckow has returned from Arivaca and Los Alamos. He likes the new lead mine and was much pleased with the works at Arivaca. He and Küstel both spoke pleased with a Patio amalgamation, on a small scale commenced. If it succeeds well, we will carry it on, also.

C. C. Monday Nov. 15. 1858.

Cold this morning and windy, but now more pleasant. The old furnace burned out the tuyere† this morning and stopped. This is the second time in ten days. They attribute it to the quartz in the lead ore, but I do to the neglect of the Mexican smelters. They are at work on the new furnace and I hope to put it in blast in the morning. There is no tuyere to be had this side of Magdalena. We expect before long to be able to make our own.

Jno. Poston got here from Arivaca at noon. He Hülseman and Brunckow are busy on accounts. We shall discharge our principal smelter and our Mexican store keeper. Neither is honest.

It is confidently asserted that the new furnace would be ready in the morning. I have been looking at it and I have my doubts.

I copied my letter to Dunbar and wrote to Margaret, and to Cheever and made a report to the Sect.

---

*Refuse of fused metals, or slag.

† The pipe through which air is forced into a blast furnace.

4½ P.M. Anton is in from Tubac, with a note from L. Akes* team not in yet. Kirkland drives for the stage co. and will not take the house. I must have Lathrop out here, as soon as the goods arrive. He must close the House. No news from Jaegers teams. They must be out 13 days if heard from the day they left.[3]

Cerro Colorado Tues. Nov. 16. 1858.

It has been warm and pleasant to-day. I moved into my tent. It feels quite comfortable now, though it may not long. It has one quality—privacy, no other place I have occupied previously had.

Hülseman got here after dinner from Arivaca and left for Tubac. I gave him my letters for the mail and a long one for Mr. Lathrop. The new furnace was promised to be done to-day, but I fear not. The bellows is ready but the front is not in the furnace. It is not dry enough I suppose. Half the lead and silver is refined and yields but 47 oz. I did hope, as there were 207 lbs H. ore that it would yield $200—but I see now it ought not to yield even $100. It is better than I expected, though I calculated so much. I thought 50 cts a pound would make $200. We have got our cart started again.

Mr. Hoppel from Mesilla, a friend of Brunckow arrived here this afternoon. Wrightson's train was at San Elizario on the 7 or 8th, this month badly broken down—the wagons overloaded. He wont be here this month. Akes team from the Colorado was at Tucson on the 13th and said Jaeger's wagons were to leave in six days after him. They should be here this week.

C. C. Wed. Nov. 17. 1858.

Mr. Hoppel went into the mine and has started for Tubac. Also our old store keeper and the arrastra maker. We will this

---

* Felix Grundy Ake and his family were farmers and teamsters.

evening discharge our principal smelter. His wages are $65 a month and the other $25. Quite a saving. We sent a wagon with ore to Arivaca. I had an old grey horse shod and went selected the road out of the valley onto a plain, from which there is no difficulty. I will try and have the road put in travelling order this week.

The new furnace was put in blast at 11½ a.m. It has been *thirty eight* days in building and might have been built in a week. I slept cold last night. The bottom of my tent is much torn.

C. C. Thurs. Nov. 18. 1858.

Night cold. Miller got back about 8 P.M. and brought me two letters from Lathrop. He has been sick again. He sent me his letter for Dunbar. It is all very well, but a buggy wagon he ordered. I told him to strike that out. He has already more personal transportation than necessary. I wrote to Ewell about his ore. From L's not sending the Ambulance I had to send up the wagon this morning, though very inconvenient. The furnace is doing well.

I went with a Mexican and pack mule nearly to the top of Cerro Colorado for stone to try to make a tuyere. Before I got back three ox carts passed for Arivaca with the tabletas for the house and Jno Streit returned with the mail. I got a letter from Hooper. Jaegers wagons did not start till the 10th. I got a letter from T. Wrightson dated 24 Sept. Hard pressed for money. I got two from Margaret, dated 24 Sept. via S. Antonio and 24 Oct. via St. Louis. She is dissatisfied and complains about the difficulty of getting money from Wrightson. It is too provoking. She has paid Colts note, she not have done, if she was in want of money. She expects Mrs. Farber from Buffalo to spend some time with her. I got her first letter from Mary. It is very well written. Her leg is not well yet. It is quite windy and rather cold and disagreeable to live in a tent. But anything to expedite work and to get off home.

C. C. Fri. Nov. 19. 1858.

I slept quite cold last night. We finished the fan, though I fear the Mexicans wont know how to use it. The carpenter Jno. Streit and Miller* left this afternoon for Arivaca. I gave them a note to Küstel he wont like. I said they were sent to complete the Amalgamation machinery and not to be taken off for any outside work. That I should make frequent visits and judge of the necessity for anything else. We cant afford to lose a day for outside work unless of great importance.[4]

I wrote a long letter to T. Wrightson and a note to Lathrop by Akes teams, on their way back. The furnace is doing well. The new stone tuyere is nearly ready. The ore from the other side the arroyo which when last assayed yielded only 150$ per ton — now it yields $600.

Cerro Colorado Sat. Nov. 20. 1858.

Cold and very windy. The wagon arrived after I got to bed. I got Lathrop's letter and answered it this morning. The wagon went to Arivaca. Gonzales is in Tubac and Pedros's wagons expected to-day. Gándara has been defeated by Pesqueira in Sinaloa.[5] The furnace does well. All the lead ore is used up. We hope to have more early next week. Mr. Lathrop got here at 3 P.M. in the Ambulance with liquor — several boxes. The wagons of Pedros will be here tonight with corn etc.

C. C. Sun. Nov. 21. 1858.

Last night had been the only night I have slept at all comfortable. I did not suffer at all from the cold. To-day is warm. I intended to go as far as we want to alter the old road (about 4 miles) with Brunckow and Louis, but the mules could not be found. We did not get them until 12. At 12½ Pedros's wagons arrived with the corn flour, frijoles, pinole and panoche etc.

---

*Possibly Fred Miller, who later worked with Methner.

Heintzelman Mine at Cerro Colorado, where a "vein of Silver ore" was discovered in late January, 1857.

In the San Antonio papers is the official report of the defeat by Major Van Dorn of the Comanches, with the loss of 56 warriors. Lt. Van Camp* was killed and Major Van Dorn wounded.[6]

C. C. Mon. Nov. 22. 1858.

Weather milder. Mr. Brunckow got back late. There are but 300 pounds lead ore and that poor. Prospect of more—bad. The Bksmith put on the tire on one of Pedros's wagons and his son left in the night with it. The mail got in still later with papers and letters. Major H. P. Heintzelman† is at Yuma Indian Agent of the Colorado Dist and wrote me a letter. In Hoopers letter I received the information of his arrival. I got a letter from T. Wrightson dated Oct. 29. Nothing special, only no money to send.[7]

Mr. Lathrop started for Tubac and goes to the Fort to try and make arrangements for more lead ore. I fear he will not succeed. We have commenced refining. I sent a wagon to Arivaca with timber etc. I must do all I can to hurry the Amalgamation works. We will try and send some ore to Sonora for smelting and thus raise a little money. We tried to get some information from Brunckow as to the ore he can get out of the mine this week, but he is entirely noncommittal. I must go over to Arivaca and see what they are doing. I fear the carpenters are wasting their time on outside work.

The Sept no. of Harper's Mag. sent by Margaret came this mail. I also got from S. Francisco the opinion of the

---

*Earl Van Dorn and Cornelius Van Camp were serving on frontier duty in Texas with the Second Cavalry when the skirmish occurred on October 1.
†Henry P. Heintzelman, Samuel's cousin, was agent for the Klamath Indian Reservation.

Judges and appointment of a receiver in the new Almaden Quicksilver mines.*[8]

We are getting out some rich ore adapted to smelting. Very little quartz in it.

C. C. Tues. Nov. 23. 1858.

I rode to Arivaca and back. They have but few men and work goes on slowly. They are in want of the timber. One of the carpenters is in Los Alamos cutting some. I got home to dinner. I road out over the ground selected for the new road. I wrote to Margaret and a note to Charlie† in answer to his of last June.

Two gentlemen [inserted: "They came for some mules left with us to keep."] rode up this afternoon and brought a letter from Mr. Lathrop. He says one is Fernandez, but it dont prove so. Miles is at Tubac and has been settled with. We were to pay him $500, but he settled without. Mr. L. goes to the Fort to-day. Wrightson was starting his teams on the 10th and wrote to Grosvenor. I wrote to T. Wrightson. Furnace started at 5½ P.M.

C. C. Wed. Nov. 24. 1858.

Got through smelting late in the afternoon—amt 215 oz. Capt. Ewell's lead was refined in the vaso and yielded 11½ oz. when there were by assay only 9 oz. in it. I sent a wagon to Tubac and one to Arivaca. I had the mules up and fed, and this morning the scamp going to Arivaca let one get away and did not leave till 10 O'Clock. We had some men after a thief who stole a horse and rifle. They found them here and recovered them. They are very good in restoring us our lost property. I told them we could not deliver the thief.

---

*These valuable mines were the subject of a title dispute that lasted twelve years. In 1858, an injunction put the mine temporarily in the category of U.S. public lands.
†Heintzelman's son.

Fernandez came this afternoon and we have made a partial agreement for his taking some ore, in place of the silver we owe him. We are getting out the richest and most abundant I have seen since I came out.

I have commenced writing my Report, or rather making copious notes. It is very warm to-day — as warm as summer. I learn now that instead of one cargo of lead ore as Brunckow said on Sunday, we have some 6 or 8 at Los Alamos. When culled there will not be over 4 or 5 fit for the furnace. This will however help us along. Fernandez came this morning. He has looked at the ore and I hope to sell him some at a fair price. We made a calculation last evening and I think it costs us near $50 to smelt a cargo of ore. I enquired of Fernandez and he says it costs them 25 to 30 dollars to smelt the same.

C. C. Thurs. Nov. 25. 1858.

Fernandez left this morning. He had some goods to sell, but was too dear. Those men left with the mules. I sent my letters by them. It is very windy and blows directly into my tent. I dont feel very well to-day. I still weigh but 124½ pounds. I dont see why I dont pick up. The furnace still goes. We got some lead ore from Los Alamos. I finished reading Harper's for Sept.

All this fine looking ore turns out poor — much copper and only $400 the ton.

C. C. Fri. Nov. 26. 1858.

Blew hard all night and the fly being a little torn flapped disagreeably. It has been blowing hard all day, first from the S.E. and now nearly veered to the S.W. with a prospect of an end of it. It was cloudy, with the clouds flying fast. Our old store keeper and his woman left in the night — about 10 or 11 P.M. A good riddance. After dark the wagon returned from Tubac. Mr. L gone to the Fort. Soon after Kirkland's ox-team with timber arrived and this morning went to Arivaca. To-morrow Akes teams with the vigas should be at Arivaca. I have not been able to do much to-day for the wind. It reminds me of Yuma. My old tent I was afraid would not stand it. It is not cold out of the wind.

I begin to feel a little homesick, as I often did at Yuma. This is however not the first time I have felt so since I have been out here. Nothing but the feeling of absolute necessity would have kept me here so long. It will take long enough to get the works in operation with me and much longer if I go away. Mr. Lathrop is a good business man, but has no idea of economy.

The peaks of the Sta. Rita have been concealed by the clouds all day.

C. C. Sat. Nov. 27. 1858.

It sounded on my tent last night as if we had a few drops of rain. To-day has been cold and windery, with several showers of rain. About 3 P.M. Mr. Lathrop and Mr. Jarvis arrived. Mr. L. bought a few tons of lead ore at $75, we to have the silver and haul. It is high but the best that could be done. Brevoort has the management of the mine from Capt. Ewell—much to the latters disgust. Jaeger's teams were heard of at the Pimas *five* days ago and should be here or rather at Tubac on Sunday.

C. C. Sun. Nov. 28. 1858.

It rained some last night. The whole rain fall is but 17/100 of an inch. The peaks of Sta Rita are white—the first time this season. L and Jarvis left at 11½ a.m. and Brunckow, to go to the Patagonia mine to select the lead ore. We have been all the morning looking for the mules to send the French carpenter to Arivaca. We made a proposition to Capt. Ewell to sell him some of our stock, to pay a pressing debt. Mr. L. and

Jarvis both have urged it. I was not disposed to accede to his proposition. They go to Tucson this week to buy blankets and great coats. I am determined to have Lathrop here this week and break up Tubac at least as a hotel. There is always an excuse to hold on to it.

Jaegers wagons should be in Tubac to-day. I send in the wag. tomorrow. Three of Akes ox wagons passed at 2½ loaded with very fine vigas for the Amalgamation works. We have hunted all day without finding our mules to send the French carpenter to Arivaca. Jno. Poston rode over. Mr. Jarvis was saying that we ought to make ourselves comfortable — that no company would want its officers to be uncomfortable. This is all true as an abstract proposition; but if last week, or any previous time I had taken some men to finish a house commenced I might as well have packed up and started for home. The furnace would have stopped and the next week the men would have left.

It has cleared off and is getting cold.

Cerro Colorado Mon. Nov. 29. 1858.

It was cold, but calm last night. I slept cold. This morning about 10 O'Clock we succeeded in making up the team to send to Tubac, in hopes our goods will be there. The other mules are not found yet. We commenced refining, but the vaso was made in the damp weather and would not stand. It has to be made over. — commenced again at 4 P.M.

We had a strike this morning. Methner knew the dissatisfaction last week and told every body but me. They think they dont get the usual rations. All they wanted was a few more frijoles and a little more salt. I granted it, but disliked to do it on compulsion. We got five new men and could not afford to risk losing a man. We yesterday gave orders to raise the frijole ration one half. They also like measure better than weight. If Methner had told it yesterday, we would at once have assented to the change. The forenoon was delightful, but now it is cloudy and cooler. At 4 P.M. found the other team mules.

C. C. Tues. Nov. 30. 1858.

A few drops rain last night. Windy and unpleasant to-day. Schuchard and the two sons of Gándara arrived at sundown. They looked at the mine and furnaces and have left for Arivaca. I have recommenced work on an unfinished building for the Director. The French carpenter I sent to Arivaca — the one who cut his foot with the adze.

Our wagon got home early. Mr. Küstel writes he has not built the blkS shop, but wants the Blk smith. It is a good sign.

December
1858

C. C. Wed. Dec. 1st. 1858.

It has blown a gale of wind all day and right into my tent. I rode to Arivaca. Are putting up the stamps.* Mr. Küstel thinks the Amal. Works will be ready in *eight* weeks—Mr. Brown says by Christmas. It goes very slowly. I am trying to get more carpenters. We want more Peons, both here and at Arivaca.

The carpenters have left their work and made themselves bunks and tables for the house—both unnecessary. Two negroes were here to-day. I hired one to drive oxen, the other is a kind of carpenter and their wives wash. They are from Texas and have been *three* years on the road, via Sinaloa and Sonora. They left their families at or near Sarica and will fetch them.

The wagon got back after dark. No goods arrived yet.

Done refining—11 lbs. 10 oz. silver. Furnace in blast since 12.

Wrote report to Secretary. Mr. Küstel can do without the BlkSmith a week or more. Every few days he gets into a fever

---

*Or stamp mill, an apparatus used to crush ore as part of the amalgamation process.

about something. The front of my tent is so rotten, to save it from blowing to pieces I had to put a large cloth over it, to keep the wind out. It surges and creaks like a ship in a gale. I dont know how much sleep I will get tonight. The weather is not cold and would be pleasant enough were it not for this wind. We had a few drops of rain just before night. Last evening a man from Altar came with a receipt for some more salt delivered at Arivaca on one of Poston's contracts, no one knows about. I told him I knew nothing about it but from him and that at present at least we did not want any more.

C. C. Thursday Dec. 2. 1858.

Heavy wind and rain storm last night, with wind, rain and snow to-day. I could not remain in my tent—could not open it, or have a fire. Have been all day in the house and wrote my monthly reports, and letters to Margaret and sister Maria. Sent wagon to Arivaca. This morning our rain gauge, (holds .6 of an inch) was full. I lay awake in the night and feared every moment the tent would come down. It is old and has but four cords to hold it.

C. C. Fri. Dec. 3. 1858.

It grew calm towards evening with snow and soon after dark the ground was quite white. I went to bed at 7 P.M. as I did not know what better to do. It was too cold to sit up in my tent.

This morning the tops of the surrounding mountains were enveloped with clouds. To the north the Mal Pais Mts. to the east the Sta Ritas and to the S.E. the Atasco range were white with snow. A range low, to the South showed patches of snow. The sun shone out occasionally, but by 10 it commenced raining again. During the night it rained but little. Yesterday morning the rain gauge was full, at 4 P.M. again and this morning. It holds but .60 of an inch of water—

entirely too little for this rainless country, according to Dr. Antisell.*[1]

Yancy and Ortiz left this morning for Tubutama. I sent by the former a letter to Küstel offering the carpenters a months wages each for a bar of silver on or before Christmas.

C. C. Sat. Dec. 4. 1858.

At 4 P.M. I emptied yesterday the rain gauge. This morning it had .5 of an inch. The whole amount of rain is 2.7 inches, not counting what was lost by the three overflows. I believe the storm is over, though there are still flying clouds. The tops of the mts all around us are quite white. The Sta Rita quite low. Its tops are still in clouds. The wind from the S. East is still quite keen.

Mr. Fernandez arrived at noon from Tucson. Jaegers wagons have arrived and must be in Tubac tomorrow. I sent off my letters this morning to Tubac and also sent in the wagon.

F. has just left here. He now proposes for a draft on Cal. for $2.000 to pay us $1.000 in gold and the balance as he gets it in Tucson—at about $100 to $150 per week. We have no smelting ore ready for him. I wrote to Mr. Lathrop to see how he can negotiate with him.

C. C. Sun. Dec. 5. 1858.

We had a cold night. I could not keep my feet warm. The day commenced beautiful, but since dinner it has clouded up and the wind has risen and is cool. The Gándaras left this morning for Tubac. This is the anniversary of my wedding day. How often I have been from home when it has occurred.

---

*Thomas Antisell (1817–1893), who served as a geologist for the railroad survey along the 32nd parallel between Doña Ana and the Pima Villages. Heintzelman, the Wrightsons, and other promoters of southwestern ventures criticized Antisell's report on the amount and character of rainfall in the Gadsden Purchase.

I will try and make this the last time. I have not a soul to even talk of it and no enjoyment. It is rather cold living in a tent. What a pleasure it would be to drop in at home to-day.

C. C. Mon. Dec. 6. 1858.

At sun down Brunckow got back. We will get our ore from the lead mine this week. We are to have *five* tons in all. It was difficult to pick out so much. The Sonoran's from Sta Cruz carted the ore away, the few days no one was in charge. There is much snow in the mountains. The houses at Sta Rita leaked badly.

Mr. Lathrop made an arrangement with Fernandez to get coin for 3 mos. drafts on S. Francisco. Jaegers wagons are expected in Tubac to-day, when he will bring out goods. The wagon I sent in got here at 1½ P.M. to-day. Brown and Miller were left in Tubac. It is too provoking that Miller should have two days, when his work is so much needed. I sent a man in to-day with a letter to Mr. L. to send and try and hire two carpenters from the soldiers, as well as try and get the one from the Pinery.

We can do but little work to-day. Cloudy, cold, windy occasionally a slight drizzle of rain. The wind is S.W. and blows from the Gulf. Refining furnace is in blast. My tent is very uncomfortable. We have failed in getting Quicksilver from Sonora and have sent $450 [$480?] to Pedros to send to Hermosillo for it. It should be here before Jan. Pedros tried to buy it on credit, but it only sells for cash. The arrangement with Fernandez fortunately gives us the cash.

C. C. Tuesday Dec. 7. 1858.

Late in the afternoon it commenced raining and this morning we had .25 of an inch of water. Soon after dark it cleared off. This morning was clear and pleasant, but afterwards clouds and a sprinkle of rain. At 1 P.M. Kirklands team with timber arrived.

Mr. Brunckow brought me the finest specimen of ore from the H. mine I have yet seen. It contains nearly or quite all the ores we find in the mine.

The silver-lead we have from the smelting of last week turns out ¾ richer than we supposed. We will get in place of $200 nearer $350 for our smelting. It is (the ore) from the neighborhood of that we were so much disappointed in. I think as we go deeper that the ore evidently improves in quality. A specimen yielded 16 per cent. But so rich ore is in very small quantities.

Mr. Lathrop got here a little after dark with a lot of goods. Our freight amounted to over $1.100. We pay part in flour and hope to get a draft from Grosvenor, for $500 sent him by Wrightson, which he cant sell and for which we can let him have coin. He is hard to deal with, as he lacks common sense. Mr. Jarvis stayed back to bring the mail—tomorrow. Wind changed to north in the afternoon and it is turning colder.

C. C. Wed. Dec. 8. 1858.

Water froze in my tent after I got up. Notwithstanding my repeated orders all our mules were turned out and this morning could not be found. After waiting sometime we took two of the Ambulance mules and Mr. Lathrop, Van Alstine and I drove to Arivaca. We found two of the carpenters over at Los Alamos getting timber. The other at work and the Peons digging a ditch for a well for the Amal. works and Küstel and Brown measuring for the horse power. The stamps are up. Most of our adobes are spoiled by the rain. When I look at the work still to be done I feel quite disheartened. We stopped to dinner and then drove home, expecting to find Jarvis with the mail, but he did not get here until near night. I got *ten* letters.

Three from Margaret, one from Mrs. Norton and one from Sister Maria—one from Cheever and the rest from Cincinnati. I hastily read them all and wrote since supper to Margaret. I had a letter from each of the children. There is some prospect of our getting some money from the States. Mr. T. Wrightson, writes quite encouragingly. Mr. Dunbar is married to a widow and 2 children and we hope wont come out.

Wind chilly.

C. Colorado Thurs. Dec. 9. 1858.

Last night was cold, but this has been a beautiful day—in fact warm. Lathrop, Jarvis & Van Alstine left about 8 a.m. for Tucson. Mr. Brunckow I sent to Los Alamos to see about lead ore. He reports more favourably. We will get some already out and there is a prospect of more coming out of the old mine. Suarez, who has long been expected came with flour. I had to pay him $100 in silver. Our furnace is doing well & we may have as much more tomorrow.

I have been trying to have a house prepared for the director, but to-day the mason I found at work on a Peon house. I ordered that he must work on the other tomorrow. Brunckow took it much to heart. It is time there should be a house for the Director.

What a nuisance it is to do business on limited means. I read over the business letters that came yesterday. We have a debt in S. Francisco of $6.292 91/100 and to meet which we have not $1.500. Unless we get prompt aid from home, we cant prevent more protests. We have already had some. Last mail gives some $1.100 Wrightson paid of Postons drafts. Part over $600 for a lot in Tubac, above our garden, some for furniture etc. of Robinson introduced chinche* here and at Tubac and a note on a gambler that will never be paid. Not a

---

*Bedbugs.

cent of it so far as I can learn was necessary and this when he was *straitened* for means.

C. C. Fri. Dec. 10. 1858 [inserted: "I wrote to cousin H. P. Heintzelman Ind agent Ft. Yuma"].

Warm and pleasant. The wagons with the last of the vigas are here and I suppose will reach Arivaca tonight. Schuchard was here and has left for Tubac. He is more reasonable about a settlement. He has promised to make me a sketch of this place for our reports. I have the masons again on the house for the Director. Got through with the litharge yesterday morning and have commenced on the H. ore. Got some more goods by those wagons from Tubac. I spent most of yesterday and evening reading the newspapers. I was quite behind.

Wrote to Hooper and cousin Heintzelman at Ft. Yuma.

Towards evening Capt. Ewell's wagon drove up with four fat hogs we bought of his company, weighing 1,359 pounds. There also came with it a soldier carpenter and another is on the way. Now I think with this aid we will soon be able to start our barrels to rolling. I also got a letter from Mr. God-frey* at the Fort who hired them for us. I have a note from Capt. Ewell, that he will have Egg nog, if I will come and my friends. I am sorry I cant come, or rather that I cant be at home to drink it. [2]

C. C. Sat. Dec. 11. 1858.

This was a beautiful morning; but clouded up, with high wind. The mason and his party had a task given them and have done more to-day, Sat. as it is than in any two days before. The carpenter from the fort has prepared the beams

---

*William J. Godfrey, postmaster for Fort Buchanan in 1858 and later superintendent of the Patagonia Mine and a partner in the Union Silver Mining Company.

for the large room and all the plank for them to rest on. Early next week, without rain the roof should be on, and in fact the house finished, so I could move in.

Küstel writes for the Blksmith monday. Akes teams are here from Arivaca. Some hands have arrived at Arivaca and the two negroes with their families.

C. C. Sun. Dec. 12. 1858.

I made arrangements to send the Blk Smith and carpenter to Arivaca to-day and all the others were going on a visit, but the worthless vaquero* let out the animals and they could not be found. Mr. Brunckow got a mule and went to dine with the *ladies* on wild ducks. About noon the carpenters came over. They give favourable accounts of the progress of the works last week. I have written a report to T. Wrightson Sec and a private letter.

After I went to bed last evening we had a violent squall lasted over an hour. I was much afraid my tent must go. There was no rain. It has been pleasant to-day, though a little windy. After tea I wrote to Cheever.

C. C. Mon. Dec. 13. 1858.

This morning, windy, cold, cloudy and threatening rain. A few drops late in the afternoon, since which it is clearing off. Mr. Lathrop and Mr. Jarvis arrived just after dinner with some blankets and other goods from Tucson.

Mr. Wrightson was seen at Cooke's springs 240 miles from Tucson and 2 feet snow in the pass this side. He gets along slowly and I fear will not be here before Christmas, if then.

It was cold, windy and cloudy this morning and threatening rain. Late in the afternoon it dropped a little and since appears to be clearing off. Our mason has gone off to Tubac and did not come back to-day, so that there has been no work

---

*A herdsman or cowboy.

done on our house and now all the adobes are used, so no more can be done, until some are made.

I took down the horse power and sent this afternoon the carpenter and Blacksmith to Arivaca. If the weather stays good the works must be done this month. A custom house officer* has arrived at Tucson and must occasion us some trouble. He made a Mexican there (Fernandez) pay duties. I fear that will interfere with us also.[3] We are now afraid Pedros will not come and may have to send down the Ambulance to get him to bring us some flour.

I got a letter from Margaret dated 16 Nov. She is getting settled for winter and is in good spirits. I also got a letter from W. T. Perkins.† He writes that Wrightson has gone East to see Colt about buying stock. If he gets money Perkins may come on with it.[4] Rain .02 of an inch.

Cerro Colorado Tues. Dec. 14. 1858.

Lathrop and Jarvis started for Tubac at 8½ a.m. Sent wagon also. Mr. Brown sent me a button of pure silver, the result of his experiment in the Mex. Patio system of Amalgamation. He thinks it will do well in the long warm summer. He wants to see me.

I got a note from Mr. Brown he wanted to see me as soon as convenient. After dinner I rode over and he told me to look out for a man to take his place, that he will leave in a month or six weeks. He thinks he can do better in a speculation of his own. I think he wants an interest in the mine Capt. Ewell has a part—the Patagonia and he expects to make $100 in 24 hours. This is the man we made an agreement with on the 8th of this month and paid his expenses out from S. Francisco.

---

*John Donaldson was appointed deputy collector of customs at Calabazas in December 1858. He later became concerned that the Sonora Exploring and Mining Company might be smuggling goods from Mexico and asked permission to inspect the roads more often.
†The clerk for the Sonora Exploring and Mining Company in Cincinnati.

He did not agree to stay any definite time, but stipulated to visit his family in the spring. This is the kind of people we have to deal with. Work goes slowly. Some of their men stayed here to-day.

The day is delightful.

Cerro Colorado Wed. Dec. 15. 1858.

A beautiful day—night was cold. Our pork is spoiling. We had the heads cut off and opened. After dinner Mr. Lathrop arrived and is now cutting the hogs up. Mr. Poston is at Tubac. His health is good, but one of his eyes has an ulcer behind and will require an operation.* He will go home soon as he can leave. He knows nothing about the markets in Sonora and in fact does not appear to have interested himself at all in company affairs. The Bishop† also came up.[5]

There is great excitement in Sonora about Filibusters. They heard those reports that were in the papers about Titus and Walker‡ and they are republished in the Gov. gazette. The Governor is disarming the people to get arms for the public service. The capt. (Davis§ of the St. Mary's) sloop of war has sent an express to Capt. Ewell to do what he can to prevent the invasion and Capt. Stone‖ has also written.[6]

---

*Poston seems to have suffered from ophthalmia, a severe inflammation of the eye.

†Pedro Loza y Pardave (1815–1898), the bishop of Sonora, who was exiled for his criticism of the 1857 Constitution.

‡William Walker (1824–1860), a filibuster, had captured the capital of Nicaragua in 1855 and had become its president in 1856. He was subsequently ousted and, during his attempt to return in 1860, was executed by the Honduran government.

§Charles Henry Davis (1807–1877), who had rescued Walker from Nicaragua when his government was overthrown.

‖Charles Pomeroy Stone (1824–1887) commanded an expedition for a Mexico City banking firm to survey the public domain in Sonora to which the governor, Ignacio Pesqueira, objected. Although Pesqueira did allow the expedition to continue, the survey was never completed. Stone was also acting consul at Guaymas.

We had quite a stampede a few minutes ago. A large drove of cattle was run on a trail from Arivaca to Sopori, or in that direction. Several insisted that the Apaches were driving them, and we ordered up animals to see, when some Mexicans who had been there told they were only a drove for a market.

Finished refining about daylight. Lit smelting fur. at 3 P.M.

C. C. Thurs. Dec. 16. 1858.

Another beautiful day. The furnace had like to have stopped if Methner had not seen it just at the time he did. The Mex. cant be trusted with the care or management of anything, without supervision. In night again something went wrong. It is doing well now.

Mr. Lathrop and I stirred up a worthless teamster and Mr. Brunckow took offense and has given his *three* months notice to quit. The man is his woman's father. He is quite worthless and B says so, but he has not been controlled — dont like to be.

We have just been getting out some of that very rich ore — silver copper glanz or Sulphurets of Silver copper. I got a few specimens and a fragment assayed yielded 50 percent.

I was going out with Schuchard to look at a mine about 3 ms. from here but the vaquero could not find me an animal to ride.

I wrote to Cheever about the mail and enclosed him a fragment of silver copper glanz that assays 50 percent silver.

C. C. Fri. Dec. 17. 1858.

The morning was beautiful and then turned very warm. In the afternoon clouds rose from the S.E. I hope they wont bring rain. We want ten days good weather. I rode out with Schuchard to look at the old S. José or Joseph mine, 2 ms or 2½ toward Baboquivera peak. There has been much more work done than at the Salero, but we could not find enough metal, in the rubbish to determine the character of the vein. The Sta Margurita mine is about a mile further. When we got back we found Küstel and Brown. They stayed to dinner. Mr. Montgomery a carpenter came and we hired him. Mr. Lathrop left at 2 P.M. We are getting out more good ore. We also found a very rare mineral—only found in Zacatecas Mexico—the Iodide of silver.

I wrote a few lines to Mr. Poston, at Tubac.

I have just obtained from Mr. Brunckow some fine specimens of Iodide of silver and chlorate. I also saw a piece of an Indian axe—made of mica slate.

C. C. Sat. Dec. 18. 1858.

Last night it was cloudy and mild at bed time [inserted: "I wrote to Margaret"] and I feared rain. It was cloudy this morning, but is now clear and looks well. It was the mildest night we have had for some time. We got from another part of the mine some fine ore, though not quite so rich as yesterday. There are over two cargos selected. I got a fine specimen of sulphuret of copper and chloride of silver. Jno. Poston left for Tubac in the little wagon to see his brother. Mr. Lathrop had him take quite a lot of fresh pork, besides what he carried with him yesterday in his saddle bags. We finished trying out our lard. Our cook and asst. have left.

Jno. Poston left and forgot my letters. Since dark the vaquero I sent after some animals returned, having been to Tubac and brought letters. The Ex. Com. have sold Col. Colt 500 shares at 25 per cent and privilege for 12 mos of 500 more— $5.000 to go by the steamer of 20th Nov. and must now be in S. Francisco to meet protested drafts. The balance after deducting the pistols, some 9.500$ goes to our credit at S. F. the next mail. This relieves us from any further embarrassment, but I would not have made such an agreement. Dunbar has resigned his place in the compy and it is accepted. He presents a large account.

I also got a letter from Margaret dated Nov. 25. The weather is bad, but she writes in good spirits, though I judge not very well. All suffer from colds. I wish Wrightson was here and as I want to start home as soon as possible. If the quicksilver comes I think we will be ready for it by the end of the month.

Wrote to T. Wrightson and to Lathrop. Jno. Poston forgot my letters to-day.

Cerro Colorado Sun. Dec. 19. 1858.

We had a most beautiful morning, but clouds soon rose and since then it has been windy and occasionally overcast and raw. I sent my letters to Tubac by a Mexican. I got Brunckow this afternoon to give me a history of the discovery of the Heintzelman mine. He did not give it in as interesting a manner as the first time he told me. Louis the Blksmith has been over and tells me the work on the Amal. Works goes on finely. A few more days of good weather and they will be ready. If only now we are not disappointed in the quicksilver.

Another carpenter has this moment reported. A discharged soldier from the Fort and I sent him to Arivaca, with a note to Brown. I think now we will get our machinery soon to work.

C. Colorado Monday Dec. 20, 1858.

Weather last night cold and clear and beautiful to-day. The carpenter, Montgomery, from Buffalo, I hired Friday has a letter from home and left, having worked one day. I asked him when he understood the works would be ready and he says Brown told him in three weeks. I dont see what *five* carpenters can find to do for so long a time. In the States they would put it up from the foundation.

Jno. Poston got here at sundown, in the Little Ex. Wag. His brother left on Sunday in the other I presume. Jarvis has gone to Tucson, to meet Major Ben. Mc'Cullough,* a Gov. emissary. He has a letter that the President will recommend 3.000 troops sent to Sonora till a stable Government is established.[7] Lathrop I dont know when he will be out. He now will wait for Poston to return and then get the papers, instead of getting them before he went and having time to examine them. His conduct is too provoking. He was when we were all in Tubac full of the Director's living at the mine and blaming Poston for not and now I cant get him here. He always contrives some excuse.

Pedros who contracted to deliver us flour, was within ten miles and met Capt. Ewell and has sold to him.

C. C. Wed. Dec. 22. 1858.

Yesterday morning I took the little Ex. Wagon and drove to Tubac. Schuchard rode his mule. I found Mr. Lathrop there. Mr. Poston got back at dusk from the Fort. He had his eye touched with nitrate of silver and the Doctor advised him not to travel. Grosvenor he say at the Fort. He went to Apache pass and there saw Wrightson and his train. Mules badly broken down. Had to double to get through the Pass and were sending back for the rest of the train. Pedros was at Fort. B. and took two of his wagons with corn to relieve Wrightson. They wont be here under 15 or 20 days. I got Mr. L. to write to him to come on, as I must see him before I go home.

Hülseman got in with the mail soon after I got there and I got letters from T. Wrightson. The overland mail will bring us $3.500 in coin. We wrote to Jarvis, who is still in Tucson to bring it in when it comes. This will relieve us from our great-

---

*Ben McCullough (1811–1862), a presidential commissioner who helped settle the 1858 Morman War, was a popular figure who had fought for Texas independence. In 1853 he was appointed marshal for the coast district of Texas, a post he resigned in the spring of 1859.

est difficulties. They are trying to buy a large stock of goods and ship across the Isthmus. We wrote immediately to them not to sell any more stock and that we dont want their goods now.

Yesterday was a beautiful day — to-day cloudy. The wagons left yesterday for our lead ore. A couple of fellows were to fight a duel up on the Sonoita. After they got on the ground and measured it Marshall,* one of the parties ran away.[8] I brought a clock out for this place. Got some Sonora oranges from Mr. Poston. [marginal note: "They are fine looking and a little sour."]

Mr. Brunckow has just assayed some black Fahl ore,† with sulphuret of copper and it yields 3.840 oz. of silver to the ton. Our ores have decidedly improved within the last week or so. Fahl ores contain silver, copper, Antimony, Zinc and arsenic and iron.

Domingo Gallo‡ was here yesterday from Los Alamos and reports the lead ore in the shaft improving in quantity and quality. I was just debating whether or not it would be well to stop work there. The fault I think has been in not pursuing one course steadily. Labor has been frittered away on other veins.

C. C. Thurs. Dec. 23. 1858.

I rode over to Arivaca. All the Mexicans have left for the Gila gold mines.§ Some persons from Sonora totled them

---

*Boyd Chittenden Marshall, who had been an expressman at Fort Buchanan, was farming on Sonoita Creek.

†Possibly Fahlband, thin beds of crystalline rock that are easily split into layers and that are impregnated with finely divided sulphides. They are not always rich enough to work.

‡Also referred to as Domingo Golio.

§Gold was discovered along the banks of the Gila River in September 1858. Gila City emerged from the ensuing emigration, but the fever quickly abated and the population declined.

off.[9] The two negroes and Mr. Brown were laying Adobes and the carpenters at work. From what one of the carpenters said they expect to be ready in about two weeks. The roof is all on but the rooms for the stamps and barrels and the wall of them have to be raised. I stayed to dinner. When I got back I found Mr. Belcher,* a brother in law of Major Allen's and agent of the San Xavier mining co. He came to see about our smelting some of their ore. I promised them and he left to bring it on. I wish he had been here a week earlier.

Late in the afternoon Lathrop and Jarvis arrived in the Ambulance. They brought a Yaqui Indian driver. Hülseman has been sent to Magdalena on some business. Mr. Lathrop has not brought his things to stay. It looks as if I would not get him out to stay, until I leave or after. Jarvis did not get the letter we wrote him and left before the mail got in. One mail is lost on account of the Express with the Presidents message.† It passed a few days ago.[10] The forenoon was beautiful. In the afternoon a cool wind and still since dark and milder. Mr. Küstel tells me it is not likely that we will have any more rain till late in January. The Mexicans wont work tomorrow and I also hear Monday.

C. C. Fri. Dec. 24. 1858.

We got up horses and mules to ride out to the St. José mina, but Jarvis had a bad cold and declined going. It got windy, cloudy and disagreeable—He took a horse, after dinner and has started for Tubac, to go to Tucson and try and meet Major Ben McCullough. Mr. Lathrop has gone to Los Alamos and Arivaca and may not be back before tomorrow.

---

*Possibly Edward H. Belcher, who signed the March 1, 1858, Memorial to Congress and the Hastings Appointment Petition.

†Buchanan's Second Annual Message of December 6, 1858, was concerned with problems along the southwestern frontier and suggested that the United States "assume a protectorate" over the northern parts of Chihuahua and Sonora.

He is here without his desk or baggage. It appears impossible to move him down here. He brought a few papers along, I suppose to satisfy me.

Mr. Jarvis read me from Col. Colts letter. It is supposed that the President will recommend ["order" crossed out] sending 3.000 troops to the frontier of Chihuahua and Sonora, to occupy if necessary. Colt wants Jarvis and I to see McCullough. Mrs. Colt has a son—born 24 Nov. It is very uncomfortable this afternoon. The furnace stopped at day light and no work doing to-day.

Mr. Lathrop got back from Arivaca after dark. On his way in he met Anton, Louis and Streit on their way to Tubac, on a frolic. The work has gone on well since I was there. The foundation for the barrels is laid.

Mr. Brunckow prepared us a hot claret punch and we spent our Christmas eve with that. Our Mexicans are very quiet. The wind has gone down and the weather is more pleasant.

Cerro Colorado Sat. Dec. 25. 1858.

This is a beautiful day. Our Mexicans are remarkably quiet. Mr. Lathrop took the little Ex. Wag and left for Tubac; with his Mex. driver, immediately after breakfast. Brunckow made a bowl of egg nog and then he and Methner and Haberman rode to Los Alamos and Arivaca. It leaves no one but Poston and I here.

We have a very simple dinner of salt fresh pork, miserable bread and as miserable pancakes made without eggs and water.

I wrote to T. Wrightson and Margaret.

Having got tired of sitting in my tent I started for a walk to see the Adobes and wells. As I approached the latter I saw a number of women half dressed run for their clothes. As it is the first time I have seen them make an attempt to wash them selves, I cut short my walk and turned back, allowing them to finish their washing without interruption.

Brunckow and Methner and Haberman got back early in the afternoon. The latter was very angry because some one rode his mule to Tubac. Every body, but the two soldier carpenters and the Frenchman are gone to Tubac. Küstel and his family they saw at Los Alamos. They also visited the lead mines and recommend moving the new from it and I think I will try the Mina Blanca.

We had a little egg nog after supper to finish off our dull Christmas. I wrote two letters and read Bayard Taylor's travels to the North.[11] The night is beautiful. You seldom see the stars so brilliant. Our whole place is remarkably quiet. Although we have over 50 Mexicans, but two bottles of whiskey were sold to-day.

Cerro Colorado Sun. Dec. 26. 1858.

This is another beautiful day, —in fact rather warm and quite so in the sunshine. The Mexicans had a game, kicking a ball called gohimire and gochimiri. A wooden ball as large as a mans fist made of hard wood. It is kicked along by the top of a mans foot. When it goes out of the road a man accompanies, whose duty it is to pick it up and place it in the road. A Mexican and Yaqui indian played, for $40. The distance from here to the Arroyo nearly half way to Arivaca, or about two leagues and back, according to the Mexican computation. I dont think it so far, but the whole distance I think about seven miles. They were gone exactly one hour. One of the assistants gave out and could not lay the ball and thus the Yaqui came in a few moments ahead. There was a dispute about the stakes, but I believe it was finally decided to give him $30.[12]

What long dull days these are, when there is no work going on. Every body complains. We are out of flour and sent a Mex. to Arivaca for a bag. We have had the most miserable bread for the last week and the cows are gone so we have no milk. To help our pork dinner, we had a very fair rice pudding.

I have just finished reading Bayard Taylor's travels in Norway, Sweden and Lapland. It is interesting; but contains too much description of the country and sky. Before this I read Gamboas mining ordinances of Spain. [13] Quite an interesting work, I bought for the company more than a year ago in Washington and sent out by mail. Books are scarce in this country.

It has been so warm that I have been setting reading in my tent without my coat.

I have felt particularly homesick to-day and so took a long nap. I very seldom sleep in day time, though I am always up before the sun.

About 8 P.M. I heard a horse approach on a gallop. A Mex. rode up and handed me a letter from Mr. Lathrop. Anton Elsner and Jno. Streit were drunk and the former shot the latter dead. Mr. L. writes in a most cowardly manner. He wants me to come in. From the Mex. account it was without any provocation. Jno. Poston rode over to Arivaca to get Miller to go to Tubac to make a coffin. Haberman is from 8 miles of Jno. Streit's fathers and will ride in with me. I was glad the other day when I heard they had gone to Tubac, as we would not have them here. I knew they all would get drunk, but I could not anticipate this.

Cerro Colorado Wed. Dec. 29. 1858.

Haberman and I rode to Tubac Monday. Anton was tied and locked up in a room. He is gone. In the night some Mexicans must have cut a hole in the wall and then cut the cords. We suspect a fellow with whom he was intimate. In the afternoon Streit was buried. He was a Catholic and is buried in the grave yard near the church. After he was buried a quite small child was buried with the drum and two violins.

[155]

I found Judge Rose, the new Consul to Guaymas* and Major Ben Mc'Cullough at the house. Yesterday after dinner they and Jarvis left in our little Exp. wag for Magdalena and Guaymas.[14]

Major Mc'Cullough is a secret agent sent to see how affairs go in Sonora and he and the Judge have also private speculations in view—amongst them a concession for a rail road. Zuloaga wishes to sell Sonora [inserted: "and part of Chihuahua"] and thinks with the money to be able to sustain himself. They expect to see Gándara. Judge Rose was in Columbus† when I was there as a. qm. and recollects my playing chess with him and McClintoc. I dont recollect him. We treated them with all the hospitality in our power and will have the Consul's aid at Guaymas. He will see if Poston can get a passage from there to meet the Steamer. He is well enough to go home now, if he only thought so. We settled with Schuchard and he leaves as soon as he sees Wrightson and gets his stock. I saw Grosvenor and he takes a message to W to come on at once as I wish to leave. His teamster stole 12 of his mules and some horses and left him at Dragoon springs—yesterday. It will take a week at least for him to get here with his train. He will leave part of it behind.

Those gentlemen and Jarvis brought up the $3.500 from Tucson. I also got a letter from T. W. Cin. He opposes sacrificing more stock for goods. I also got an order about the Actions with the Indians—and six companies of 1st Cav. to Riley, Washita and Fort Smith. These gentlemen think my Regt. may be ordered on this frontier. On some accounts I would like it; but then I will not be with my family. I have been separated enough already. The weather was tolerably pleasant yesterday, but cloudy towards night. In the night it

*Robert Rose, who arrived at his post in January 1859.
†Georgia.

commenced rain, then wind and snow. The rain gauge overflowed — .6 of an inch it registers.

Mr. Lathrop has been to Arivaca. They want Peons. Domingues is here. The mina Blanca he has cleared out and he thinks it not worth following up. Very little better prospect at Arenia. The vaso is going and the furnace has started late this afternoon. It has cleared off, but still windy. Wind North. Yesterday was Charlies thirteenth birthday. He is quite a large boy.

Cerro Colorado Thurs. Dec. 30. 1858.

I have determined not to wait for the Amalgamation works, but leave as soon as Wrightson comes here. The works may not be done under a month. I cant carry my trunk and am trying to have a bag made of "Vacate"* to hold my clothes. What I will have to carry will weigh about 25 or 30 pounds and my trunk weighs 36 pounds. I am only allowed 40 pounds baggage with the Overland stages.

The weather to-day is a little cool, but pleasant. The sheep Poston bought at Magdalena are here. They are not what we wanted and I dont believe he saw them when he bought. We have just bought a lot of cheese and oranges. The latter for about $1^{50} a hundred. They are not quite ripe enough and a little sour.

Cerro Colorado Gads. Purch Fri. Dec. 31. 1858.

Last night was quite cold. The water in my pail froze. To-day has been quite pleasant, though a slight chill in the air. We sent a flock of nearly a hundred sheep to Arivaca, or Los Alamos and another carpenter. The ore we take from the mine to-day, not so good as the last. Got the lead ore from the Patagonia mine at sun-down.

---

*Cowhide.

I have had Brunckow in my tent giving me material about the management of affairs at the mines. I want it to be prepared if anything is said about what the company did in Cincinnati. Affairs were much better managed than at the mines. Wrote to Margaret.

Mr. Brunckow prepared a hot orange punch. The oranges are not a good variety and it was rather bitter.

The Mexicans are very quiet for the close of the year. Our people always make a great noise, by firing guns etc.

Fri. — when Mr. Lathrop got to Arivaca Anton was gone. No one but Louis the Blk smith would speak to him and he scarcely. He took his horse and tried to get his rifle, but they would not give it to him.

January
1859

Cerro Colorado Gadsden Purchase
Sat. Jan. 1st. 1859.

I wrote to Margaret last evening and said I would leave in a week or ten days—only waiting for Wrightson. I added a postscript this morning. Mr. Lathrop got back from Arivaca at 9½ a.m. and left in a few minutes for Tubac. When he got to Arivaca last evening Anton Elsner had left. None but Louis the Bk smith spoke to him and he scarcely. He got his horse and sent Louis for his rifle, but Mr. Brown would not give it up to him.

A little before dinner several persons from Arivaca came in. Louis went to Arivaca, taking a weeks leave. He may find it a much longer one. If the other Blk smith does as well as we expect and the work gets on well, we may not need him any more.

I have my "vacate" port manteau finished, all but a string to lace. It weighs but 4¾ pounds and will more than hold my clothes. Not so cold as the night before and quite pleasant to-day. Our Mexicans are at work, but no one at Arivaca.

Suarez with flour from Sonora arrived. Left it at Arivaca

and came here to settle. In the night he left. I had the benefit of him at my fire after I went to bed.

Cerro Colorado Sun. Jan. 2. 1859.

One of our men, who has been to Sarica returned yesterday and reports that our cook and his assistant fell into the hands of the Apaches. The boy was killed and the man is missing. They are Opate Indians and were on their way to Opodepe, on a branch of the Sonora river, to visit their relations. Sonora is overrun with Apaches. They live in the mountains and kill and steal at liberty and seldom meet with any resistance. The Governor has disarmed the people and taken all the troops South to fight his battles.

Schuchard and Dunbar, when in the service of the Gadsona company* were *six* months in the Arizona Mts. but I cannot learn that they prospected much. Schuchard had not even a blowpipe with him. The most they did was to hunt and eat and when the game gave out, they went to the Ajo copper mines.† Near Sarica is where Count de Boulbon‡ built houses and prepared to locate, some 18 miles from the Planchas de Plata.§ These have since been examined, but only ore lump, or plancha of near 20 pounds and some quite small pieces were found. Gonzales of Magdalena spent some

---

*Heintzelman may be referring to Schuchard's work before he joined the Sonora Exploring and Mining Company. He had worked for the Arizona Mining and Trading Company and traveled throughout the border area looking for mines.

†In 1855, the Arizona Mining and Trading Company began to reopen the copper mines in Ajo, about 110 miles east of Fort Yuma and 25 miles north of the Mexican border.

‡Gaston Raoul de Raousset-Boulbon (1817–1854) led two unsuccessful filibuster expeditions into Sonora, one in 1852 and the second in 1854. He was captured at Guaymas and executed on August 12, 1854.

§In Sonora, west of present-day Nogales, these mines were discovered in the early eighteenth century and accounts of their potential wealth became legendary. In the 1850s several attempts were made to locate them; Schuchard was among the searchers.

$2.000 and abandoned the work. The remains of former extensive workings are to be seen.[1]

Mr. Brunckow pointed out to me a spot he says is the place indicated in old records, where the Planchas were found. It is between the two sharpest peaks of the range of Mts. between Tubac and Cerro Colorado, called the "Calaveras" and 15 miles from here. The northern peak is quite conical. It is a few degrees south of east from C. C. and is also said to be 13 miles from Tumacacori and 30 from Calabazas. These were discovered by a soldier from Tubac. He found a piece of metal, dark and malleable, in the Mts. and took it to mould bullets, supposing it lead. It was silver. He afterwards got more, but the other people could not find the spot.

When the California gold discoveries were drawing people that way the priest of Tumacacori told his people, why go to Cal. when they had such mines near at hand. I have no doubt but that there can with proper examination be found rich mines in this vicinity. The country has not been thoroughly explored.

Cerro Colorado Sun. Jan. 2. 1859.

The weather has been clear but a little chilly. I have been examining papers and writing on my report. Mr. Brown and our new Blk smith Rogers were over from Arivaca. The latter and the only one, worked yesterday. Brown thinks it will take *eight* weeks to finish the Amalgamation works. There is undoubtedly much to do and still a scarcity of Mexican labor.

C. C. Monday Jan. 3. 1859.

Two of our smelters went off last night, in debt and also stole some of our silver-lead ore. I rode over to Arivaca and sent two men after them. The work is going on there, but I still see that there is a great deal to do. I got a note from Mr.

Lathrop last night. Wrightson and Grosvenor are to be in Tubac to-day and we may see them here tomorrow.

I have been busy all the afternoon writing on my report. When I get home I will not have much time and may then find I want some data. Last night was warmer than the night before and pleasant to-day. The refining furnace is in operation. We were out of flour again through Mr. J. Poston's negligence. Some of the Mex. refused to work.

Cerro Colorado Tues. Jan. 4. 1859.

Pleasant this morning, but mild and cloudy in the afternoon. It threatens rain. Got through refining and started smelting at 5 P.M. The two men I sent after the smelters got back, after going as far as Busani without overtaking the thieves. They were close on them, but it was across the Line. Our salt man from Altar was here this afternoon. Left more salt at Arivaca.

I have packed up all my things, but my clothes in the wash at Arivaca. I have all the afternoon been looking for Lathrop and Wrightson. I will go to Arivaca in the morning and the next day to Tubac.

I tried my Colt's pistol this forenoon and split off an inch and a half of the side of the barrel, near the cylinder. It does not appear to affect its firing. I have seen a number of barrels fail like this.

Cerro Colorado Wed. Jan. 5. 1859.

I intended going to Arivaca this morning, but the animals were out, so I wrote a note and sent a burro for my clothes. I spent the morning making various little preparations and soon after dinner Schuchard and Grosvenor arrived in the little express wagon. They report Wrightson and Lathrop to be here and only waiting for the mail.

I went down the main shaft and into the "fronton." The latter is 26 feet and will soon reach the vein—in 5 or 6 feet. I then went all through the mine and got a couple of specimens. Mr. Brunckow assayed a piece of the smaller one and it yields 2.320 ounces.

About the middle of the afternoon Mr. Lathrop and Mr. Wrightson arrived. They brought the mail and I got six letters. I have one from Margaret dated 13 Dec. All well and expecting me. One from cousin H. P. Heintzelman, two or three old ones from Conkling in N. Y. one from Dunbar — one from Eddy, returning the draft, as the bill was paid. Colemans have bought the wine. Major Ringgold* paid my account. [2]

Mr. Brunckow made a bowl of egg-nog for us. We, Wrightson, Lathrop and I have been sitting in my tent and at my fire till near midnight, transacting business and talking. Wrightson is a little impracticable and has not yet found out that he dont know much about this country and its people. We start for Tubac in the morning.

Tubac Thurs. Jan. 6. 1859.

We got off at 9½ a.m. in the ambulance — Lathrop, Wrightson, Grosvenor and —Schuchard rode a horse. The latter and I leave in the morning for Tucson. We did not get here until 3 P.M. Our Mexican driver is slow, with lazy mules. There was no one at Sopori as we passed. I have never had time to visit, Mowry's *famous* mine at Sopori.

I got $225 from Mr. Lathrop to pay my expenses to the States. I am afraid that I have too much baggage. I have a few specimens of ore and a plancha of silver.

I have with Mr. Wrightson appointed Mr. Lathrop acting Director at the Mines and we have signed and filled up the Stock due the members of the company not here. I got my spyglass sent by Mr. Wrightson — rather late to be of much use.

---

*George H. Ringgold, a paymaster on the Pacific Coast.

Tucson Sat. Jan. 8. 1859.

Schuchard and I left Tubac in the Ambulance with two Mexican drivers for this place. It was 8½ a.m. before we got our breakfast and could leave. The day was quite pleasant, though a little cool. At the "Canoa" we stopped to water. As we were there Anton and Carriso, a Mexican rode up from the Pinery. The former spoke to us, but I would not notice him. We got to the Punta del Agua at 3½ P.M. —38 miles, where we stayed all night. We got a good supper and break-fast but I slept cold.

The night was very cold and all the morning. We reached here at 10½ a.m. and immediately went to the stage office and secured seats in the stage. It is not due till 3 P.M. tomor-row, but they tell us may be here before day light, though not probably until after dinner. It dont run full now. I paid $150, to Tipton the Western rail road terminus. The time is 16 days to St. Louis. An hour after the stage from the East got in, with Robinson and his wife* from Mesilla. [3]

I got several letters with copies of others from Cin. which I sent with a note to Mr. Lathrop. The action of the Ex. Com. at Cin. agrees with mine here. Our conveyance, has started back to go to the Punta del Agua this afternoon.

I hear that if the President's suggestion with regard to So-nora is acted on, many persons from Cal. will go there.

I added a postscript to my letter to Margaret and will mail it this evening. There are many more Americans here and the town looks more lively than when I was here last summer.

There is a report here, that a German and Mexican arrived from Sonora with letters to the Gándaras from their father, that he had landed at Guaymas with 5.000 men—Mexicans

---

*Palatine and Sarah Robinson were returning to Mesilla. He was a farmer, merchant, and landowner who was later charged with several serious crimes, including illegal confiscation of the property of the So-nora Exploring and Mining Company.

and 125 or 130 Americans etc. and would be half across the State before they could join him. We saw the German at our table in Tubac and he had no news. He was searched by Pesqueiras troops for letters.

Newport Ky. Wed. Jan. 26th. 1859.

On Sunday after dinner (2½ P.M.) the Overland stage arrived, with three passengers. Mr. Schuchard and I got seats. We had no trouble about our baggage, though both of us had a little over the 40 pounds allowed.

There were in the stage three rather hard looking characters. I afterwards learned that one was a butcher and I think a common gambler; another a broken down Fourth ward N.Y. politician and the third a green farmer from Arkansas, who took cattle to Cal. They did not make the most agreeable companions.

We had pleasant weather most of the way, but cold this side of Fort Smith. A little rain and snow near the Rio Grande and some ice at the Apache Pass. We saw a few Apaches near there and a number at the station. Not a Comanche on the road.

We passed Forts Chadbourne and Belknap in the night and arrived at Fort Smith about 11 P.M. and left at day light. Here I went to bed for a few hours. At Franklin, we stopped for dinner and I there saw Capt. Llewellyn Jones of the Rifles who commands Ft. Bliss a mile and a half on the road. He told me that the Navajo war was closed satisfactorily.[4]

From Belknap to Ft. Smith we had Glover the Sup of the road along the Pecos and Pardee,* who brought out the coin for our company. They crowded us very much. At

---

*William L. Pardee, formerly employed by Wells, Fargo, was an express rider for the Butterfield Overland Mail Company. He is credited with making the fastest run on the route when he delivered a copy of Buchanan's Second Annual Message from St. Louis to San Francisco in 19 days, 15 hours.

Springfield Mr. Butterfield* the President of the Mail company got into the stage and rode with us to Warsaw. He and I talked about the company's carrying our silver. He will arrange to do it. Pardee also expressed a willingness.[5]

At Tipton we arrived at 10 P.M. and took the Rail Road, Monday for St. Louis, where I arrived at 11 P.M.

The trip across the Continent is not a bad one. The roads west of Ft. Smith are generally excellent and very bad this side. The road on the Llano Estacada is most excellent. The stations until we got to the Indian nations are very indifferent, but at all they expected to furnish us with coffee bread and meat at all hours, whilst horses were changed. The stations and country along the Pecos very bad — the worst part of the route. Some of the animals there were poor. Generally very good this side of Ft. Smith.

We found the weather generally cold at nights. I never in my life suffered so much from cold as this side Ft. Smith. On Friday morning I got some apples and put them into my overcoat pockets. They froze. The mer. I hear was −5°. I slightly froze my feet and hands.

Col. F. Lee 2 Infy was buried on Saturday at St. Louis. I met Ruggles his Adjutant, Major Longstreet and Col. Rich† at the Planters Hotel.[6]

I telegraphed from St. Louis and found all well at home and expecting me. Matilda and her mother are here. Mary is still lame, but has grown much. Charlies health is better. Margaret is well, but thin.

This morning Major Macrae‡ called. I went to the Garri-

---

*John Butterfield (1801–1869), one of the founders of the American Express Company.

†Francis Lee (1804–1859); George D. Ruggles, acting adjutant general of the Department of the West; James "Old Pete" Longstreet (1821–1904); Rich has not been identified.

‡Nathaniel Chapman Macrae (1804–1878), a classmate of Heintzelman's at West Point, was commanding officer of Jefferson Barracks, Missouri, from 1859–1861.

[166]

son,* but the Doctor's people were all over in Cin. Col Buchanan not returned from Washington and Lts. Mason and McLean in Cin.† I then walked to Cin. and saw T. Wrightson. With him I called on Mr. Park.‡ W. then drove me home. The weather is pleasant, but I feel the cold. I wrote a few lines to Mr. Lathrop, to let him know my arrival home. [7]

Newport Ky Sat. Jan. 29. 1859.

Thursday it rained and I did not step outside the door. Yesterday I walked to town and met Wrightson. I also in the afternoon called on Col. Whistler, at Macrae's and went with Margaret to the Doctor's and called at Col. Buchanan's, who with his wife got home the night before. He was at dinner. Lts. Mason and McLean called. The night before we went to the Band's concert at the Garrison. After the concert they gave me a fine serenade. Col. Kennett§ called. [8]

I feel more tired since I got home than before. I sat up—did not lay down, except an hour on the seat on the staked plain// and two hours before we got to Tipton. I am satisfied that I frosted my feet in the stage. Yesterday was delightful but overcast to-day.

---

*Newport Barracks.
†Robert Christie Buchanan (1811–1878); John Sanford Mason (1824–1897); Nathaniel Henry McLean (1827–1884).
‡John D. Park, a stockholder in the Sonora Exploring and Mining Company and a director of the Santa Rita Silver Mining Company.
§Possibly Henry G. Kennett.
//The "Staked plain," *Llano Estacado*, 30,000 square miles of high plains in western Texas and eastern New Mexico.

Part III

Epilogue

A Hole to
Bury Money In

One of Heintzelman's last official duties as president of the Sonora Exploring and Mining Company was to report on his activities in Arizona.[1] At the stockholders' meeting in Cincinnati on March 21, 1859, it was decided to dissolve the original corporation and relocate and incorporate the company under the laws of another state. Wrightson and Company, Henry Howe and John Park (two Ohio investors), and Heintzelman protested the move.[2] However, Samuel Colt, by now the largest stockholder, was elected president of the company in April. Four new officers were chosen from among his business associates: William T. Coleman, a New York and California merchant, was elected vice-president; Richard W. H. Jarvis, Colt's brother-in-law, was elected treasurer; and the new directors included New Yorkers Augustus Belknap and William M. B. Hartley. Charles Debrille Poston was elected as a director and as secretary pro tem; Edgar Conkling and Henry Howe were the only two Cincinnati men represented on the board of directors.[3] Colt preferred to incorporate the company under the laws of Connecticut, but he met with opposition; on February 9, 1860, the Sonora Exploring and Mining Company was incorporated under the laws of the state of New York.[4]

[171]

By the time Colt was elected president, Heintzelman was serving on frontier duty in Texas. Thomas Wrightson kept him informed of events and acted as his attorney in submitting the protest. Heintzelman was distressed to learn "about a nefarious scheme of Colts" to purchase the remainder of the Sonora Exploring and Mining Company stock "at a nominal price" and "control the company." He hoped that Wrightson and Poston would prevent this.[5]

By June 1859, Colt's agent in Cincinnati, Erastus Smith, who had been "busy two days among the mining men here without exciting any suspicion," related, "No one will sell stock at present for less than $25." The agent informed Colt that the men in Cincinnati believed that Colt "was trying to get the control of the company but there was no doubt the old Directors would get it back."[6] Colt did, however, succeed in assuming control of the company. Large amounts of capital were needed to develop the mines, and as an established eastern industrialist, Colt had access to such funds.

The new president urged one of his associates, Charles S. Brown of Boston, to go to Ohio "and put a quietus to the foul plottings and movements of those bad fellows." Colt sent Brown a bar of silver from the Heintzelman Mine and instructed him to "show it in a quiet way to Gentlemen in whom you have confidence." If Brown managed to interest "a few Gentlemen of good standing" who would authorize him "to purchase all the stock of the Western owners," Colt would help Brown finance the arrangement. The arms manufacturer asserted, "After we have got over this Cincinnati humbugging, and these Western men find themselves without power, they I think will be glad to get out of the scrape for 10 or 15 per cent at most on the par value of their stock." Colt speculated:

All we have now to do, if we wish to get rid of these Western people, that are so Troublesome to us is to decline to purchase stock at any price for the present, and let them flounder about or wallow for a while in their filth, and then to aid in cleansing them will be a great, and more lasting blessing to them than the same thing done at an earlier day.[7]

A sequence of dubious legal maneuvers surrounded the ownership of the Arivaca estate and the mines. On October 16, 1860, the Sonora Exploring and Mining Company of Ohio (which by this time had been reincorporated in New York) leased all its real estate, mines, and property for ten years and two and one-half months to Poston for a reported annual rent of $10,000 for the first five years and $15,000 for the next five years. Poston was to account for any property he sold, and he could pay off the company's debts. The agreement was signed by John Kennett, A. M. Searles, and Poston. On November 6, 1860, Andrew Talcott, a Colt representative who was acting as agent for the company, "delivered" the real estate, mines, and property to Poston. On February 2, 1861, Poston transferred this lease to Colt and agreed to turn over the property by May 1, 1861.[8]

The arms manufacturer worked aggressively to reorganize the company. He paid debts, sent men of his choosing to manage the mines, and bought thousands of dollars worth of machinery and supplies. Among the items Colt sent to Arizona were boilers, two twenty-five-horsepower steam engines with crushers and amalgamators, a turning lathe, guns, boots and brandy—the latter, Colt instructed, "for madicenal [sic] purposes and must not be used in any other way."[9] At the same time he tried to encourage Congress to send more troops to protect the citizens. He believed that the Heintzelman Mine was a "good one," and that "with energy and capital it may be made to pay." He warned that if the mine were placed "in the hands of a half-horse concern, pulling all ways, and dragging its slow length along, it is but a hole to bury money in."[10]

Colt's assessment was accurate; even he was unable to overcome numerous obstacles. Faulty, crude equipment, unskilled labor, high costs for supplies and transportation, the inferior quality of the secondary ores, and the careless methods of refining all contributed to the failure of the Sonora Exploring and Mining Company. When the Butterfield Overland Mail Company discontinued its services through Arizona in April 1861, Apache depredations increased. The American Civil War forced the evacuation of Forts Breckenridge and Buchanan, and workers at the mines were left without military protection. Tensions between the Mexican and American residents heightened. By August 1861, Poston and Raphael Pumpelly, a mining engineer, were forced to flee to Fort Yuma after the murder of Poston's brother, John, by Mexican laborers. The properties of both the Sonora Exploring and Mining Company and the Santa Rita Silver Mining Company were abandoned.[11] The Civil War, Indian uprisings, and banditry temporarily halted the quest for mineral riches. The initial demands of southern New Mexico residents for a separate territorial government had not been met. A Confederate Territory of Arizona was organized in January 1862, but it was soon toppled by the Union Army under the command of Colonel James H. Carleton, who declared martial law and established himself as military governor.

Samuel Colt died in 1862, but his representatives struggled for several years to overcome these handicaps and operate the mines. One employee, George W. Pierce, described the living conditions at Cerro Colorado in August 1862:

As far as I can learn, Arizona has ever been a resort for the outlaws from California and the East and has begotten such a mob-law and shot gun state of things that an honest man to give no offence etc. must either leave or acquiesce in wrong. So much for the whites. The Apaches, ever taking advantage of a loose state of affairs—the withdrawal of troops and Overland Mail, which they boastingly assert they compelled — become emboldened to kill, steal and make desolate to a miserable degree. During our brief residence here perhaps 100 men have been killed by the Apaches. The Mexicans, of which people I presume the worst class live just over our line in Sonora, are always plotting to rob and kill.[12]

In 1863, Colt's associates formed the Arizona Mining Company. On August 13, 1863, Heintzelman, in trust for the Sonora Exploring and Mining Company, made an agreement with the new company for the sale of the Arivaca estate, mines, and property. The recorded sum was $500,000.[13] Stockholders were invited to exchange stock certificates. On October 22, 1863, Colt's executors and Poston sold their interests and conveyed the lease of the Sonora Exploring and Mining Company to William M. B. Hartley for a recorded sum of $70,000. Hartley, for a purported $2.5 million, conveyed his interest in the Arivaca Ranch, and the mines and property, to the Arizona Mining Company.[14]

Several reports were issued,[15] and the company was incorporated in New York.[16] In 1870 the Arizona Mining Company transferred the property to Poston, who later tried to lure European investors.[17] Thereafter many other transactions took place, and numerous individuals laid claim to the real estate, mines, and property.[18]

Although Heintzelman was no longer involved in southwestern ventures, two of his associates, Charles Debrille Poston and Herman Ehrenberg, remained committed to the nineteenth-century expansionist ideals of economic progress and self-betterment and eagerly sought to find in Arizona the wealth that had lured thousands to California. Poston's friends, in 1863, 1866, and 1881, were unsuccessful in their efforts to have the president appoint Poston as territorial governor, although in 1863 Lincoln did appoint him to serve as the territory's first superintendent of Indian affairs. In 1864 Poston was elected the territory's first delegate to Congress but was defeated for reelection in 1865 and again in 1866. He practiced law in Washington and traveled through Europe with the writer J. Ross Browne. When Browne was appointed minister to China, Poston journeyed with him, serving as a delegate from the Department of Agriculture.

The last thirty years of Poston's life were filled with rash, unsuccessful schemes and a pathetic quest for a variety of jobs. In the 1870s Poston tried but failed to interest London financiers in Arizona mining ventures. In 1877 he returned to Arizona and worked for a pittance as the register of the U.S. Land Office at Florence but was forced to resign in 1879. He subsequently held numerous jobs, including that of consular clerk in Nogales, Mexico, military agent in El Paso, and statistical agent for the Department of Agriculture in Phoenix. In 1884 he founded the Society of Arizona Pioneers, which became the Arizona Historical Society. He was disheartened and embittered by his inability to secure title to the Arivaca Ranch and to convince the government to award him compensation for Indian depredations. In 1899 the Arizona Territorial Legislature granted him a monthly pension of $25 (later $35) and voted him "Father of Arizona." He died in poverty in a Phoenix hovel in 1902.[19]

Herman Ehrenberg's efforts were devoted to exploration, mining, and mapmaking. He drafted a set of mining laws and wrote articles for the *Mining Magazine and Journal of Geology* and for the *Weekly Arizonian.* By October 1862, he was mining for gold on the Colorado River at La Paz, and from 1862 to 1866 he filed, sold, and transferred numerous mining claims, formed several companies, and helped establish the La Paz Town Association. He blazed and mapped a trail from La Paz to Prescott, and the "Ehrenberg Road" became the main wagon route between the two towns. As a special Indian agent for the Mohave Indians he provided the federal government with an enlarged and detailed map of the territory.

Unhappily, he was shot to death during the night of October 9, 1866, at the desert stage station of Dos Palmas, between San Bernardino and La Paz. An important and neglected pioneer, Ehrenberg made a significant contribution to the cartographic history of the American West.[20]

Mining was the foundation of Arizona's wealth. The mining frontiers—Tubac, Cerro Colorado, Arivaca, Santa Rita—provided a source of employment for a growing, diverse, and often fragmented community. The mining entrepreneurs—Heintzelman, Poston, Colt, the Wrightsons, and others—succeeded in convincing Congress to create a separate Territory of Arizona in 1863. That legislative act did not bring immediate peace and stability. The quest for mineral riches and the expansion of the dominion of the United States threatened the Indian tribes and gave new directions to the federal government's frontier policy. As emigrants pushed westward, they demanded protection. Military action, the development of the railroad, the financial resources of American and European capitalists, and the energy and hopes of countless pioneers combined to promote the exploration, exploitation, and settlement of Arizona.

The Benefit
of My Abilities

Upon his return from the Arizona mines in early 1859, Major
Samuel Peter Heintzelman was reunited with his family but
was soon ordered to Texas, where he engaged in campaigns
against the Indians. He also commanded operations along
the Rio Grande border against the Mexican bandit Juan Cor-
tinas.[1] Once he rejoined his regiment, Heintzelman was unable to influence the management of the Sonora Exploring
and Mining Company. Colt replaced him as president in
April 1859. The soldier's journals from 1859 to 1870 mention
the company infrequently—to comment on the mounting
debts, to note the conversion of stock certificates to those of
the Arizona Mining Company, and to record the deaths of
John Poston, William Wrightson, and Herman Ehrenberg.
Heintzelman also urged the goverment to station more troops
near the mines. Finally, he was instrumental in securing the
passage of the bill to establish the Territory of Arizona, details
of which have been thoroughly studied by Benjamin Sacks.[2]

The American Civil War was approaching, but Heintzelman was at first unprepared to believe that the other southern states would join South Carolina in its secession.[3] By

December 20, 1860, he sadly recorded: "I fear the Union is gone. The Southern States appear to be determined and the Blk Republicans are not disposed to make any concessions —at least until they will be too late." At the outbreak of the war he was called to the nation's capital to serve as acting inspector of the Department of Washington and was promoted to colonel of the Seventeenth Infantry. Shortly thereafter he received a commission as brigadier general in the Volunteer Service and was placed in command of the forces that occupied Arlington and Alexandria, Virginia. Assigned to command the third division of Major General Irwin McDowell's army, he took part in the Manassas campaign. During the first Battle of Bull Run he fought desperately, but unsuccessfully, and was severely wounded in the right elbow. Refusing to dismount, he demanded that his arm be treated while he remained in the saddle. By March 1862, he was in command of the Third Army Corps and fought under Major General George B. McClellan's direction for the next seven months in the Peninsula campaign. In May he was promoted to major general in the Volunteer Service. Later he received brevets, in the regular army, of brigadier general for gallant and meritorious conduct in the Battle of Fair Oaks, and of major general for gallant and meritorious service in the Battle of Williamsburg. From September 1862 to February 1863, he commanded the defenses of Washington, D.C., south of the Potomac; and from February to October 1863, he was commander of the Department of Washington and the Twenty-second Army Corps. [4]

McClellan's unwillingness to consult with him and the other corps commanders was a source of dissatisfaction. As pressure intensified to replace McClellan, Heintzelman transmitted his feelings privately and publicly to members of the Senate. He expressed concern that the army suffered most because of the events surrounding the change in McClellan's command. However, he refused to accuse McClellan of disloyalty, treachery, or treason, for he knew the charges were false. Claiming that no one in the army knew more about the details of the service than he, Heintzelman asserted: "I never commanded an expedition that failed and in Mc'Clellan's campaign my Corps always sustained its high character." He added, "I think I could have commanded Armies too if they had given me the opportunity, or rather, if I had met the intrigue that wished me to throw myself in the arms of the Radicals."[5]

The vindictive actions of the radical Republicans, the policy of arbitrary arrests, and the 1864 election year dissension between Lincoln and the Democratic nominee, McClellan, contributed to Heintzelman's dilemma. In January 1864, he was transferred to Columbus, Ohio, to command the Northern Department, which consisted of parts of the states of Michigan, Ohio, Indiana, and Illinois. These states were a hotbed of peace advocates or so-called Copperheads. Radical Republicans exaggerated the danger these forces posed to the political and military situation, and Heintzelman was pressed by state and federal officials and by officers within his command to take sterner actions against the dissident Democrats. He resisted these pressures.

By October 1864, he was relieved of this command and "kept for a month in exile" at Wheeling, West Virginia, awaiting orders. On the day he was relieved of his command of the Northern Department he declared:

I have not been radical enough — wont arrest people without orders — will not take the responsibility of doing what Mr. Stanton [Secretary of War Edwin M. Stanton] would do without Mr. Lincoln's orders. They cant make me radical. I will do what I think best for the country and not for a party. I have served my country too long to now commence to serve a party.[6]

As a soldier he believed, "When your country is in trouble you must stand by it whether you like the way it is administered or not." Although he considered the Mexican War to have been "a great outrage on our part" and stated that he had observed many "outrageous things" in the course of the Civil War, he declared, "As it was the Government of the Country I gave it the benefit of my abilities." Writing at the end of the Civil War he expressed a desire that those radical Republicans who had committed "arbitrary and tyrannical things" be "called to account for those violations of law."[7]

For the remainder of the war Heintzelman served on court-martial duty. He was mustered out of the Volunteer Service in August 1865 and resumed command of the Seventeenth Infantry, serving briefly in New York and in Texas. Returning to New York in 1867 he served as a member of the examining and retiring boards.[8]

Heintzelman was a good officer, but not a great leader. Descriptions of his strategic endeavors during the Civil War indicate that, at times, he lacked initiative and was impractical, too hasty or premature, and disorganized.[9] Bruce Catton described Heintzelman as "an old-timer, and Indian fighter from the plains, rugged and stiff and hard, still a regimental officer at heart, brave enough for a dozen men but unfitted for any problem of leadership that extended beyond men he could reach with his own voice." Catton thought that Heintzelman "somehow just missed being an effective corps commander."[10]

There are more favorable accounts. In September 1862, a fellow officer referred to Heintzelman's corps as "one of the very best in the Army."[11] R. H. Beattie, Jr., asserted: "Heintzelman performed best of all four division com-

[182]

manders. He pressed his column hard at every chance, his tactical judgment was sound and his efforts were not too personalized."[12] That he was eager to test new techniques is witnessed by his interest in the use of balloons for strategic observation. Making numerous ascensions with the army's chief aeronaut, he once "narrowly escaped death" when his balloon was shelled by the Confederates.[13]

Heintzelman's Washington home was a popular meeting place for army officers. He was especially fond of oyster and champagne suppers, and the Heintzelmans were hosts for such a party several days prior to the passage of the Arizona territorial bill in 1863. The military officer's journals detail innumerable visits, teas, suppers, and official functions. Heintzelman adhered to a rigid code of social behavior. As a member of an established male elite he maintained a sense of social class and was disdainful of those who did not. Passengers bound for California in 1858 were described as "not very refined looking."[14] Sharp criticisms were leveled at women. Commenting on the appearance of guests at a White House party, he wrote, "I was disappointed in not seeing so much beauty as I expected and some badly dressed and others badly painted."[15]

Eager to receive a commission as a general in the regular army, and to retire as such, he labored arduously for four years to secure this promotion. Although Heintzelman strongly resented those officers who sought favors for promotion—and succeeded—he, too, was ambitious and used every ploy at his command. His efforts were successful. After having spent forty-seven of his sixty-three years as a brave and dedicated soldier, he retired from the army with the full rank of major general in February, 1869.[16] Assured of an annual income of over $7,000, he did not think his financial obligations had ceased. At the end of 1869 he disclosed that his financial position was precarious, but that with a new position his circumstances might improve. Besides his pension, the general now held the post of president of the Mutual Guarantee Life Insurance Company of Englewood, New Jersey.[17] Although he became dissatisfied with this arrangement within two years, his financial situation appears to have improved, for there were no more entries in his journal about concerns over money. He began to think about a permanent home, "for the few remaining years I can expect to live."[18] Wishing to retire to the growing community of San Diego, where he owned real estate, he instead settled for the city spaces of the nation's capital.[19]

Heintzelman rarely complained of ill health. Occasionally throughout his journals he mentions having a sore throat or influenza and, in later years, rheumatism. While at the Arizona mines, he — along with many others — suffered from fevers and chills. His last journal entry, written at the age of sixty-seven, noted that his health had improved but there were "a thousand and one disagreements" over the arrangements for his new house.[20]

Samuel Peter Heintzelman died at the age of seventy-four at his home in Washington, D.C., in the early morning of the first of May 1880. The nation's flag was displayed at half-mast. His body was accompanied by a military escort to Buffalo, New York, and conveyed to City Hall, where it remained in state for half a day. He was buried with military honors in Buffalo's Forest Lawn Cemetery, in his wife's family plot.[21]

From the initiation of his military career he strove to be recognized, not so much for personal power, fame, or great wealth, but more for the chance to prove himself. As an elitist he sought political preferment commensurate with his abilities and loyalties. He was embittered and outraged by some events of his life, especially during the Civil War. Yet his life was not confined to the military. Heintzelman's personal ambitions expanded along with the growth of his nation, but without the large sums of capital needed to finance mineral exploitation, the time, or the administrative talent, he did not become a wealthy man. As a soldier, speculator, and promoter he contributed significantly to the settlement of the frontier. Indeed, the record of nineteenth-century America is greatly enhanced by his finely detailed observations. Heintzelman seems to have lacked a broad sense of humor, but he was rich in admirable qualities — integrity, self-reliance, courage, and endurance. As a loyal soldier and enterprising southwestern pioneer, he never ceased to strive or to care for himself, his family, and his country.

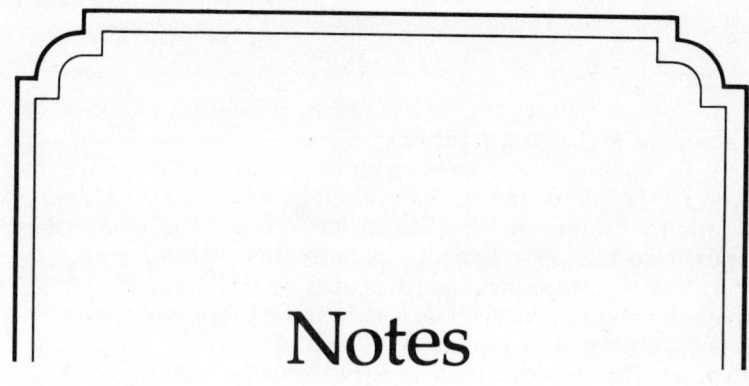

Notes

Preface

1. (Phoenix: Arizona Historical Foundation, 1964).

2. For a few sources that provide descriptions different from those in this study consult the references to Poston in the text and see also Hubert Howe Bancroft, *History of Arizona and New Mexico, 1830–1888*, vol. XVII of *The Works of Hubert Howe Bancroft* (San Francisco: The History Company, 1889), p. 498; Ray A. Billington, *The Far Western Frontier, 1830–1860*, New American Nation Series, ed. H. S. Commager and R. D. Morris (New York: Harper and Brothers, 1956), p. 250; Thomas E. Farish, *History of Arizona*, 8 vols. (Phoenix: Filmer Brothers, 1915), II, 16, 60; Odie B. Faulk, *Land of Many Frontiers: A History of the American Southwest* (New York: Oxford University Press, 1968), p. 164; John A. Hawgood, *America's Western Frontiers: The Exploration and Settlement of the Trans-Mississippi West* (New York: A. A. Knopf, 1967), pp. 230–31; W. Eugene Hollon, *The Southwest: Old and New* (Lincoln: University of Nebraska Press, Bison Books, 1961), pp. 190–91; Howard R. Lamar, *The Far Southwest, 1846–1912: A Territorial History*, Yale Western Americana Series, no. 12 (New Haven, 1966), pp. 418–19, 423; and Rufus K. Wyllys, *Arizona: The History of a Frontier State* (Phoenix: Hobson and Herr, 1950), p. 121.

3. Roy P. Basler, Chief, Manuscript Division, Library of Congress, to the editor, July 19, 1972.

4. In addition, five manuscript diaries for June 1, 1825, to August 12, 1831, are in the collection of the U.S. Military Academy Library at West Point, New York. The USMA Library also has miscellaneous papers and reports, a map of Fort Yuma, and pencil sketches and seventy-nine drawings made by Heintzelman while a cadet. The Library of Congress has seven boxes of materials containing original pocket diaries, notebooks, cashbooks, survey books, limited correspondence, orders, and military materials for his entire career. It is obvious after a thorough study of these papers that only certain ones were retained. For example, where are the numerous letters Heintzelman received from his family, especially from his wife? Where is the correspondence received from Poston, Colt, and Wrightson?

A Southwestern Pioneer

1. Samuel Peter Heintzelman Papers, Library of Congress, July 4, 1850, Special Orders No. 33. These papers will be cited hereafter as SPH, LC, or the diary date will be given in the text. Unless otherwise noted, the citations refer to the bound journals.

2. Paul Neff Garber, *The Gadsden Treaty* (Gloucester, Mass.: Peter Smith, 1959), pp. 3–4.

3. SPH, LC, 1848–1850.

4. Ibid., November 27, 1850.

5. Ibid., March 20, 1851. He commenced the move on March 17.

6. Joseph King Fenno Mansfield, *On the Condition of the Western Forts*, edited with an introduction by Robert W. Frazer, The American Exploration and Travel Series (Norman: University of Oklahoma Press, 1963), pp. 107–08. See also Robert W. Frazer, *Forts of the West* (Norman: University of Oklahoma Press, 1965), p. 34; *Soldier and Brave: Historic Places Associated with Indian Affairs and the Indian Wars in the Trans-Mississippi West*, The National Survey of Historic Sites and Buildings, ed. R. G. Ferris, vol. XII (Washington, D.C.: National Park Service, 1971), pp. 81–85.

7. SPH, LC, December 1851–March 1852. When the site was reoccupied it was referred to as Fort Yuma. See also *Journal of Lt. Thomas W. Sweeny, 1849–1853,* ed. Arthur Woodward, Great West and Indian Series, vol. VII (Los Angeles: Westernlore Press, 1956). The lieutenant moved his men six miles below Camp Yuma to a spot he called Camp Independence.

8. Sweeny, *Journal*, p. 55.

9. Ibid., p. 117. See also *The California Diary of General E. D. Townsend*, ed. Malcolm Edwards (Los Angeles: Ward Ritchie Press, 1970), p. 39. Townsend warned against maintaining small outposts and hence providing the Indians with an opportunity to attack.

10. SPH, LC, December 21, 1851; and "Expedition Against the Indians of Los Coyotes and Destruction of Their Village, Dec. 21, 1851," Records of the U.S. Army Continental Commands, RG 393, NARS, Pacific Division, H-4, 1851; and "Proceedings of a Council of War Convened in the Valley of Los Coyotes, Dec. 23, 1851," H-4, 1852. For a comprehensive description see George H. Phillips, *Chiefs and Challengers: Indian Resistance and Cooperation in Southern California* (Berkeley: University of California Press, 1975).

11. Townsend to Heintzelman, January 16, 1852, AD, USMA.

12. Captain Rufus Ingalls, Denmark, Maine, to Major General Thomas Jesup, Quartermaster General, USA, September 9, 1853, Records of the Office of the Quartermaster General, RG 92, NARS, Consolidated Correspondence File, 1794–1915, Box 1273.

13. U.S. Congress, House, *Message from the President ...,* *transmitting Report in regard to Indian Affairs on the Pacific,* H. Exec. Doc. #76, 34th Cong., 3rd sess., 1857, pp. 34–58, cited hereafter as HED #76, 1857.

14. Ibid., p. 50. See also Jack Forbes, *Warriors of the Colorado: The Yumas of the Quechan Nation and Their Neighbors,* Civilization of the American Indian Series (Norman: University of Oklahoma Press, 1965).

15. SPH, LC, December 29, 1831. See also George L. Heiges, "General S. P. Heintzelman Visits His Hometown of Manheim," *Journal of the Lancaster County Historical Society,* 68 (Trinity, 1964), 88.

16. SPH, LC. Heintzelman's appointment as a cadet is dated March 23, 1822, and is signed by the Secretary of War, John C. Calhoun.

17. Heintzelman file, AD, USMA.

18. Heintzelman to George W. Cullum, December 18, 1865, AD, USMA. See also George W. Cullum, *Biographical Register of the Officers and Graduates of the United States Military Academy*, 3rd ed., rev., 3 vols. (Boston: Houghton Mifflin and Company, 1891), I, 372.

19. SPH, LC, April 6, 1832, Special Order No. 47; and Cullum, *Biographical Register*, I, 372.

20. SPH, LC, August 4, 1835, Special Order No. 114; and January 15, 1836, Special Order No. 6. He vacated his staff commission in 1846, when staff officers and regular line regiments were separated.

21. Ibid., December 31, 1840.

22. Ibid., January 1, 1839.

23. Ibid., October 15, 1844. Margaret Stuart was born December 1, 1819, and died August 9, 1893. Little is known of her or her family. See also ibid., December 4, 1844, May 6, 1845, and December 1, 1867.

24. Ibid., December 29, 1845.

25. Francis B. Heitman, *Historical Register and Dictionary of the United States Army*, 2 vols. (Washington, D.C.: GPO, 1903), I, 521. Lincoln's endorsement is written on an envelope containing recommendations in Charles's favor. See Records of the Adjutant General's Office, RG 94, NARS, USMA 1861, No. 373, Box 78.

26. SPH, LC, February 28, 1848, February 28, 1851, and February 28, 1856. In his journal for 1858, Heintzelman describes how Mary underwent surgery for the removal of a tumor on her leg. She seems to have remained with her parents, and after her father's death she resided in Washington, D.C., and frequently submitted letters to the editors of magazines defending her father's Civil War record. She died March 24, 1927.

27. Ibid., February 9, 1858.

28. Ibid., March 9, 1851.

29. Ibid., December 5, 1852.

30. Ibid., October 8, November 27, December 3, 1847. See also Cullum, *Biographical Register*, I, 372.

31. SPH, LC, January 5, 1859, February 26, 1864, August 9, 1864, January 9, 1865, December 22, 1867, July 12, 1872.

32. Ibid., September 16, 1858, January 1, 1861.

33. *Memoirs of General William T. Sherman*, Civil War Centennial Series (Bloomington: Indiana University Press, 1957), p. 191; and *Autobiography of Oliver Otis Howard*, 2 vols. (New York: Baker and Taylor Company, 1907), I, 142.

34. SPH, LC, November 22, 1851, July 31, 1854, December 30, 1872. See also SCF on Heintzelman.

35. SPH, LC, December 23, 1850, January 8 and 27, 1851, January 28 and 29, 1852, July 19, 1852, April 5, 1853. George F. Hooper (1826–1901), a native of Virginia, went west after serving in the Mexican War and worked as a subassistant surveyor for the U.S.-Mexican Boundary Commission. By 1851 he was settled in San Diego as a wholesale, retail, and general commission merchant and served as a councilman. Hooper became the sutler at Fort Yuma in 1852. In 1853, along with Dr. George McKinstry and later Francis Hinton, he established the mercantile firm of George F. Hooper and Company that became known as Hinton and Hooper. By 1868 he had retired from the mercantile business. He was elected president of the First National Gold Bank in San Francisco, a position he held until 1876, when he retired to his 900-acre ranch in the Sonoma Valley. Sweeny, *Journal*, p. 263, n. 113; *San Diego Herald*, May 29, 1851, 1:1; July 24, 1851,2:2; *Weekly Arizonian*, November 10, 1859, 3:4; *Weekly Arizona Miner*, December 12, 1868, 3:1, 2; *Daily Arizona Citizen*, September 25, 1875, 3:5; *Arizona Sentinel*, February 8, 1879, 3:2; *History of Sonoma County* (San Francisco: Alley, Bowen and Company, 1880), p. 677; *An Illustrated History of Sonoma County, Calif.* (Chicago: The Lewis Publishing Co., 1889), p. 647.

George Alonzo Johnson (1824–1903) was a native New Yorker who came to California in 1849; by 1854 he had organized a company that operated the first steamboat to navigate the Colorado River. In 1866 the Johnson Company was incorporated as the Colorado Steam Navigation Company, and Johnson continued in the business until 1877, dominating transportation on the Colorado until the arrival of the Southern Pacific Railroad, when he sold his vessels. In 1863 he was elected to the California State Legislature as a representative for San Diego County; and in 1882 he served as the collector for the port of San Diego. *Arizona Sentinel*, August 12, 1882, 3:1; *Los Angeles Star*, September 20, 1862, 2:2; *Weekly Arizona Miner*, February 14, 1866, 3:4; Arthur Woodward, *Feud on the Colorado*, Great West and Indian Series, IV (Los Angeles: Westernlore Press, 1955), p. 31; and Francis H. Leavitt, "Steam Navigation on the Colorado River," *California Historical Society Quarterly*, XXII, 1 (Mar. 1943), 1, 4–7, 21, n. 32.

36. Sweeny, *Journal*, p. 117.

37. Janet Lee Hargett, "Louis John Frederick Jaeger: Entrepreneur at Yuma Crossing" (M.A. thesis, University of Arizona, 1967), p. 34.

Louis Jaeger (or Iaeger, Yaeger, 1824–1892), a native of Pennsylvania, arrived in San Francisco in 1850 and by August operated a ferry service across the Colorado River at its junction with the Gila. The service continued until 1877, when the Southern Pacific Railroad built a bridge. When the army arrived, Jaeger managed a mercantile and freighting business, secured government contracts for supplies, and transported ore and equipment for miners. He was a stationkeeper for the Butterfield Overland Mail.

38. SPH, LC, July 12, 1853, January 3, 1854.

39. Ibid., January 4, 1851.

40. HED #76, 1857, pp. 51–53.

41. Mansfield, *Western Forts*, pp. 146, 147, 189.

42. Assistant Adjutant General E. R. S. Canby, Headquarters 10th Military Department, Monterey, to Heintzelman, September 26, 1849, William H. Emory Papers, YWA.

43. Hubert Howe Bancroft, *History of Arizona and New Mexico, 1830–1888*, vol. XVII of *The Works of Hubert Howe Bancroft* (San Francisco: The History Company, 1889), pp. 484–85. Heintzelman reported that Le Conte left the Oatmans on the 17th. See SPH, LC, March 27, 1851.

44. HED #76, 1857, p. 45.

45. SPH, LC, January 27–March 29, 1851. See also Edward J. Pettid, "Henry Stuart Hewit, M.D.," *Arizona Medicine*, January 1969, pp. 62–70.

46. SPH, LC, March 7–10, 1851, and March 27, 1851.

47. Ibid., March 15–29, 1851. The author is preparing an article that examines this controversial story.

48. Garber, *Gadsden Treaty*, pp. 62–131. The treaty was proclaimed law by President Franklin Pierce on June 30, 1854. However, the ratified treaty was dissimilar in important details from the one James Gadsden negotiated (and which is ordinarily dated December 30, 1853): the sum paid to Mexico was reduced; the southern boundary was altered; prior claims were not mentioned; and the United States would no longer protect Mexico from filibuster and Indian raids.

49. *Survey of a Route on the 32nd Parallel for the Texas Western Railroad, 1854, The A. B. Gray Report and including the Reminiscences of Peter R. Brady who Accompanied the Expedition*, with introduction and notes by L. R. Bailey, Great West and Indian Series, vol. XXIV, Western Survey Series II (Los Angeles; Westernlore Press, 1863), cited hereafter as *Gray Report*.

50. SPH, LC, August 22, November 4, 1855.

51. Ibid., April 26, 1856.

52. Ibid., October 13, 1856.

53. *Railroad Record Supplement*, February 18, 1856, p. 3.

54. For a detailed history of Heintzelman's role as a leading advocate for the creation of the Territory of Arizona, see Benjamin Sacks, *Be It Enacted: The Creation of the Territory of Arizona* (Phoenix: Arizona Historical Foundation, 1964).

55. Raphael Pumpelly, *My Reminiscences*, 2 vols. (New York: Henry Holt and Company, 1918), I, 257–58.

56. SPH, LC, May 5, 1865; see also SCF on Colorado City.

The Sonora Exploring and Mining Company

1. SPH, LC, July 11, 1854; Charles Debrille Poston, "Reconnaissance in Sonora," manuscript, AHS; "Southwestern Chronicle: The Journal of Charles Debrille Poston," ed. Byrd Granger, *The Arizona Quarterly*, XIII, 3 (Fall 1957), 254; B. Sacks, "Charles Debrille Poston, Prince of Arizona Pioneers," *The Smoke Signal*, no. 7 (Spring 1963), 4; and SCF on Poston.

2. Diane M. T. Rose, "The Maps, Plans, and Sketches of Herman Ehrenberg," *Prologue: The Journal of the National Archives*, IX, 3 (Fall 1977), 162–70.

3. SPH, LC, February 7 and 15, 1855. Poston also lobbied

for the establishment of a southern route for the Pacific Railroad (from El Paso to the Colorado) and noted that, if the effort failed, the secretary of war would consider designating a military road from El Paso to Colorado City. See also Sacks, "Charles Debrille Poston," pp. 4–5.

4. SPH, LC, February 26–March 5, 1855; and Charles D. Poston, "Building a State in Apache Land," *Overland Monthly*, XXIV, 2nd series (August 1894), 203.

5. SPH, LC, March 7, 1856. See also Mario De Blasio, "Sonora Exploring and Mining Co., 1856–1861" M.A. thesis, University of San Diego, 1971). De Blasio relied on the company's stockholders' reports.

6. SPH, LC, March 7, 1856; and *Railroad Record*, September 15, 1859, pp. 355–56. Born in England, the Wrightson brothers (Thomas, 1822–1897; William, 1827–1865) arrived in the United States in 1832. Educated in Albany, New York, they moved to Cincinnati, where they edited and published the *Railroad Record*. Thomas was, in addition, superintendent of the Cincinnati Enquirer Company. As organizers of the Sonora Exploring and Mining Company, they also established the Santa Rita Silver Mining Company. On September 6, 1858, William arrived in San Antonio, Texas, and from there traveled overland with mining equipment and goods for use by both companies. He reached Tubac in early January 1859. The publication of Arizona's first newspaper, the Tubac *Weekly Arizonian*, was made possible through the support of both companies and because William brought a printing press with him, and an editor, Edward E. Cross. William helped Heintzelman promote the bill establishing the Arizona Territory. Upon his return to Arizona, he was murdered by Indians on February 17, 1865. Mt. Wrightson in Arizona is named for him. Thomas died in Newport, Kentucky, on August 7, 1897. Unfortunately the records of the printing firm were destroyed in a fire. SPH, LC, 1856–1865; Benjamin Sacks, *Be It Enacted: The Creation of the Territory of Arizona* (Phoenix: Arizona Historical Foundation, 1964), pp. 34, 89–91; and *Railroad Record*, September 2, 1858, p. 236; November 11, 1858, p. 351; April 20, 1865, p. 105. William Duffen, the editor of Phocion Way's diary, is preparing a book on the Wrightsons' southwestern adventures.

7. SPH, LC, March 11, 1856.

8. Ibid., March 14, 1856.

9. Ibid., March 12, 1856. See also Hubert Howe Bancroft, *History of Arizona and New Mexico,* vol. XVII of *The Works of Hubert Howe Bancroft* (San Francisco: The History Company, 1889), pp. 399–400.

10. SPH, LC, March 27, 1856. See also *Sonora and the Value of its Silver Mines, Report of the Sonora Exploring and Mining Co., Made to the Stockholders, Dec. 1856* (Cincinnati: Railroad Record Print, 1856), cited hereafter as 1856 *Report.*

11. SPH, LC, May 1, 1856. See also: Texas Western Railway Company. *Circular to the Stockholders of the Texas Western Railroad Company, Issued by Authority of the Executive Committee, New York, June, 1856* (New York: W. H. Arthur and Co., 1856), p. 26.

12. SPH, LC, April 26, 1856.

13. Poston, "Building a State in Apache Land," pp. 203–4.

14. SPH, LC, June 28, 1856.
The venture to establish the Southern Pacific Railroad Company, an outgrowth of the Texas Western Railroad Company, was beset with difficulties. The latter was incorporated in 1852 and purchased in 1854 by the Atlantic and Pacific Railroad Co. The original name was maintained until 1856, when the Texas Western was changed to the Southern Pacific Railroad Company. By 1857 the company was troubled by rumors of fraud. In 1872 the Texas and Pacific Railway Company purchased the Southern Pacific.

15. Ibid., July 3, 1856. Park (1816–1894), who sold "patent family medicines," was also a director of the Santa Rita Silver Mining Company. See *Weekly Arizonian,* April 28, 1859, 4:4; and *Cincinnati Enquirer,* September 19, 1894, 5:7.

16. SPH, LC, November 17, 1856.

17. 1856 *Report.* Ehrenberg was listed as "Christian Ehrenberg, Topographical Engineer and Surveyor." Frederick Brunckow was listed as "Frederick Brunchow, Geologist, Mineralogist and Mining Engineer."

18. Sacks, "Charles Debrille Poston," p. 6.

19. Sacks, *Be It Enacted,* pp. 10–11.

20. 1856 *Report,* p. 41; Robert W. Frazer, *Forts of the West* (Norman: University of Oklahoma Press, 1965), p. 13; *Railroad Record,* February 3, 1859, 494–96.

21. The Treaty of Guadalupe Hidalgo and the Gadsden

Purchase Treaty stipulated that the United States would honor Mexican and Spanish claims for land in the areas acquired if valid evidence of the title could be located in the Mexican archives. Fraud, confusion, the withholding of lands, congressional delays, and in some instances years of litigation resulted when individuals tried to present claims for land in the Southwest. For further details consult Ray H. Mattison, "Early Spanish and Mexican Settlements in Arizona," *New Mexico Historical Review*, XXI, 4 (October 1946), 273–327; and B. Sacks, "The Plats of Private Land Claims in Arizona," 2 vols., map collection presented to the Arizona Historical Foundation (Phoenix: Arizona Historical Foundation, 1965, typewritten).

22. Pima County, Arizona, Recorder's Office, *Old Records, Book No. A*, pp. 11–14, cited hereafter as *Old Records Book A*. This document is often referred to as Poston's Record Book.

23. Sacks, "Plats," 1, 6–10.

24. *Possessions and Prospects of the Sonora Silver Mining Company, Report of the Sonora Exploring and Mining Company, Made to the Stockholders, Sept. 1857* (Cincinnati: Railroad Record Print, 1857), p. 7, cited hereafter as 1857 *Report*.

25. *Old Records Book A*, p. 189. For example, on December 7, 1856, the company reportedly paid Anton Elsner $1,000 for land in the Santa Rita Mountains.

26. Ibid., pp. 194–95.

27. Frederick Brunckow (Brunchow, Bronkow, Bronco, Bronckow, c. 1820–1860), a native of Prussia and a graduate of the Royal Mining Academy, came to the United States, possibly after the 1848 revolution. By 1856 he was settled near New Braunfels, Texas. Poston hired him to work for the company in exchange for a share in the venture, and by 1858 he was the administrator at Cerro Colorado. In 1859 he left to work his own claim, the San Pedro Silver Mines (near Tombstone) and was murdered on July 23, 1860, by his Mexican employees. SCF on Brunckow; SPH, LC, May 18, 1856, February 7, 1857, May 4, 10, 18, 1859; Raphael Pumpelly, *My Reminiscences*, 2 vols. (New York: Henry Holt and Co., 1918), I, 202; *San Francisco Bulletin*, August 21, 1860, 3:5.

Charles Schuchard (Shuchard, Shuardt, 1827–1883), a German mining engineer and artist, joined A. B. Gray's railroad survey team in Texas in 1853 and served as the expedition's artist. In 1854 he was a member of the Arizona Mining and Trading Company, and by 1857 he went to work for the Sonora Exploring and Mining Company as an engineer in charge of the smelting operations. He drew sketches and made maps of southwestern Arizona, and these were printed in the company's reports. He moved to Texas in 1859. In March 1860, he offered to sell his 100 shares of stock in the company to Samuel Colt for "25¢ per $" and would "take the amount in Navy and Army Revolvers." Schuchard raised sheep for awhile but became interested in mining operations in Texas and Mexico. He died in Mexico on May 4, 1883. SPH, LC, May 13, 1859, September 6, 1860; Schuchard to Samuel Colt, March 11, 1860, Samuel Colt Papers, CHS; *Old Records Book A*, p. 199; *Gray Report*, pp. xvi, 183, 226; Charles Schuchard, "Ajo Mines, Arizona Argonauts," typescript, AC; "The First Silver Mines on the Coast, Some Scraps of Early History," *Mining and Scientific Press*, XLVI (February 1883), 126.

Located at 110° 16' West longitude 31° 41' North latitude, 41 miles southwest of Tucson and 15 miles west of Tubac, at the foot of the Atasco Range, the altitude of Cerro Colorado ("red hill") is 4202'; see *Old Records Book A*, p. 197. Title to the property at the base of the hill has changed hands numerous times. The present owner of the mine is searching for mercury.

28. 1856 *Report*, p. 1.

29. *Railroad Record*, April 19, 1857, p. 107.

30. Heintzelman to Emory, March 13, 1857, William H. Emory Papers, YWA.

31. SPH, LC, May 2, 1858.

32. Ohio, Office of the Secretary of State, *Records of Incorporation*, I, 418.

33. SPH, LC, August 25, 1857.

34. *Second Annual Report of the Sonora Exploring and Mining Co., Made to the Stockholders, March 29, 1858* (Cincinnati: Railroad Record Print, 1858), pp. 8–9, cited hereafter as 1858 *Report*. For a full discussion of the economic crisis of 1857, see George W. Van Vleck, *The Panic of 1857: An Analytical Study* (New York: Columbia University Press, 1943).

35. SPH, LC, September 5, 7, 1857.

36. Ibid., December 18, 1857. Colt (1814–1862) also invested

in mining and railroad ventures in Mexico. He spent considerable time in Washington lobbying for the sale of his firearms, and while he promoted his patents, he also urged the government to send troops to the Southwest to protect U.S. citizens and their investments. SPH, LC, 1857–1862; *Hartford Daily Courant,* January 11, 1862, p. 2; "Col. Samuel Colt, 1814–1862," *Bulletin of the Wadsworth Atheneum,* III, 4 (October 1925), 31–33; William B. Edwards, *The Biography of Col. Samuel Colt* (Harrisburg, Pa.: The Stackpole Co., 1953).

37. SPH, LC, December 18, 1857. Sylvester Mowry (1832–1871) was a native of Providence, Rhode Island, and a West Point graduate who served in the Northwest and in the Territory of Utah before going to Fort Yuma in 1855. The ambitious lieutenant became involved in the movement to organize the territory of Arizona; in 1858 he resigned his commission to devote time to lobbying in Congress, delivering lectures, and writing books and articles on the proposed territory. He was thrice elected to serve as Arizona's delegate to Congress, but was not seated. In 1859 the Bureau of Indian Affairs chose Mowry to supervise the survey of Pima and Maricopa lands for a reservation site and to distribute gifts to the Indians. Mowry also became publisher of the Tubac *Weekly Arizonian* and moved the press to Tucson. He promoted mining ventures and invested in silver mines, notably the Patagonia (later Mowry) Silver Mine. The Civil War brought discredit to him and ushered in a period of difficulty and bitterness, ending in an early death. B. Sacks, "Sylvester Mowry: Artilleryman, Libertine, Entrepreneur," *The American West,* I, 3 (Summer 1964), 14–25, 79; and Mowry's publications, listed in the bibliography.

38. SPH, LC, December 19, 1857.

39. Ibid.

40. Ibid.

41. Ibid., December 20, 1857. A draft copy of Colt's agreement dated Washington, D.C., December 20, 1857, appears in the Samuel Colt Papers, CHS.

42. SPH, LC, December 20, 1857.

43. In 1858, Sylvester Mowry and John Russell Bartlett were instrumental in encouraging New England businessmen to organize two separate companies, the Sopori Land and Mining Company and the Arizona Land and Min-

ing Company. Mowry had earlier convinced certain Sonoran landowners to allow him to represent them as their attorney. The land to which Mowry, the Astiazaran family, Juan A. Robinson, Manuel Cubillas, and others supposedly held title was four square leagues south of the mission of San Xavier del Bac, land known as the Sopori Ranch. In addition, Robinson, a former consul at Guaymas, had sent Bartlett the title to an additional thirty-odd leagues that included the Sopori Mine and surrounding lands. Mowry reportedly sold the deed of the four square leagues to the Sopori Land and Mining Company for $25,000 and an interest for himself and his clients in the Arizona Land and Mining Company. The Sopori Land and Mining Company also held title to what they considered to be the preemption rights, or 160 acres, including the Sopori Mine. The Arizona Land and Mining Company held title to thirty-one square leagues. Together the two companies had purchased the three titles and owned 160,000 acres of land, according to their stockholders' reports.

The two companies were incorporated in Rhode Island in 1859. Welcome B. Sayles served as their agent in Arizona. The executive officers were the same for both companies, and Mowry, Sayles, and Colt served on the board of both companies. Little work was done, and the Civil War interrupted the companies' efforts. The question of the validity of these titles was unsettled for years, and the testimonies (perhaps misleading) of various individuals may be found in U.S. Congress, Senate, Committee on Private Land Claims, S.E.D. no. 93, 48th Cong., 1st sess., 1884. Consult the reports of both companies listed in the bibliography and SPH, LC, March 16, 26, and April 3, 4, 5, 7, 19, 21, 1858.

44. SPH, LC, December 24, 1857.

45. Ibid., December 27, 1857.

46. Ibid., January 1, 2, 4, 1858. He wrote that he paid "$865 for which Poston was arrested and let off by drawing on us." The arms arrived in San Francisco and were sold at a loss because they had been damaged in shipment; ibid., June 28, 1858.

47. Ibid., January 15, 1858.

48. On Crabb's venture, see U.S. Congress, House, H.E.D. #64, Serial 955, *Execution of Col. Crabb and Associates*, 35th Cong., 1st sess., 1858; *New York Evening Post,* July 7, 1857, 2:5.

49. 1858 *Report*, p. 12.

50. "Population Schedule of the Eighth Census of the United States, 1860," Roll 712, New Mexico, vol. I, part I, County of Arizona, pp. 1–185, on Microcopy no. 653, Records of the Bureau of Census, RG 29, NARS. It is important for students of Arizona history to use the original census lists (which unfortunately have errors but are as complete as possible), and not the printed excerpts that Senator Carl Hayden had his clerks prepare (U.S. Congress, Senate, *Federal Census, Territory of New Mexico and Territory of Arizona, Excerpts from the Decennial Federal Census, 1860 for Arizona County,* Sen. Doc. 13, 89th Cong., 1st sess., 1965). When the transcriptions were made (nearly twenty years before the document was published), a number of entries were omitted, and with the conversion from actual place of residence to alphabetical order, the evidence of living relationships was negated, not only as to sites but as to family or marital associations also.

51. SPH, LC, December 21, 1857.

52. 1858 *Report*, p. 4.

53. SPH, LC, July 10, 1857; *Railroad Record,* April 22, 1858, p. 103.

54. *San Diego Herald,* May 1, 1858, 1:4; August 21, 1858, 2:2; SPH, LC, September 8, 9, 10, 25, 28, 1858.

55. SPH, LC, July 2, 21, 1858.

56. 1857 *Report*, pp. 8–9.

57. Ibid., p. 10.

58. 1858 *Report*, p. 10.

59. SPH, LC, December 17, 1857.

60. Ibid., March 14, 1858.

61. Ibid., June 1, 1858. Sacks thought that one of the reasons Ehrenberg resigned was Poston's exaggerated representations of the richness of the mines. See SCF on Ehrenberg.

Guido Küstel (Kostel, Kuestel), a metallurgist, mining engineer, and writer, was born in Austria and educated in Germany. By 1857 he was working as an agent for the San Francisco smelting firm of Wass, Uznay, and Warwick, and after examining the mines owned by the Sonora Exploring and Mining Company, he resigned his position with the former and went to work for the latter. He introduced and improved the barrel amalgamation process for the company and was "one of the pioneers of the use of chloride and lixiviation" (the separation of a soluble substance from an insoluble one by washing with a solvent.). His text, *Nevada and California Process of Silver and Gold Extraction* (San Francisco: Carlton, 1863), has been described as "a standard reference in his day." When he moved back to California, Küstel formed partnerships for a metallurgical and assaying firm first with Ottaker Hoffman and later with Eugene N. Riotte. *San Francisco Bulletin*, November 6, 1858, 2:3; *Daily Alta California*, September 12, 1859, 1:6; *Weekly Arizona Miner*, December 12, 1863, 3:3; Clark C. Spence, *Mining Engineers and the American West: The Lace-Boot Brigade, 1849–1933*, Yale Western Americana Series, vol. 22 (New Haven, 1970), pp. 238–39, 361, 364. A later edition of his book was entitled *Roasting of Gold and Silver Ores and the Extraction of their Respective Metals without Quicksilver* (San Francisco: A. J. Leary, 1880).

62. Phocion R. Way (1826–1898), arrived in Arizona in June 1858. He remained in Arizona for about two years, returned to Ohio, enlisted in the Union Army, and after the war worked as an engraver, worked in a wagon factory, and sold insurance.

Horace Chipman Grosvenor (1820–1861), whose illustrations appeared in *Harper's Magazine,* was described by Raphael Pumpelly as "a strong and lovable character," and by Phocion Way as a man with "an inquiring turn of mind." He supervised the company's operations in the Santa Rita Mountains until he was murdered by Apaches on April 25, 1861.

By 1859, the Santa Rita Mining Company had erected buildings and was working seven mines. Pumpelly was forced to abandon the mines after Grosvenor's death. William Wrightson returned to reopen them in 1864 but he, too, was murdered. In 1869, the major stockholders agreed to allow James Eldredge to purchase the company. The stockholders would receive 100,000 pounds sterling of the stock of the "La Mancha Irrigation and Land Co. — Ltd," a foreign enterprise. At that time Heintzelman held 3,500 shares of Santa Rita stock. SPH, LC, March 9, 13, 28, 1858; *Railroad Record,* March 4, 1858; Pumpelly, *My Reminiscences,* I, 197–99, 213; Phocion R. Way, "Overland via 'Jackass Mail' in 1858: The Diary of Phocion R. Way," edited and annotated by William A.

Duffen, *Arizona and the West,* II, 1–4 (Spring–Winter 1960), 35–54, 147–64, 279–93, 353–71; and the annual reports of the company cited in the bibliography.

63. SPH, LC, March 28, 29, 1858. Other directors were Thomas Wrightson and Poston. William Wrightson served as secretary.

64. Ibid., April 10, 12, 16, 1858. It is not known whether Colt's suggestions were agreed to, because the Cincinnati officials objected to the terms. Colt wrote later that he sold all his stock in the Santa Rita Silver Mining Company for $1.00 per share; Colt to Messrs. Smith Crane and Co., n.d., n.p., Samuel Colt Papers, CHS.

65. SPH, LC, May 1, 2, 1858. The money was returned before November 18, 1858.

66. Ibid., May 1, 1858.

67. Colt to Heintzelman, May 2, 1858, Samuel Colt Papers, CHS.

68. On Jarvis, consult the correspondence of the Rev. William Jarvis and Richard W. H. Jarvis, CHS; *Hartford Times,* January 21, 1903, 11:6; Connecticut Historical Society Obituary Scrapbook Collection, 1881–1923, comp. Mrs. Anna M. Perry, vol. 48, p. 2, CHS.

69. Raphael Pumpelly, "Mineralogical Sketch of The Silver Mines in Arizona," in Sylvester Mowry, *Arizona and Sonora: The Geography, History, and Resources of the Silver Region of North America,* 3rd ed., rev. and enl. (New York: Harper and Brothers, 1864), p. 166.

70. "Processes for the Extraction of Silver, Followed at the Reducing Establishments of the Heintzelman Mines, Arizona, and the Real del Monte Mines, Mexico," *The Mining Magazine and Journal of Geology,* 2nd ser., I, 1 (November 1859), 17–19; Pumpelly, "Mineralogical Sketch," pp. 163–68; *Report of Frederick Brunckow, Geologist, Mineralogist and Mining Engineer, To A Committee of the Stockholders of the Sonora Exploring and Mining Co., upon the History, Resources and Prospects of the Company in Arizona, With an Appendix by the Committee* (Cincinnati: Railroad Record Print, 1859), pp. 9–14, cited hereafter as Brunckow's *Report;* "Silver and Copper Mining in Arizona," *The Mining Magazine and Journal of Geology,* 2nd

ser., I, 1(November 1859), 1–15; Otis E. Young, with the technical assistance of Robert Lenon, *Western Mining: An Informal Account* (Norman: University of Oklahoma Press, 1970).

Editor's Note

1. Solon Huntington Lathrop (1823–1867), was born in New Hampshire but moved to Buffalo, New York. He worked for the firm of Jewett, Thomas and Company, publishers of the *Commercial Advertiser* and several other papers. By 1855, he and C. F. S. Thomas were in charge of the establishment, and the firm's name was changed to Thomas and Lathrop, but they were forced out of business by the 1857 depression. He married Elizabeth Stuart, the sister of Heintzelman's wife. In 1858 he was elected treasurer of the Sonora Exploring and Mining Company with a salary of $2,000 a year, including board, lodging, and a dividend of ten shares of stock. In July 1858, Lathrop joined Heintzelman in San Francisco and together they traveled across the desert to Tubac. When Heintzelman left Arizona in January 1859, Lathrop became the superintendent of the company's operations. While living in Tubac he contracted to carry mail from Tubac to Tucson until the regular service was established. By January 1861, he was in Cincinnati, and the company's directors had voted him an increase in pay for the preceding year and a half of service. He died of yellow fever in 1867. *The Commercial Advertiser Directory for the City of Buffalo, 1847–1848* (Buffalo: Jewett, Thomas and Co., and T. S. Cutting, 1847), p. 90; *The Commercial Advertiser Directory for the City of Buffalo, 1854* (Buffalo: Jewett, Thomas and Co., 1854), p. 297; *The Commercial Advertiser Directory for the City of Buffalo, 1855* (Buffalo: Thomas and Lathrop, 1855); SPH, LC, December 11, 1860, January 12, 1861, and frequent references from 1857 through 1868; *San Diego Herald,* July 10, 1858, 2:4; *Weekly Arizonian,* March 10, 1859, p. 2; and Francis B. Heitman, *Historical Register and Dictionary of the United States Army,* 2 vols. (Washington, D.C.: GPO, 1903), I, 517.

August 1858

1. See Francis H. Leavitt, "Steam Navigation on the Colorado River," *California Historical Society Quarterly*, XXII, 1–2 (March, June 1943), 1–7.

2. On the San Xavier Silver Mining Company see *Old Records Book A*, p. 204; and *Railroad Record*, December 20, 1863, p. 33.

3. On Hammond see *San Deigo Herald*, March 14, 1857, 2:2; and T. H. S. Hamersly, *Complete Regular Army Register* (Washington, D.C.: T. H. S. Hamersly, 1880), p. 488. The "Petition to His Excellency the President of the United States of the Residents of the Western Division of the Proposed Territory of Arizona," YWA, is cited hereafter as the Hastings Appointment Petition.

4. On Hamilton, see his letter (recording Heintzelman's arrival) to Frank Ames, Fort Yuma, Calif., August 12, 1858, in AHS. See also *1970 Cullum Memorial Edition* (West Point, N.Y.: West Point Alumni Foundation, Inc., 1970), p. 239.

5. On Nauman, see *1970 Cullum Memorial Edition*, p. 213; Hamersly, *Army Register*, pp. 658–59. For Summers, consult Hamersly, *Army Register*, p. 791; and Francis B. Heitman, *Historical Register and Dictionary of the United States Army*, 2 vols. (Washington, D.C.: GPO, 1903), II, 625.

6. On Elder, see Constance W. Altshuler, ed., *Latest From Arizona: The Hesperian Letters, 1859–1861* (Tucson: Arizona Pioneer's Historical Society, 1969), pp. 249–50.

7. On Congressman McKibbin, see U.S. Congress, Senate, Senate Doc. #92-8, *Biographical Directory of the American Congress, 1774–1971*, 92nd. Cong., 1st sess. (Washington, D.C.: GPO, 1971), p. 1383. On Walker, see Edward E. Hill, "The Tucson Agency: The Use of Federal Records in the National Archives," *Prologue: The Journal of the National Archives*, IV, 2 (Summer 1972), 77–82; *Weekly Arizonian*, March 24, 1859, 3:1.

8. On Aldrich, see Mark. A. Aldrich Papers in AHS; SCF on Aldrich; Benjamin Sacks, *Be It Enacted: The Creation of the Territory of Arizona* (Phoenix: Arizona Historical Foundation, 1964), pp. 11, 36, 59, 98, n. 194; *Weekly Arizona Miner*, October 11, 1873, 4:2.

For the Overland Mail Company, see Roscoe P. and Margaret B. Conkling, *The Butterfield Overland Mail, 1857–1869*, 3 vols. (Glendale, Calif.: Arthur H. Clark Company, 1947).

9. On Steen and the Dragoons, see B. Sacks, "The Origins of Fort Buchanan: Myth and Fact," *Arizona and the West*, VII, 3 (Autumn 1965), 207–26.

10. On Carson, see Phocion R. Way, "Overland via 'Jackass Mail' in 1858: The Diary of Phocion R. Way," ed. William A. Duffen, *Arizona and the West*, II, 2 (Summer 1960), 159.

11. *La Paloma Blanca del Desierto* was built by the Franciscans, aided by the Gaona brothers, between 1772 and 1783; the remarkably rich details were added in the 1790s. B. L. Fontana, "Biography of a Desert Church: The Story of Mission San Xavier del Bac," *The Smoke Signal*, no. 3 (1961); and J. A. Donohue, "The Unlucky Jesuit Mission of Bac," *Arizona and the West*, II, 2 (Summer 1960), 127–40.

12. On Douglass, see Way, "Overland," pp. 285–86; *Los Angeles Star*, April 4, 1857, 2:2. On Sayles, see Jack L. Cross, "The El Paso-Fort Yuma Wagon Road, 1857–1860," *Password*, IV, 1, 2 (1959), 4–18, 58–70; and SCF on Sayles. On the title dispute, see U.S. Congress, Senate, Committee on Private Land Claims, S.E.D. no. 93, 48th Cong., 1st sess., 1884.

13. See J. C. Ives, *Report Upon the Colorado River of the West, Explored in 1857 and 1858* (Washington, D.C.: GPO, 1861), p. 21; and *San Diego Herald*, July 31, 1858, 2:1.

14. On Dunbar, see U.S. Congress, House, H.E.D. #64, Serial 955, *Execution of Col. Crabb and Associates*, 35th Cong., 1st sess., 1858, pp. 58–61; *Pacific News*, December 5, 1849, 2:2; *Daily Alta California*, October 12, 1853, 4:2; *New York Evening Post*, May 8, 1858, 1:2; "Memorial and Petition to Congress, Citizens of Arizona, Tubac, March 1, 1858," *Records of the United States Senate*, 35th Cong., 2nd sess., RG 46, NARS, cited hereafter as March 1, 1858, Memorial; Catherine North, *History of Berlin, Conn.*, ed. A. B. Benson (New Haven: Tuttle, Morehouse and Taylor, 1916), pp. 147–48. Dunbar wrote a series of articles for the *New York Times* in 1859 and was the author of *The Romance of the Age, or the Discovery of Gold in California* (New York: D. Appleton and Co., 1867).

15. On Cheever, see SPH, LC, March 16, April 4, 7, 12, May 1, 2, 4, 9, 10, 14, 18, 20, 25, 1858.

16. On dealings with Conklin, consult SPH, LC, July 8–10, 12, 13, 23, 1858.

17. On Fitzgerald, see Heitman, *Historical Register*, I, 422; Edward S. Wallace, *The Great Reconnaissance: Soldiers, Artists and Scientists on the Frontier, 1848–1861* (Boston: Little, Brown and Co., 1955), p. 146; *Los Angeles Star*, January 14, 1860, 2:3.

On Ewell, see *The Making of a Soldier: Letters of General R. S. Ewell*, ed. Percy G. Hamlin (Richmond: Whittet and Shepperson, 1935), pp. 82, 84, 86.

18. For information about the Ainsa brothers' involvement in Crabb's expedition, see J. Y. Ainsa, *History of the Crabb Expedition into Northern Sonora* (Phoenix, 1951); Robert H. Forbes, *Crabb's Filibustering Expedition into Sonora, 1857: An Historical Account* (Tucson: Arizona Silhouettes, 1952).

19. Pierce's visit was noted by the *New York Evening Post*, May 8, 1858, 1:2. See also Way, "Overland," p. 358.

20. On the meteorite, see R. J. McGough, "References on the Early History of the Tucson, Arizona, Meteorites: The 'Irwin-Ainsa' and the 'Carleton' Irons," *Popular Astronomy*, LI (November–December 1943), 511–18, 563–67; John R. Bartlett, *Personal Narrative of Exploration and Incidents in Texas, New Mexico, California, Sonora, and Chihuahua Connected with the United States and Mexican Boundary Commission*, 2 vols. (New York: D. Appleton-Century, 1854).

21. On Stevens, see Sen. Doc. #92-8, *Biographical Directory*, p. 1752; *Daily Arizona Citizen*, March 21, 1893, 1:4; March 22, 1893, 4:2; August 29, 1916, 2:5; H. S. Stevens Papers, AHS; SCF on Stevens. The information about Stevens's baptism and marriage was provided by Francis J. Fox, S. J., Archivist, Diocese of Tucson, using notes provided by Henry F. Dobyns from the Magdalena Parish Archives, Baptisms Book, #2, 1850–1860, Entry 1475.

An illustration of San Augustín del Tucson, showing two bells hanging from poles in the churchyard, appears in J. W. Barber and H. Howe, *All the Western States and Territories* (Cincinnati: Howe's Subscription Book Concern, 1867), p. 565. The crude engraving bears the date 1860. See also "Map of Tucson, A. T. Surveyed by Order of Major D. Fergusson ... 1862," in HPF.

22. On McCarty and the election, see *Santa Fe Weekly Gazette*, May 1, 1858, 2:4; *Daily Alta California*, October 11,

1858, 1:7; SPH, LC, March 20, 1858; Sacks, *Be It Enacted,* pp. 31–32, 51, n. 105.

23. Brevoort was the author of *New Mexico: Her Natural Resources and Attractions* (Santa Fe: E. Brevoort, 1874). See also SCF on Brevoort; *Weekly Arizonian,* March 3, 1859, 3:2; July 7, 1859, 3:2; and Way, "Overland," p. 365, n. 17.

24. Heintzelman wrote in his pocket diary for Monday, August 30, 1858, that he "Saw Conner shot by Van Alstine." On the latter, see Sacks, *Be It Enacted,* pp. 119, 121; Way, "Overland," p. 344, n. 15; *Weekly Arizonian,* June 30, 1859, 3:1; August 4, 1859, 2:2; *Daily Arizona Citizen,* November 5, 1870, 2:2; July 18, 1874, 3:3; October 16, 1875, 2:5; March 16, 1898, 4:3.

September 1858

1. On Tripler and Whistler, see T. H. S. Hamersly, ed., *Complete Regular Army Register* (Washington, D.C.: T. H. S. Hamersly, 1880), p. 817; and Francis B. Heitman, *Historical Register and Dictionary of the United States Army,* 2 vols. (Washington, D.C.: GPO, 1903), II, 689.

2. Heintzelman gave Bull's address as "no. 3 Nassau St., N.Y." and wrote that Bull and his associates could raise "60 to 70,000$." SPH, LC, June 5, 1858.

3. Captain Henry Heth's proposal for a "System of Target Practice" was approved and adopted on March 1, 1858, for instruction of troops "when armed with Musket, Rifle, Musket Rifle or Carbine." Letters Received by the Office of the Adjutant General, Main Series, 1822–1860, in Records of the Adjutant General, RG 94, NARS, H:1858.

4. On Hendershott and McLean, see Heitman, *Historical Register,* II, 625; and Hamersly, *Army Register,* pp. 506, 626, 791.

5. On the so-called Mormon War (1857–1859), see Norman F. Furniss, *The Mormon Conflict, 1850–1859* (New Haven: Yale University Press, 1960).

6. For information on the Mexican civil war, see Walter F. Scholes, "Mexican Politics During the Juárez Regime, 1855–1872," *University of Missouri Studies,* XXX (1957), 29–43. The

earthquake is reported in "Monthly Record of Current Events," *Harper's New Monthly Magazine*, XVII, 100 (September 1858), 546.

7. For Townsend, see his journal, *The California Diary of General E. D. Townsend*, ed. Malcolm Edwards (Los Angeles: Ward Ritchie Press, 1970).

8. On Coleman, see Alonzo Phelps, *Contemporary Biographies of California's Representative Men* (San Francisco: A. L. Bancroft and Co., 1881), I, 272–80; SCF on Coleman; W. J. Ghent, "William Tell Coleman," *Dictionary of American Biography*, 22 vols. in 12 (New York: Charles Scribner's Sons, 1958), II, 2, pp. 295–96.

9. For John Poston, see SCF on Poston; Raphael Pumpelly, *My Reminiscences*, 2 vols. (New York: Henry Holt an Co., 1918), I, 242–44.

On Fuller, see Phocion R. Way, "Overland via 'Jackass Mail' in 1858: The Diary of Phocion R. Way," ed. William A. Duffen, *Arizona and the West*, II, 1–4 (Spring–Winter 1960), 287, n. 28; Frank C. Lockwood, *More Arizona Characters* (Tucson: University of Arizona Press, 1943), p. 10; *Old Records Book A*, p. 195; *Daily Missouri Republican*, December 5, 1858, 2:4.

On Doss, see Constance W. Altshuler, ed., *Latest from Arizona! The Hesperian Letters, 1859–1861* (Tucson: Arizona Pioneer's Historical Society, 1969), p. 248; SCF on Doss; *Weekly Arizonian*, September 15, 1859, 3:3; *Daily Arizona Citizen*, April 8, 1871, 2:5; and John and Lillian Theobald, *Arizona Territory: Post Offices and Postmasters* (Phoenix: Arizona Historical Foundation, 1961), p. 118.

10. On Irwin see Heitman, *Historical Register*, I, 564; Hamersly, *Army Register*, p. 536; *Weekly Arizonian*, July 7, 1859, 3:2; October 25, 1859, 3:1; *American Decorations: A List of Awards* (Washington, D.C.: GPO, 1927), p. 206; and B. I. D. Irwin, "Sanitary Report, Fort Buchanan, Feb., 1859," in U.S. Congress, Senate, Sen. Exec. Doc. #52, *Statistical Report on the Sickness and Mortality in the Army of the U.S. Compiled from the Records of the Surgeon General's Office, 1855–1860*, 36th Cong., 1st sess., 1860 (Washington: G. W. Bowman, 1860), pp. 207–20.

For Lord, see Hamersly, *Army Register*, p. 587; and George W. Cullum, *Biographical Register of the Officers and Graduates of the United States Military Academy,* 3rd ed. rev., 3 vols. (Boston: Houghton Mifflin and Co., 1891), II, 441–42.

For a later history of the Patagonia Mine, see Bernard L. Fontana, "The Mowry Mine, 1858–1958," *Kiva,* 23, 3 (February 1958), pp. 14–16; Sylvester Mowry, *Arizona and Sonora,* 3rd ed., rev. and enl. (New York: Harper and Brothers, 1864), pp. 27, 61–78; *Weekly Arizonian,* April 28, 1859, 3:2; June 30, 1859, 3:3; Georgia Wehrman, "Harshaw: Mining Camp of the Patagonias," *Journal of Arizona History.* VI (Spring 1965), 23–24.

11. On Steen, see Heitman, *Historical Register,* II, 613. On Hastings, see Hamersly, *Army Register,* p. 498.

12. On the Salero Mine, see Way, "Overland," p. 290, no. 35.

13. See SCF on Thompson.

14. The only reference located to date for Mrs. Klein and her daughter is that provided by Poston in his poem, "Apache-Land." Poston noted their relationship to Guido Küstel and said: "His sister, and niece the fraulein Kline, / Were Company for those at the mine. / The fraulein, a most accomplished person, / Inspired, somehow, a great aversion." Charles D. Poston, *Apache-Land* (San Francisco: A. L. Bancroft Co., 1878), p. 53.

On Sloan, see Hamersly, *Army Register,* p. 762.

15. On the Concord Coach, see H. N. Scheiber, "Coach, Wagon, and Motor-Truck Manufacture, 1813–1928: The Abbot-Downing Co. of Concord," in "Abbot Downing and the Concord Coach," *Historical New Hampshire,* XX, 3 (Autumn 1965), 3–25.

For the mission of San José de Tumacacori, consult B. Sacks, "The Plats of Private Land Claims in Arizona," 2 vols. (Phoenix: Arizona Historical Foundation, 1965, typewritten), I, 52–54; H. F. Dobyns, "Indian Extinction in the Middle Santa Cruz River Valley, Arizona," *New Mexico Historical Review,* XXXVIII, 2 (April 1963), 165–66; and "Tumacacori National Monument," a pamphlet prepared by the U.S. National Park Service, 1969.

16. On Streit, see *Weekly Arizonian,* April 28, 1859, 4:2.

17. On the Donati comet, see Charles P. Olivier, *Comets* (Baltimore: Williams and Wilkins Co., 1930), pp. 149–53.

18. On Garland, see Hamersly, *Army Register,* p. 456.

19. On Hülseman, see his letter of June 25, 1855, to William H. Emory, YWA; *Old Records Book A,* pp. 203, 209–10, 220; *Weekly Arizonian,* April 22, 1859, 3:4; Julius Froebel, *Seven Years' Travel in Central America, Northern Mexico, and the Far West of the U.S.* (London: Richard Bentley, 1859), pp. 495–96, 501.

20. On Miles, see Benjamin Sacks; *Be It Enacted: The Creation of the Territory of Arizona* (Phoenix: Arizona Historical Foundation, 1964), p. 11; Way, "Overland," p. 354, n. 2; *Daily Missouri Republican,* September 10, 1858, 2:2.

21. On Ronstadt and the claims to his title, see SPH, LC, March–April 1858; SCF on Ronstadt and the Sopori Land and Mining Company. It is doubtful that much of the testimony on the "El Sopori Land Claims" in U.S. Congress, Senate, Committee on Private Land Claims, S.E.D. no. 93, 48th Cong., 1st sess., 1884, is accurate.

22. On the Magdalena pilgrimage, see Alice Joseph, Rosamond Spicer, and Jane Chesky, *The Desert People* (Chicago: University of Chicago Press, 1949), pp. 85–86.

23. On Moohrmann, see SCF on Moohrmann; Moohrmann to William H. Emory, May 24, 1855, Wiliam H. Emory Papers, YWA; Froebel, *Seven Years' Travel,* pp. 495, 497, 501; Pima County, Arizona, Recorder's Office, *Deeds of Real Estate,* I, 65–68.

October 1858

1. See SCF on Meyer; C. H. Meyer Papers, AHS.

2. See Louis Quesse Papers, AHS.

3. On Allen, see T. H. S. Hamersly, ed., *Complete Regular Army Register* (Washington, D.C.: T. H. S. Hamersly, 1880), pp. 256–57; *Daily California Chronicle,* May 15, 1855, 3:2; SCF on Allen.

4. Consult SCF on Kirkland; HPF. On the Canoa Ranch, see B. Sacks, "The Plats of Private Land Claims in Arizona," 2 vols. (Phoenix: Arizona Historical Foundation, 1965, typewritten), I, 31–33; Raphael Pumpelly, *Across America and Asia* (New York: Leypoldt and Holt, 1870), p. 7; *Weekly Alta Cali-*

fornia, March 2, 1861, 5:2; *Weekly Arizonian*, September 9, 1859, 3:2.

5. On Titus, see John W. Geary to Henry Titus, November 8, 1856, Geary Papers, YWA; undated statement by Henry Titus, Geary Papers, YWA; W. H. Stephenson, *Publication of the Kansas State Historical Society, Embracing the Political Career of General James H. Lane* (Topeka, 1930), III, 68, 76–78; *Railroad Record*, February 3, 1859, pp. 494–96; *Weekly Arizonian*, March 3, 1859, 2:4; April 7, 1859, 2:4; June 30, 1859, 3:2; *San Francisco Weekly Bulletin*, March 31, 1860, 1:5,6.

6. On Peck, see *The Commercial Advertiser Directory for the City of Buffalo, 1847–1848*, (Buffalo: Jewett, Thomas and Co., 1847), p. 119.

7. On Elsner, see *Old Records Book A*, pp. 188–90; *Weekly Arizonian*, April 28, 1859, 4:2.

8. On Brown, see *Third Annual Report of the Sonora Exploring and Mining Company, Made to the Stockholders, March, 1859* (New York: W. Minns and Co., 1859), p. 13.

9. For Grosvenor's description of the pinery, see *Railroad Record*, August 12, 1858, p. 293.

10. On Gándara's family, consult Franciso Almada, *Diccionario de historia, geografia, y biografia sonorenses* (Chihuahua: Impresora Ruiz Sandoval, 1952), pp. 287–88.

11. On Buckley, see *Weekly Arizonian*, March 3, 1859, 2:2; Roscoe P. and Margaret B. Conkling, *The Butterfield Overland Mail, 1857–1869*, 3 vols. (Glendale, Calif.: Arthur H. Clark Company, 1947), I, 127; and SCF on Buckley.

12. Notice of Olds's death was published in the *Weekly Arizonian*, April 28, 1859, 4:2.

13. For details on the military reorganization, consult Francis Paul Prucha, *A Guide to Military Posts of the United States: 1789–1895* (Madison: State Historical Society of Wisconsin, 1964), pp. 145–47, 150–57.

November 1858

1. See SCF on Fernandez; *Weekly Arizonian*, June 19, 1869, 3:1; November 27, 1869, 3:2.

2. On Kitchen, see March 1, 1858, Memorial to Congress;

John and Lillian Theobald, *Arizona Territory: Post Offices and Postmasters* (Phoenix: Arizona Historical Foundation, 1961), p. 114; Raymond W. Thorp, "Pete Kitchen's Road," *True West*, XII, 2 (November–December 1964), 6–8, 66–67; *Prospector, Cowhand, and Sodbuster: Historic Places Associated With Mining, Ranching, and Farming Frontiers in the Trans-Mississippi West*, The National Survey of Historic Sites and Buildings, ed. Robert G. Ferris, vol. XI (Washington, D.C.: National Park Service, 1967), p. 150.

On Carothers, see Sylvester Mowry to Howell Cobb, Secretary of the Treasury, September 24, 1858, in General Records of the Department of the Treasury, RG 56, NARS, Vol. K, Custom House Nominations, Texas, September 1858–December 1881, Box 450, vol. 10; SCF on Carothers.

3. On the Ake family, see Constance W. Altshuler, ed., *Latest From Arizona! The Hesperian Letters, 1859–1861* (Tucson: Arizona Pioneer's Historical Society, 1969), p. 241; *Mesilla Times*, January 15, 1862, 2:1. A popular story of Ake's son Jeff has been written by James B. O'Neill, *They Die But Once: The Story of a Tejano* (New York: Knight Publications, Inc., 1935).

4. See SCF on Miller.

5. On Ignacio Pesqueira (1820–1886), see *Diccionario Porrua de historia, biografia y geografia de Mexico*, 2 vols. (Republica Argentina, Mex.: Editorial Porrua, S.A., 1970–1971), II, 1622–23; and Rodolfo Acuña, *Sonoran Strongman: Ignacio Pesqueira and His Times* (Tucson: University of Arizona Press, 1974).

6. On Van Dorn and Van Camp, see Francis B. Heitman, *Historical Register and Dictionary of the United States Army*, 2 vols. (Washington, D.C.: GPO, 1903), II, 657; George W. Cullum, *Biographical Register of the Officers and Graduates of the United States Military Academy*, 3rd ed. rev., 3 vols. (Boston: Houghton Mifflin and Co., 1891), II, 149–50; and Robert G. Hartje, *Van Dorn: The Life and Times of a Confederate General* (Nashville: Vanderbilt University Press, 1967).

7. On Henry Heintzelman, see SPH, LC, February 19, 1855; T. Gregory, *History of Sonoma County, California with Biographical Sketches* (Los Angeles: Historic Record Co., 1911), pp. 177–78, 249–51; *Report of the Commissioner of Indian Affairs, Accompanying the Annual Report of the Secretary of the Interior, for the Year 1858* (Washington: W. A. Harris, 1859), pp. 286–87.

8. On the Almaden mines, see Miscellaneous letters and documents relating to the land claim and the mine at New Almaden, California, YWA; "California's Oldest Mine: The Quicksilver of New Almaden, A Calico Print Folio," *Calico Print*, July 1953, pp. 27–38: *Prospector, Cowhand, and Sodbuster*, pp. 114–15; and Henry W. Splitter, "Quicksilver at New Almaden," *Pacific Historical Review*, XXVI, 1 (February 1957), 33–51.

December 1858

1. On Antisell, see Lt. John G. Parke, *Report of Explorations for that Portion of a Railway Route, Near the Thirty-Second Parallel* (Washington, D.C.: Nicholson, 1855), pp. 171 f.; *The National Cyclopedia of American Biography*, 54 vols. (New York: James T. White and Co., 1926), XIX, 448; and *Railroad Record*, January 22, 1857, p. 754.

2. On Godfrey, see John and Lillian Theobald, *Arizona Territory: Post Offices and Postmasters* (Phoenix: Arizona Historical Foundation, 1961), p. 76; *Weekly Arizonian*, April 28, 1859, 3:2; July 17, 1859, 3:2.

3. On Donaldson, see his letter to Sam Jones, July 25, 1859, General Records of the Department of the Treasury, RG 56, NARS, Custom House Nominations, September 1858– December 1881; SPH, LC, May 17, 1859.

4. On Perkins, see SPH, LC, January 11, February 13, February 22, March 5, April 12, 1858.

5. On Loza y Pardave, see *Diccionario Porrua de historia, biografia, y geografia de Mexico*, 2 vols. (Republica Argentina, Mex.: Editorial Porrua, S.A., 1970–1971), I, 1217; Francisco Almada, *Diccionario de historia, geografia, y biografia sonorenses* (Chihuahua: Impresora Ruiz Sandoval, 1952), pp. 436–38.

6. On Walker, see his *War in Nicaragua* (Mobile, Ala.: S. H. Goetzel and Co., 1860); and Albert Carr, *The World and William Walker* (New York: Harper and Row, 1963).

On Davis, see Allan Westcott, "Charles Henry Davis," *Dictionary of American Biography* (New York: Charles Scribner's Sons, 1958), vol. III, pt. 1, pp. 106–07; L. B. Miller, F. Voss, and J. Hussey, "Charles Henry Davis," in *The Lazzaroni: Science and Scientist in Mid-Nineteenth Century America*

(Washington, D.C.: National Portrait Gallery, Smithsonian Institution Press, 1972), pp. 43–48.

On Stone, see his *Notes on the State of Sonora, 1860* (Washington, D.C.: Henry Polkinhorn, 1861); H. H. Bancroft, *History of the North Mexican States and Texas,* vol. XVI of the *Works of Hubert Howe Bancroft* (San Francisco: The History Company, 1889), II, 695.

7. On McCullough, see Robert G. Caldwell, "Ben McCullough," *Dictionary of American Biography,* 1961, vol. VI, pt. 2, pp. 5–6; Victor M. Rose, *The Life and Services of Ben McCullough* (1888; rpt. ed., Austin: The Steck Co., 1958).

8. See SCF on Marshall; *Weekly Arizonian,* March 3, 1859, 2:4; April 14, 1859, 3:3.

9. On the Gila River gold discovery, see *Daily Missouri Republican,* November 30, 1858, 2:4; December 13, 1858, 2:2; December 22, 1858, 2:5; *Railroad Record,* December 20, 1860, p. 533; Sylvester Mowry, *Arizona and Sonora,* 3rd ed., rev. and enl. (New York: Harper and Brothers, 1864), p. 38.

10. Buchanan's message is in *A Compilation of the Messages and Papers of the Presidents, 1789–1897,* comp. J. D. Richardson, 10 vols. (Washington, D.C.: GPO, 1897), V. 497–529.

11. Bayard Taylor, *Northern Travel: Summer and Winter Pictures of Sweden, Denmark, and Lapland* (New York: G. P. Putnam, 1858).

12. For a description of this and other Sonoran Indian games, see Wendell C. Bennett and Robert M. Zingg, *The Tarahumaras: An Indian Tribe of Northern Mexico,* University of Chicago Publications in Anthropology, Ethnological Series (Chicago, 1935), pp. 335, 339, 391–97.

13. Francisco Xavier de Gamboa (1717–1794), the inventor of the cazo reduction process for refracting silver ore, wrote *Comentarios a las ordenanzas de minas* (Madrid: J. Ibarra, 1761). A two-volumes-in-one English translation by Richard Heathfield was published in London in 1830 by Longman, Rees, Orme, Brown, and Green.

14. On Rose, see his letter to Lewis Cass, January 17, 1859, General Records of the Department of State, RG 59, NARS, U.S. Consul in Guaymas, Mexico, 1832–1896, vol. I; see also

the letters of Rev. William Jarvis to William Jarvis, January 25, January 31, and February 21, 1859, in the correspondence of Richard W. H. Jarvis, CHS.

January 1859

1. On Schuchard and the Ajo mines, see Charles Schuchard, "Ajo Mine, Arizona Argonauts," typescript, AC; Sylvester Mowry, *Memoir of the Proposed Territory of Arizona* (Washington, D.C.: Henry Polkinhorn, 1857), p. 11; *Railroad Record*, December 20, 1860, p. 533; "Silver and Copper Mining in Arizona," *The Mining Magazine and Journal of Geology*, 2nd ser., I, 1 (November 1859), 15.

On Boulbon, see Rufus K. Wyllys, *The French in Sonora, 1850–1854: The Story of French Adventurers from California into Mexico*, University of California Publications in History, ed. H. E. Bolton et al., vol. XXI (Berkeley, 1932), pp. 220–36; Paul Neff Garber, The Gadsden Treaty (Gloucester, Mass.: Peter Smith, 1959), pp. 162–64; *Weekly Alta California*, October 21, 1854, 6:3–5.

On the Planchas de Plata mines, see *San Francisco Herald*, April 16, 1855, 2:2, April 28, 1855, 2:3; *Weekly Alta California*, August 4, 1860, 6:3–5.

2. On Ringgold, see Francis B. Heitman, *Historical Register and Dictionary of the United States Army*, 2 vols. (Washington, D.C.: GPO, 1903), II, 550; and *San Diego Herald*, March 14, 1857, 2:2.

3. On the Robinsons, see Phocion Way, "Overland via 'Jackass Mail' in 1858: The Diary of Phocion Way," ed. William A. Duffen, *Arizona and the West*, II, 1–4 (Spring–Winter 1960), 50; *Weekly Arizonian*, March 24, 1859, 3:1; March 31, 1859, 3:3; June 2, 1859, 2:2; June 15, 1859, 3:4; *Sacramento Daily Union*, September 23, 1859, 2:2; August 9, 1862, 3:2; *Old Records Book A*, pp. 183–84; SCF on Robinson; Robinson Papers, AHS; and the notes of Roy L. Goodale, AC.

4. On Jones, see *1970 Cullum Memorial Edition* (West Point, N.Y.: West Point Alumni Foundation, Inc., 1970), p. 223; T. H. S. Hamersly, ed., *Complete Regular Army Register* (Washington, D.C.: T. H. S. Hamersly, 1880), p. 546.

5. On Pardee, see D. N. Barney to E. B. Morgan, January 8, 1853; R. W. Washburn to E. B. Morgan, July 14, 1853; Henry Morgan to E. B. Morgan, January 23, 1854; and Alpheus Reynolds to E. B. Morgan, February 15, 1855; all in the E. B. Morgan Papers, LJL. See also Roscoe P. and Margaret B. Conkling, *The Butterfield Overland Mail, 1857–1869,* 3 vols. (Glendale, Calif.: Arthur H. Clark Company, 1947), I, 129.

On Butterfield, see LeRoy R. Hafen, "John Butterfield," *Dictionary of American Biography* (New York: Charles Scribner's Sons, 1957), vol. 2, pt. 1, pp. 374–75.

6. On Lee, see Heitman, *Historical Register,* I, 623–24. On Ruggles, see *1970 Cullum Memorial Edition,* p. 249. On Longstreet, see his *From Manassas to Appomatox: Memoirs of the Civil War in America,* 2nd ed. rev. (Philadelphia: J. B. Lippincott, 1903).

7. On Macrae, see Hamersly, *Army Register,* p. 597. On Buchanan, see Charles D. Rhodes, "Robert Christie Buchanan," *Dictionary of American Biography,* 1957, vol. II, pt. 1, pp. 217–18. On Mason, see *1970 Cullum Memorial Edition,* p. 239. On McLean, see Hamersly, *Army Register,* 6, 626.

8. On Kennett, see Hamersly, *Army Register,* p. 909.

A Hole to Bury Money In

1. Sonora Exploring and Mining Company, 1859 *Report.*

2. Ohio, Office of the Secretary of State, *Records of Incorporation,* I, 418 f. The protest was filed on May 12, 1859. On February 27, 1860, two protests were filed in the office of New York's secretary of state; additional signatures on the protest included those of Samuel Flickinger, S. H. Burton, E. C. Middleton, and John Reeves(?). Consult New York, Office of the Secretary of State, *Miscellaneous Papers,* IV, 23.

3. *Letter to the Stockholders Only, Report to the Stockholders of the Sonora Exploring and Mining Company, New York, May 1, 1859* (New York: n.p., 1859), p. 14, cited hereafter as Colt's *Report.*

4. Ibid., pp. 15, 16. See also Colt to William Hartley or Charles S. Brown, n.d., Samuel Colt Papers, CHS; and New York, Office of the Secretary of State, *Business Records,* VII, 16. The seven trustees were William M. B. Hartley, Charles S.

Brown, James P. Kilbreth, William T. Coleman, William H. Fogg, Augustus Belknap, and William W. Howe. On February 23, 1860, these men and Granville Y. Jenks were listed as the trustees of a newly formed organization, the Sonora Mining Company, with operations in the Territory of New Mexico; ibid., VII, 25.

5. SPH, LC, May 13, 1859.

6. Erastus Smith to Colt, June 4, 1859, Samuel Colt Papers, CHS.

7. Colt to Charles S. Brown, March 8, 1860, Samuel Colt Papers, CHS. The letter is marked "Confidential."

8. *Old Records Book A,* pp. 215–21. See also SPH, LC, March 9 and 15, 1861.

9. Colt to J. Deane Alden, Feburary 20, 1860, Samuel Colt Papers, CHS. See also *Fourth Annual Report of the Sonora Exploring and Mining Company, Made to the Stockholders, March, 1860* (New York: W. Minns and Co., 1860); cited hereafter as 1860 *Report.*

10. Colt's *Report,* p. 17.

11. Raphael Pumpelly, *My Reminiscences,* 2 vols. (New York: Henry Holt and Co., 1918), I, 208–38. See also *Weekly Arizonian,* June 2, 1859, 3:2; July 21, 1859, 3:1,2.

12. George W. Pierce, Cerro Colorado Mine, to Col. Seymour, August 29, 1862, Thomas H. Seymour Papers, CHS. See also 1860 *Report,* pp. 7–16.

13. Pima County, Arizona, Recorder's Office, *Deeds of Mines,* I, 1–4, 225–26.

14. Pima County, Arizona, Recorder's Office, *Miscellaneous Records,* I, 1–3. See also B. Sacks, "The Plats of Private Land Claims in Arizona," 2 vols. (Phoenix: Arizona Historical Foundation, 1965, typewritten), I, 9.

15. *The Arizona Mining Company, Its Mines, Property and Organization, 1863* (Jersey City: Davison and Ward, 1863); W. M. B. Hartley, *Heintzelman Mine, Arizona* (New York, 1863); and *Arizona Mining Company, Reports of Sam F. Butterworth and Guido Küstel* (n.p., 1864).

16. New York, Office of the Secretary of State, *Business Records,* LII, 235–42.

17. *Brief Description of the Arivaca Estate in the Territory of Arizona, U.S.A.* (London: Charles Carter and Co., c. 1875); SCF on Poston.

18. *Statement. The Cerro Colorado Mine* (San Francisco: Charles Coolidge, 1876).

19. Benjamin Sacks, *Be It Enacted: The Creation of the Territory of Arizona* (Phoenix: Arizona Historical Foundation, 1964), pp. 6–70; SCF on Poston; Charles Debrille Poston Papers, AHS. The town of Poston is named for him.

20. Diane M. T. Rose, "The Maps, Plans, and Sketches of Herman Ehrenberg," *Prologue: The Journal of the National Archives*, IX, 3 (Fall 1977), 162–70. The town of Ehrenberg, several miles south of La Paz, was named for him by his friend, Michael Goldwater; and the U.S. Board on Geographic Names, Department of Interior, designated Ehrenberg Point, in the northeast corner of the Grand Canyon National Park (about two miles southwest of Point Imperial).

The Benefit of My Abilities

1. U.S. Congress, House, *Letter from the Secretary of War, Communicating . . . information in relation to troubles on the Texas frontier*, House Exec. Doc. #81, 36th Cong., 1st sess., 1860. Heintzelman's account reads like a Zane Grey thriller.

2. Benjamin Sacks, *Be It Enacted: The Creation of the Territory of Arizona* (Phoenix: Arizona Historical Foundation, 1964).

3. SPH, LC, November 21, 1860.

4. George W. Cullum, *Biographical Register of the Officers and Graduates of the United States Military Academy*, 3rd ed. rev., 3 vols. (Boston: Houghton Mifflin and Co., 1891), I, 372–74. Heintzelman's Civil War activities require a separate study. For additional details consult his journals, especially a small notebook dated January 9, 1861–October 27, 1863, and Frederick H. Dyer, *A Compendium of the War of the Rebellion*, 3 vols. (New York: Thomas Yoseloff, 1959), I, 272–80.

5. SPH, LC, August 11, 1862, October 12, 1864, January 16, 1866.

6. Ibid., September 30, 1864. See also Frank L. Klement, *The Copperheads in the Middle West* (Chicago: University of Chicago Press, 1959).

7. SPH, LC, January 5, 1866.

8. SPH, LC, Special Order No. 380, July 27, 1867.

[218]

9. Ezra J. Warner, *Generals in Blue: Lives of the Union Commanders* (Baton Rouge: Louisiana State University Press, 1964), p. 228.

10. Bruce Catton, *The Army of the Potomac: Mr. Lincoln's Army* (Garden City, N.Y.: Doubleday and Co., Inc., 1951), pp. 114–30.

11. *The Civil War Letters of General Robert McAllister*, ed. James L. Robertson, Jr. (New Brunswick: Rutgers University Press, 1965), p. 204.

12. R. H. Beattie, Jr., *Road to Manassas: The Growth of Union Command* (New York: Cooper Square Publishers, Inc., 1961), p. 208.

13. F. Stansbury Haydon, *Aeronautics in the Union and Confederate Armies*, 2 vols. (Baltimore: Johns Hopkins Press, 1941), I, 343.

14. SPH, LC, June 9, 1858.

15. Ibid., January 12, 1858.

16. SPH, LC, General Orders No. 47, April 29, 1869.

17. SPH, LC, December 31, 1869.

18. Ibid., December 31, 1870.

19. Ibid., November 1, 1871.

20. Ibid., December 31, 1872. His last residence was 1123 Fourteenth Street, N.W., Washington D.C.

21. *New York Times*, May 2, 1880, p. 5, and May 4, 1880, p. 5. See also J. C. Robinson and J. W. De Peyster, *Obituary Notices of Major Generals Heintzelman and Hooker* (New York: Charles H. Ludwig, 1881). The Heintzelman family wills and related court papers for Samuel, Margaret, Charles, and Mary are filed in the District of Columbia. These documents gave little information about the extent of the family's financial assets. Although there was no indication of great wealth, each succeeding family member seems to have been provided for adequately.

Bibliography

Manuscript and Archival Collections

Arizona Collection, Charles Trumbull Hayden Memorial Library, Arizona State University, Tempe, Arizona
    Hayden Pioneer Files
    Map Collection
    Charles Schuchard, "Ajo Mine, Arizona Argonauts"
Arizona Historical Society, Tucson, Arizona
    Mark A. Aldrich Papers
    Wiliam P. Blake Papers
    Charles H. Meyer Papers
    Charles Debrille Poston Papers
    Louis Quesse Papers
    Palatine Robinson Papers
    Ronstadt Family Papers
    Schneider Papers
    Hiram S. Stevens Papers
Connecticut Historical Society, Hartford, Connecticut
    Samuel Colt Papers, including the correspondence of J. Deane Alden, Reverend William Jarvis, and Richard W. H. Jarvis
    Obituary Scrapbook Collection, compiled by A. M. Perry
    Thomas H. Seymour Papers
Library of Congress, Washington, D.C.
    Samuel Peter Heintzelman Papers

Louis Jefferson Long Library, Wells College, Aurora, New York
  Temple R. Hollcroft Papers
  Edwin Barber Morgan Papers
National Archives and Record Service, Washington, D.C.
  RG 28, Records of the Post Office Department
  RG 29, Records of the Bureau of Census
  RG 46, Records of the United States Senate
  RG 48, Records of the Office of the Secretary of the Interior
  RG 56, General Records of the Department of the Treasury
  RG 59, General Records of the Department of State
  RG 75, Records of the Bureau of Indian Affairs
  RG 76, Records of Boundary and Claims Commissions and
    Arbitrations
  RG 77, Records of the Office of the Chief of Engineers
  RG 92, Records of the Office of the Quartermaster General
  RG 94, Records of the Adjutant General's Office
Office of the Secretary of State, New York
  Business Records, VII
  Miscellaneous Papers, IV
Office of the Secretary of State, Ohio
  Records of Incorporation, I
Probate Court of the First Judicial District, Pima County, Arizona
  Record of Denunciation of Mines
Recorder's Office, Pima County, Arizona
  Deeds of Real Estate, I
  Miscellaneous Records, I, III, X, XXVII, XXIX
  Old Records Book No. A
  Records of Mines, I, II, A, B, F, G, K, L
Benjamin Sacks Collection, Arizona Historical Foundation, Arizona State University, Tempe, Arizona
  Files on: Felix G. Ake; Mark Aldrich; Robert Allen; Elias
    Brevoort; Frederick Brunckow; William Buckley; James
    Carothers; William Coleman; Colorado City; Samuel Colt;
    Richard Doss; Edward Dunbar; Herman Ehrenberg; Juan
    Fernandez; Samuel Heintzelman; Bernard Irwin; Louis
    Jaeger; William Kirkland; Justus McCarty; Boyle C. Mar-
    shall; Charles Meyer; Fred Miller; Theodore Moohrmann;

Bibliography

Sylvester Mowry; Ramon Pacheco; Charles D. Poston; Palatine Robinson; Frederick Ronstadt; Santa Rita Silver Mining Company; Sonora Exploring and Mining Company; Solomon Warner. Also "Map Collection Presented to the Arizona State University at Tempe by the Arizona Historical Foundation, Part I: The Plats of the Private Land Claims in Arizona." Compiled by B. Sacks. Phoenix: Arizona Historical Foundation, 1965 (typewritten).

Western Americana Collection, Beinecke Rare Book and Manuscript Library, Yale University, New Haven, Connecticut

Diary of Richard Dallam

William Hemsley Emory Papers

John W. Geary Papers

Miscellaneous letters and documents relating to the land claim and quicksilver mine at New Almaden, California

"Petition, to His Excellency, the President of the United States, of the Residents of the Western Division of the Proposed Territory of Arizona"

Printed Sources

Ainsa, J. Y. *History of the Crabb Expedition into Northern Sonora. Decapitation of the State Senator of California, Henry A. Crabb and Massacre of Ninety-eight of His Friends at Caborca and Sonoita, Sonora, Mexico, 1857.* Phoenix, 1951.

Altshuler, Constance W., ed. *Latest from Arizona! The Hesperian Letters, 1859–1861.* Tucson: Arizona Pioneer's Historical Society, 1969.

Arizona Land and Mining Company. *Charter and By-Laws of the Arizona Land and Mining Company, Incorporated by the State of Rhode Island, June, 1859. With a Statement Giving the Particulars of the Estates of the Company and of the Mineral Regions in the Territory of Arizona.* Providence: Knowles, Anthony and Co., 1859.

Arizona Mining Company. *Reports of Sam F. Butterworth and Guido Küstel.* N., 1864.

The Arizona Mining Company, Its Mines, Property and Organization, 1863. Jersey City: Davison and Ward, 1863.

Atlantic and Pacific Railroad Company. *Circular to the Stockholders of the Atlantic and Pacific Railroad Company.* New York: G. F. Nesbitt and Co., 1855.

Bancroft, Hubert Howe. *The Works of Hubert Howe Bancroft.* Vol. II, *1801–1889;* vol. V, *1824–1861;* vol. VI, *1848–1859;* vol. XIII, *History of Mexico;* vol. XVI, *History of the North Mexican States and Texas;* vol. XVII, *History of Arizona and New Mexico, 1830–1888;* vol. XXIII, *History of California.* San Francisco: The History Company, 1885–1889.

Barber, John Warner, and Howe, Henry. *All the Western States and Territories from the Alleghanies to the Pacific.* Cincinnati: Howe's Subscription Book Concern, 1867.

Barnes, Will C. "Arizona Place Names." *University of Arizona Bulletin* No. 2., VI, 1 (January 1935).

Bartlett, John Russell. *Personal Narrative of Explorations and Incidents in Texas, New Mexico, California, Sonora, and Chihuahua, Connected with the United States and Mexican Boundary Commission During the Years 1850, '51, '52, and '53.* 2 vols. New York: D. Appleton-Century, 1854.

Bender, Averam. "Frontier Defense in the Territory of New Mexico, 1853–1861." *New Mexico Historical Review,* IX (October 1934), 1–32.

Billington, Ray A. *The Far Western Frontier, 1830–1860.* The New American Nation Series, edited by H. S. Commager and R. B. Morris. New York: Harper and Brothers, 1956.

Brevoort, Elias. *New Mexico: Her Natural Resources and Attractions, Being a Collection of Facts, Mainly Concerning her Geography, Climate, Population, Schools, Mines and Minerals.* Santa Fe: E. Brevoort, 1874.

Brief Description of the Arivaca Estate in the Territory of Arizona, U.S.A. London: Charles Carter and Co., [1875].

Brown, J. Cabell. *Calabazas or Amusing Recollections of an Arizona City.* San Francisco: Valleau and Peterman, 1892.

Browne, J. Ross. *Adventures in the Apache Country: A Tour Through Arizona and Sonora, with Notes on the Silver Regions of Nevada.* New York: Harper and Brothers, 1874.

Calabasas Land and Mining Company. *Prospectus and Reports of the Property of the Calabasas Land and Mining Co., Located in*

Pima County, Arizona Territory. San Francisco: Francis and Valentine, 1878.

Coffin, George M. *Silver: From 1849 to 1892.* New York: Greenwood Press, 1969.

"Col. Samuel Colt, 1814–1862," *Bulletin of the Wadsworth Atheneum*, III, 4 (October 1925), 31–33.

Colton, Ray C. *The Civil War in the Western Territories, Arizona, Colorado, New Mexico and Utah.* Norman: University of Oklahoma Press, 1959.

Conkling, Roscoe P. and Margaret B. *The Butterfield Overland Mail, 1857–1869, Its Organization and Operation over the Southern Route to 1861, Subsequently over the Central Route to 1866, and under Wells, Fargo & Co., in 1869.* 3 vols. Glendale, Calif.: Arthur H. Clark Company, 1947.

Cooke, Philip St. George. *The Conquest of New Mexico and California, An Historical Narrative.* New York: G. P. Putnam's Sons, 1878.
———. *Scenes and Adventures in the Army or Romance of Military Life.* Philadelphia: Lindsay and Blakiston, 1857.

"Copper Mines and Mining in Arizona." *The Mining Magazine and Journal of Geology,* 2nd ser., I, 4 (February 1860), 321–22.

Corle, Edwin. *The Gila: River of the Southwest.* Rivers of America, edited by H. Allen and C. Carmer. New York: Rinehart and Co., Inc., 1951.

Cozzens, Samuel Woodworth. *The Ancient Cibola, The Marvellous Country, or Three Years in Arizona and New Mexico. Containing an Authentic History of this Wonderful Country ... with Strange Events and Startling Adventures.* Boston: Shephard and Gill, 1873.

Cram, Thomas Jefferson. *Memoir Showing How to Bring the Lead, Copper, Silver & Gold of Arizona into the Marts of the World, and Project of a Railroad Through Sonora To Connect with the Pacific Rail Road in Arizona.* Troy, N.Y.: R. V. Wilson, 1857 or 1858.

Cross, Jack L. "The El Paso-Fort Yuma Wagon Road, 1857–1860." *Password,* IV, 1, 2 (1959), 4–18, 58–70.

Cullum, George W. *Biographical Register of the Officers and Graduates of the United States Military Academy.* 2 vols. New York: D. Van Nostrand, 1868.
_____. *Biographical Register of the Officers and Graduates of the United States Military Academy* 3rd. ed. rev. 3 vols. Boston: Houghton Mifflin and Co., 1891.
_____. *1970 Cullum Memorial Edition. Register of Graduates and Former Cadets of the United States Military Academy.* West Point, N.Y.: West Point Alumni Foundation, Inc., 1970.

Darton, N. H. *A Resume of Arizona Geology. University of Arizona Bulletin,* no. 19, College of Mines and Engineering. Tucson: University of Arizona, n.d.

Donohue, J. Augustine. "The Unlucky Jesuit Mission of Bac," *Arizona and the West,* II, 2 (Summer 1960), 127–40.

Dunbrier, Roger. *The Sonoran Desert.* Tucson: University of Arizona Press, 1968.

Eaton, Clement. "Frontier Life in Southern Arizona, 1858–1861." *Southwestern Historical Quarterly,* XXXVI (1933), 173–92.

Eckhart, George B. "A Guide to the History of the Missions of Sonora, 1614–1826." *Arizona and the West,* II, 2 (Summer 1960), 165–83.

Edwards, E. I., *Lost Oases Along the Carrizo.* Los Angeles: Westernlore Press, 1961.

Edwards, William B. *The Biography of Col. Samuel Colt.* Harrisburg, Pa.: The Stackpole Co., 1953.

Ehrenberg, Herman. *With Milam and Fannin: Adventures of a German Boy in Texas' Revolution.* Edited by Henry Smith, translated by Charlotte Churchille. Dallas: Tandy Publishing Company. 1935.

Ewell, R. S. *The Making of a Soldier: Letters of General R S. Ewell.* Edited by Percy G. Hamlin. Richmond: Whittet and Shepperson, 1935.

Ewing, R. C. "The Pima Outbreak in November, 1751." *New Mexico Historical Review,* XII (1938), 337–46.

Farish, Thomas Edwin. *History of Arizona.* 8 vols. Phoenix: Filmer Brothers, 1915–1918.

Faulk, Odie B. *Destiny Road: The Gila Trail and the Opening of the Southwest*. New York: Oxford University Press, 1973.
_____. *Land of Many Frontiers: A History of the American Southwest*. New York: Oxford University Press, 1968.
_____. *Too Far North . . . Too Far South*. Los Angeles: Westernlore Press, 1967.

Fontana, Bernard L. "Biography of a Desert Church: The Story of Mission San Xavier del Bac." *The Smoke Signal*, no. 3 (1961).
_____. "The Mowry Mine, 1858–1958." *Kiva*, 23, no. 3 (February 1958), 14–16.

Forbes, Jack D. *Apache, Navaho, and Spaniard*. Norman: University of Oklahoma Press, 1960.

Forbes, Robert H. *Crabb's Filibustering Expedition into Sonora, 1857: An Historical Account*. Tucson: Arizona Silhouettes, 1952.

Frazer, Robert W. *Forts of the West: Military Forts and Presidios and Posts Commonly Called Forts West of the Mississippi River to 1898*. Norman: University of Oklahoma Press, 1965.

Froebel, Julius. *Seven Years' Travel in Central America, Northern Mexico, and the Far West of the United States*. London: Richard Bentley, 1859.

Frontain, D. *San Xavier del Bac, A Living Mission*. Tucson: Los Amigos, 1968.

Furniss, Norman F. *The Mormon Conflict, 1850–1859*. New Haven: Yale University Press, 1960.

Galbraith, Frederick W., and Brennan, Daniel J. *Minerals of Arizona*. Tucson: University of Arizona Press, 1959.

Garber, Paul Neff. *The Gadsden Treaty*. Gloucester, Mass.: Peter Smith, 1959.

Gerald, Rex E. *Spanish Presidios of the Late Eighteenth Century in Northern New Spain*. Museum of New Mexico Research Records, no. 7. Santa Fe. Museum of New Mexico Press, 1968.

Goetzmann, William H. *Army Exploration in the American West, 1803–1863*. Yale Publications in American Studies, no. 4. New Haven, 1959.

Goetzmann, William H. *(Continued)*
_____. *Exploration and Empire: The Explorer and the Scientist in the Winning of the American West.* New York: A. A. Knopf, 1966.

Granger, Byrd. *Arizona Place Names.* 2nd ed., rev. and enl. Tucson: University of Arizona Press, 1960.

Greever, William S. *The Bonanza West: The Story of the Western Mining Rushes, 1848–1900.* Norman: University of Oklahoma Press, 1963.

Gressinger, A. W. *Charles D. Poston: Sunland Seer.* Globe, Ariz.: Dale Stuart King, 1961.

Hafen, LeRoy. *The Overland Mail, 1849–1869, Promoter of Settlement, Precursor of Railroads.* Cleveland: Arthur H. Clark Co., 1926.

Hall, John Denton. *Sonora: Travels and Adventures in Sonora Containing a Description of Its Mining and Agriculture Resources and Narrative of a Residence of Fifteen Years.* Chicago: J. M. W. Jones, 1881.

Hamersly. T. H. S., ed. *Complete Regular Army Register of the United States for 100 Years, 1779 to 1879.* Washington, D.C.: T. H. S. Hamersly, 1880.

Hamilton, Patrick. *The Resources of Arizona: A Description of Its Mineral, Farming, Grazing and Timber Lands, Its Rivers, Mountains, Valleys and Plains.* 2nd ed., enl. San Francisco: A. L. Bancroft & Co., 1883.

Hamlin, Percy G. *Old Bald Head, The Portrait of a Soldier.* Strasburg, Va.: Shenandoah Publishing House, Inc., 1940.

Hart, Herbert M. *Old Forts of the Southwest.* Seattle: Superior Publishing Co., 1964.

Hartley, W. M. B. *Heintzelman Mine, Arizona.* New York, 1863.

Hawgood, John A. *America's Western Frontiers: The Exploration and Settlement of the Trans-Mississippi West.* New York: A. A. Knopf, 1967.

Heiges, George L. "General S. P. Heintzelman Visits His Hometown of Manheim," *Journal of the Lancaster County Historical Society,* 68 (1964), 85–109.

Heitman, Francis B. *Historical Register and Dictionary of the United States Army.* 2 vols. Washington, D.C.: GPO, 1903.

Hill, Edward E. "The Tucson Agency: The Use of Federal Records in the National Archives." *Prologue: The Journal of the National Archives*, IV, 2 (Summer 1972), 77–82.

Hine, Robert V. *Bartlett's West: Drawing the Mexican Boundary.* New Haven: Yale University Press, 1968.

Hinton, Richard J. *The Hand-Book to Arizona: Its Resources, History, Towns, Mines, Ruins and Scenery.* 1878. Reprint ed. Tucson: Arizona Silhouettes, 1954.

Hollon, W. Eugene. *The Great American Desert Then and Now.* New York: Oxford University Press, 1966.
————. *The Southwest: Old and New.* Lincoln: University of Nebraska Press, Bison Books, 1961.

Hostetter, A. K. "Major General Samuel Peter Heintzel-man." *Papers Read Before the Lancaster County Historical Society*, XVII, 2 (1913), 57–78.

Ives, Lt. Joseph Christmas. *Report upon the Colorado River of West, explored in 1857 and 1858 by Lt. Joseph C. Ives, Corps of Topographical Engineers, under the direction of the Office of Exploration and Surveys, A. A. Humphreys, Captain, Topographical Engineers, in charge.* Washington, D.C.: GPO, 1861.

Jackson, Earl. *Tumacacori's Yesterdays.* Santa Fe: Southwestern Monuments Association, 1951.

Jackson, W. Turrentine. *Wagon Roads West: A Study of the Federal Road Surveys and Construction in the Trans-Mississippi West, 1846–1869.* Yale Western Americana Series, no. 9. New Haven, 1965.

"Journal of Copper Mining Operations — Arizona Copper Mines." *Mining and Statistical Magazine*, X (April 1858), 335–36.

Keleher, William A. *Turmoil in New Mexico, 1846–1868.* Santa Fe: The Rydal Press, 1952.

Keller, B. C. *Where to Go To Become Rich: Farmer's, Miner's and Tourist's Guide.* Chicago: Belford, Clarke and Co., 1880.

Küstel, Guido. *Nevada and California Process of Silver and Gold Extraction.* San Francisco: Carlton, 1863.

Küstel, Guido *(Continued)*
————. *Roasting of Gold and Silver Ores and the Extraction of their Respective Metals without Quicksilver.* New ed. San Francisco: A. J. Leary, 1880.

Lamar, Howard R. *The Far Southwest, 1846–1912: A Territorial History.* Yale Western Americana Series, no. 12. New Haven, 1966.

Leavitt, Francis H. "Steam Navigation on the Colorado River," *California Historical Society Quarterly,* XXII, 1–2 (March, June 1943), 1–26, 151–75.

Lockwood, Frank C. *Arizona Characters.* Los Angeles: Times-Mirror Press, 1928.
————. *Life in Old Tucson, 1854–1864, As Remembered by the Little Maid, Atanacia Santa Cruz.* Los Angeles: Ward Ritchie Press, 1943.
————. *More Arizona Characters.* Tucson: University of Arizona Press, 1943.

Longstreet, James. *From Manassas to Appomattox.* Philadelphia: J. B. Lippincott Co., 1896.

McClintock, James H. *Arizona: Prehistoric, Aboriginal, Pioneer, Modern.* 3 vols. Chicago: S. J. Clarke Publishing Co., 1916.

McKay, S. "Texas and the Southern Pacific Railroad, 1848–1860." *Southwestern Historical Quarterly,* XXXV (July 1931), 1–27.

Mansfield, Joseph King Fenno. *On the Condition of the Western Forts.* Edited with an Introduction by Robert W. Frazer. The American Exploration and Travel Series. Norman: University of Oklahoma Press, 1963.

Martin, Douglass D. *An Arizona Chronology: The Territorial Years, 1846–1912.* Tucson: The University of Arizona Press, 1963.

Mattison, Ray H. "Early Spanish and Mexican Settlements in Arizona." *New Mexico Historical Review,* XXI, 4 (October 1946), 273–327.

"The Mines of Northern Mexico." *Knickerbocker,* LVII, 6 (June 1861), 577–87.

Mowry, Sylvester. *Arizona and Sonora: The Geography, His-*

tory, and Resources of the Silver Region of North America. 3rd ed., rev. and enl. New York: Harper and Brothers, 1864.

_____. *The Geography and Resources of Arizona and Sonora, An Address Before the American Geographical and Statistical Society.* Washington, D.C.: Henry Polkinhorn, 1859.

_____. *Memoir of the Proposed Territory of Arizona.* Washington, D.C.: Henry Polkinhorn, 1857.

_____. *The Mines of the West, Shall the Government Seize Them? The Mining States, How Shall They Be Taxed?* New York: G. E. Currie, 1864.

Ogle, Ralph Hedrick. *Federal Control of the Western Apaches, 1848–1886.* Historical Society of New Mexico, Publications in History. Albuquerque: University of New Mexico Press, 1940.

Parke, Lt. John G. *Report of Explorations for that Portion of a Railway Route, Near the Thirty-Second Parallel of Latitude, Lying Between Doña Ana, on the Rio Grande, and Pimas Villages, on the Gila.* Washington, D.C.: Nicholson, 1855.

Paul, Rodman. *Mining Frontiers of the Far West, 1848–1880.* History of the American Frontier, edited by Ray A. Billington. New York: Holt, Rinehart and Winston, 1963.

Pettid, Edward J. "Henry Stuart Hewit, M.D." *Arizona Medicine,* January 1969, pp. 62–70.

Portrait and Biographical Record of Arizona. Chicago: Chapman Publishing Co., 1901.

Poston, Charles D. *Apache-Land.* San Francisco: A. L. Bancroft and Co., 1878.

_____. "Building a State in Apache Land." *Overland Monthly,* XXIV, 2nd ser. (July–December 1894), 87–93, 203–13, 291–97, 403–08.

_____. "Southwestern Chronicle: The Journal of Charles Debrille Poston." Edited by Byrd Granger. *The Arizona Quarterly.* XII, 2, 3, 4, (Summer–Winter 1957), 152–63; 251–61; 353–62.

"Processes for the Extraction of Silver." *The Mining Magazine and Journal of Geology,* 2nd ser., I, 1 (November 1859), 16–22.

Prospector, Cowhand, and Sodbuster: Historic Places Associated with the Mining, Ranching, and Farming Frontiers in the Trans-Mississippi West. The National Survey of Historic Sites and Buildings, edited by Robert G. Ferris, vol. XI. Washington, D.C.: National Park Service, 1967.

Pumpelly, Raphael. *Across America and Asia. Notes of a Five Years' Journey Around the World and of Residence in Arizona, Japan, and China.* New York: Leypoldt and Holt, 1870.

———. *My Reminiscences.* 2 vols. New York: Henry Holt and Co., 1918.

Reed, St. Clair Griffin. *A History of the Texas Railroads and of Transportation Conditions Under Spain and Mexico and the Republic of the State of Texas.* Houston: St. Clair Publishing Co., 1941.

Rickard, T. A. *A History of American Mining.* New York: McGraw Hill Book Co., Inc., 1932.

Robinson, John C., and De Peyster, J. W. *Obituary Notices of Maj. Gens. Heintzelman and Hooker ... Members of the Third Army Corps Union.* New York: Charles H. Ludwig, 1881.

Rose, Diane M. T. "The Maps, Plans, and Sketches of Herman Ehrenberg." *Prologue: The Journal of the National Archives,* IX, 3 (Fall 1977), 162–70.

Sacks, Benjamin. *Be It Enacted: The Creation of the Territory of Arizona.* Phoenix: Arizona Historical Foundation, 1964.

———. "Charles Debrille Poston: Prince of Arizona Pioneers." *The Smoke Signal,* no. 7 (Spring 1963).

———. "The Origins of Fort Buchanan: Myth and Fact." *Arizona and the West,* VII, 3 (Autumn 1965), 207–26.

———. "Sylvester Mowry: Artilleryman, Libertine, Entrepreneur." *The American West,* I, 3 (Summer 1964), 14–25, 79.

Santa Rita Silver Mining Company. *First Annual Report of the Santa Rita Silver Mining Company, Made to the Stockholders, March 21st, 1859.* Cincinnati: Railroad Record Print, 1859.

———. *Second Annual Report of the Santa Rita Silver Mining Company, Made to the Stockholders, March 19, 1860.* Cincinnati: Railroad Record Print, 1860.

———. *Third Annual Report of the Santa Rita Silver Mining*

Company, Made to the Stockholders, March 18, 1861. Cincinnati: Wrightson and Co., 1861.

_____. *Fourth Annual Report of the Santa Rita Silver Mining Company, Made to the Stockholders, March 17, 1862.* Cincinnati: Wrightson and Co., 1862.

San Xavier Mining and Smelting Company. *Prospectus with Estimates and Reports of the Property of the San Xavier Mining and Smelting Company.* San Francisco: Francis, Valentine and Co., 1879.

Schmidt, Louis Bernard. "Manifest Opportunity and the Gadsden Purchase." *Arizona and the West,* III (Autumn 1961), 245–64.

Scholes, Walter F. "Mexican Politics During the Juárez Regime, 1855–1872." *University of Missouri Studies,* XXX (1957), 29–43.

Scroogs, William O. *Filibusters and Financiers: The Story of William Walker and His Associates.* New York: Macmillan Co., 1916.

"Silver and Copper Mining in Arizona." *The Mining Magazine and Journal of Geology,* 2nd ser., I, 1 (November 1859), 1–15.

"Silver Mining in Arizona." *The Mining Magazine and Journal of Geology,* 2nd ser., I, 3 (January 1860), 243.

Sloan, R. E., ed. *History of Arizona.* 4 vols. Phoenix: Record Publishing Co., 1930.

Soldier and Brave: Historic Places Associated with Indian Affairs and the Indian Wars in the Trans-Mississippi West. The National Survey of Historic Sites and Buildings, edited by Robert G. Ferris, vol. XII. New ed. Washington, D.C.:National Park Service, 1971.

Sonora Exploring and Mining Company. *Sonora and the Value of its Silver Mines, Report of the Sonora Exploring and Mining Co., Made to the Stockholders, December, 1856.* Cincinnati: Railroad Record Print, 1856.

_____. *Possessions and Prospects of the Sonora Silver Mining Company, Report of the Sonora Exploring and Mining Company, Made to the Stockholders, September, 1857.* Cincinnati: Railroad Record Print, 1857.

Sonora Exploring and Mining Co. *(Continued)*

_____. *Second Annual Report of the Sonora Exploring and Mining Company, Made to the Stockholders, March 29, 1858.* Cincinnati: Railroad Record, 1858.

_____. *Third Annual Report of the Sonora Exploring and Mining Company, Made to the Stockholders, March, 1859.* New York: W. Minns and Co., 1859.

_____. *Report of Frederick Brunckow, Geologist, Mineralogist and Mining Engineer, To a Committee of the Stockholders of the Sonora Exploring and Mining Co., upon the History, Resources and Prospects of the Company in Arizona, With an Appendix by the Committee.* Cincinnati: Railroad Record Print, 1859.

_____. *Letter to the Stockholders Only, Report to the Stockholders of the Sonora Exploring and Mining Company, New York, May 1, 1859.* New York: n.p., 1859.

_____. *Fourth Annual Report of the Sonora Exploring and Mining Company, Made to the Stockholders, March, 1860.* New York: W. Minns and Co., 1860.

Sopori Land and Mining Company. *Charter and By-Laws of the Sopori Land and Mining Company, Incorporated by the State of Rhode Island, June, 1859. With a statement Giving the Particulars of the Estates of the Company and of the Mineral Regions in the Territory of Arizona.* Providence: Knowles, Anthony and Co., 1859.

Southern Pacific Railroad Company. *Convention of the Stockholders of the Southern Pacific Railroad Company, held at Memphis, Sept. 17, 1858.*

_____. *First Annual Report to the Board of Directors of the Southern Pacific Railroad Company.* New York: American Railroad Journal Office, 1856.

_____. *Proceedings of the Meeting of the Stockholders of the Southern Pacific Railroad Company, Held in Louisville, Kentucky, November 25th and November 27th, 1858.*

Spence, Clark C. *British Investments and the American Mining Frontier, 1860–1901.* Ithaca, N.Y.: Cornell University Press, 1958.

_____. *Mining Engineers and the American West, The Lace-*

Boot Brigade, 1849–1933. Yale Western Americana Series, no. 22. New Haven, 1970.

Statement. The Cerro-Colorado Mine. San Francisco: Charles Coolidge, 1876.

Stone, Charles P. *Notes on the State of Sonora, 1860.* Washington, D.C.: Henry Polkinhorn, 1861.

Stratton, R. B. *Captivity of the Oatman Girls.* 3rd ed. New York: Carlton and Porter, 1858.

Survey of a Route on the 32nd Parallel for the Texas Western Railroad, 1854, The A. B. Gray Report and including the Reminiscences of Peter R. Brady who Accompanied the Expedition. With Introduction and notes by L. R. Bailey. Great West and Indian Series, no. XXIV, Western Survey Series, no. II. Los Angeles: Westernlore Press, 1963.

Sutherland, Robert Q., and Wilson, R. L. *The Book of Colt Firearms.* Kansas City, Mo.: R. Q. Sutherland, 1971.

Sweeny, Thomas W. *Journal of Lt. Thomas W. Sweeny, 1849–1853.* Edited by Arthur Woodward. Great West and Indian Series, no. VII. Los Angeles: Westernlore Press, 1956.

Tevis, James H. *Arizona in the '50's.* Albuquerque: University of New Mexico Press, 1954.

Texas Western Railroad Company. *Circular to the Stockholders of the Texas Western Railroad Company, Issued by Authority of the Executive Committee, New York, June 1856.* New York: W. H. Arthur and Co., 1856.

Theobald, John and Lillian. *Arizona Territory: Post Offices and Postmasters.* Phoenix: Arizona Historical Foundation, 1961.

Thorp, Raymond W. "Pete Kitchen's Road." *True West,* XII, 2 (November–December 1964), 6–8, 66–67.

Townsend, E. D. *The California Diary of General E. D. Townsend.* Edited by Malcolm Edwards. Los Angeles: Ward Ritchie Press, 1970.

U.S. Congress. House. *Letter from the Secretary of War, Communicating, in Compliance with a resolution of the House, information in relation to troubles on the Texas frontier.* House Exec. Doc. No. 81. 36th Cong., 1st sess., 1860.

U.S. Congress. House (Continued)

———. *Message from the President of the United States, Communicating Official Information in relation to the "Execution of Colonel Crabb and his Associates."* House Exec. Doc. No. 64, Serial 955. 35th Cong., 1st sess., 1858.

———. *Message from the President of the United States, transmitting Report in Regard to Indian Affairs on the Pacific.* House Exec. Doc. No. 76. 34th Cong., 3d sess., 1857.

U.S. Congress. Senate. *Committee on Private Land Claims.* Senate Exec. Doc. No. 93. 48th Cong., 1st sess., 1884.

Utley, Robert M. *Frontiersmen in Blue, 1848–1865.* The Wars of the United States, General Editor, Louis Morton. New York: Columbia University Press, 1943.

Velasco, Francisco. *Sonora: Its Extent, Population, Natural Productions, Indian Tribes, Mines.* Translated by William F. Nye. San Francisco: H. H. Bancroft and Co., 1861.

Villa, Eduardo W. *Compendio de historia del Estado de Sonora.* Mexico, D.F., 1937.

Wagoner, Jay J. *Arizona Territory, 1863–1912: A Political History.* Tucson: University of Arizona Press, 1970.

———. *Early Arizona: Prehistory to Civil War.* Tucson: University of Arizona Press, 1975.

Wallace, Edward S. *The Great Reconnaissance: Soldiers, Artists and Scientists on the Frontier, 1848–1861.* Boston: Little, Brown and Co., 1955.

Way, Phocion R. "Overland via 'Jackass Mail' in 1858: The Diary of Phocion R. Way." Edited and annotated by William A. Duffen. *Arizona and the West,* II, 1–4 (Spring–Winter 1960), 35–54, 147–64, 279–93, 353–71.

Wehrman, Georgia. "Harshaw: Mining Camp of the Patagonias." *Journal of Arizona History,* VI (Spring 1965), 21–36.

Westphall, Victor. *The Public Domain in New Mexico, 1854–1891.* Albuquerque: University of New Mexico Press, 1965.

Wheat, Marvin. *Travels on the Western Slope of the Mexican Cordillera, in the Form of Fifty-One Letters Descriptive of*

Much of this Portion of the Republic of Mexico. San Francisco: Whitton, Towne and Co., 1857.

Wilson, Eldred. "Early Mining in Arizona." *Kiva,* II (May 1946), 39–47.

———. "History of Mining in Pima County." Tucson: Chamber of Commerce, 1943.

———. *A Resume of the Geology of Arizona.* Bulletin 171, the Arizona Bureau of Mines. Tucson: University of Arizona Press, 1962.

Witherell, W. *Arizona as a Silver Country.* St. Louis, Mo.: McKittrick and Co., 1879.

Woodward, Arthur. *Feud on the Colorado River.* Great West and Indian Series, no. IV. Los Angeles: Westernlore Press, 1955.

Wyllys, Rufus K. *Arizona: The History of a Frontier State.* Phoenix: Hobson and Herr, 1950.

———. *The French in Sonora, 1850–1854: The Story of French Adventurers from California into Mexico.* University of California Publications in History, vol. XXI, edited by H. Bolton et al. Berkeley, 1932.

Yerger, Geo., and Lawrason, Geo. *Circular to the Stockholders of the Southern Pacific Railroad Company.* New Orleans, December 22, 1857.

Young, Otis E. *How They Dug the Gold: An Informal History of Frontier Prospecting, Lode-Mining, and Milling in Arizona and the Southwest.* Tucson: Arizona Historical Society, 1967.

Young, Otis E., with the technical assistance of Robert Lenon. *Black Powder and Hand Steel: Miners and Machines on the Old Western Frontier.* Norman: University of Oklahoma Press, 1975.

———. *Western Mining: An Informal Account of Precious Metals, Prospecting, Placering, Lode Mining, and Milling on the American Frontier from Spanish Times to 1893.* Norman: University of Oklahoma Press, 1970.

Theses and Dissertations

Acuña, Rudolph F. "The Times of Ignacio Pesqueira, Sonora, Mexico, 1856–1876." Ph.D. dissertation, University of Southern California, 1968.

Bents, Doris. "The History of Tubac, 1752–1948." M.A. thesis, University of Arizona, 1949.

De Blasio, Mario. "Sonora Exploring and Mining Co., 1856–1861." M.A. thesis, University of San Diego, 1971.

Hargett, Janet Lee. "Louis John Frederick Jaeger: Entrepreneur at Yuma Crossing." M.A. thesis, University of Arizona, 1967.

Jones, Richard D. "Geology of the Cerro Colorado Mining District, Pima County, Arizona." M.S. thesis, University of Arizona, 1957.

Park, Joseph F. "The History of Mexican Labor in Arizona During the Territorial Period." M.A. thesis, University of Arizona, 1961.

Whalen, Norman H. "The Catholic Church in Arizona, 1820–1870." M.A. thesis, University of Arizona, 1964.

Newspapers

Arizona Sentinel
Cincinnati Daily Gazette
Cincinnati Enquirer
Daily Alta California
Daily Arizona Citizen
Daily California Chronicle
Daily Missouri Republican
Hartford Daily Courant
Hartford Times
Los Angeles Star
Mesilla Times
New York Evening Post
New York Times
Pacific News
Railroad Record
Sacramento Daily Union
San Diego Herald
San Francisco Bulletin
San Francisco Herald
San Francisco Weekly Bulletin
San Joaquin Republican
Santa Fe Weekly Gazette
Weekly Alta California
Weekly Arizona Miner
Weekly Arizonian

Index

[239]

San Augustín del Tucson, 54,
 67, 206
San Coyetano mines, 30
San Diego (California), xii, 4, 10,
 14–15, 48–49, 77
San Elizario (Texas), 127
San Francisco (California), 12, 29,
 33, 37–38, 47, 70, 90, 117, 142
San José mine, 147, 152
San Pedro River, 124
Santa Cruz River, 24, 85, 98
Santa Cruz Valley, 33, 74
Santa Isabel (California), 5
Santa Margarita mine, 148
Santa Rita Mountains (Arizona), 25,
 30, 36, 39, 56, 134, 138–39
Santa Rita Silver mines, 36, 70,
 73–75, 86, 111, 140, 177
Santa Rita Silver Mining Company,
 xii, 39, 44, 61, 87, 167, 174, 201
San Xavier del Bac, 55
San Xavier mines, 50, 55
San Xavier Mining Company, 55,
 97, 153
Sarica, Sonora, Mexico, 137, 160
Sayles, Welcome B., 56, 62, 113, 199
Schuchard, Charles, 25, 37, 57, 82,
 88, 90–93, 96–97, 101, 110, 116–17,
 136, 143, 147, 156, 160, 162, 164–
 65, 196–97
Scott, Winfield (General), 11
Searles, A.M., 172
Seminole Indians, 8
Senator (steamboat), 48
Sherman, William T. (General), 10
Shootings: Elsner kills Streit, 155,
 158; at grog shop, Tucson, 68–69;
 murders, Dragoon Springs, 84;
 on the Sonoita, 151
Silver mining techniques, xiii, 37,
 41–44, 57–58, 76, 81, 84, 89–92,
 94, 97, 99–108, 110–30, 132–33,
 135–37, 151, 153, 157, 161–63, 173;
 arrastras, 42, 81–82; barrel amalgamation process, 42–43; dry
 stamp mills, 42; Fahlband, 151;
 firestone, 108; liquation, 119;
 litharge, 113; patio amalgamation

process, 42; quicksilver, 42, 90,
 117, 140, 149; reverberatory fur-
 nace, 42, 44; smelting process,
 43–44; stamp mill, 137
Sinaloa, Mexico, 19, 129, 137
Sloan, William James (Doctor), 80
Smelting process, 43–44
Smith, Erastus, 172
Smith, Fort, 156, 165–66
Snelling, Fort, 51
Society of Arizona Pioneers, 176
Sonoita Valley, 74, 76, 151
Sonora (Mexico), xiii, 3, 11, 19, 33,
 89–90, 120, 123, 137, 146, 150, 156,
 160, 164–65
Sonora Exploring and Mining
 Company, xii–xiv, 17, 19–177;
 coining money, 75–76; conditions
 at mines, xii–xiv, 27–29, 33,
 37–38, 40–44, 57–59, 69–70, 73,
 81–82, 84, 86, 88, 96–97, 99–108,
 110–30, 132–64, 173–75; directors,
 22, 28, 148, 171, 173, 202; establishment of xii, 17, 21–22;
 finances, 28–29, 40–41, 44–45,
 59–61, 72, 75, 79, 81, 88, 91–94,
 97, 100, 105, 107, 110, 116–20, 123,
 125–130, 132–35, 139–42, 145, 148,
 151, 156, 163, 165, 172–75; incorporators, 28, 171, 173, 175, 217–18;
 individual mines, xii, 25, 30, 38,
 56–58, 63, 70, 73, 82, 84, 101; investors, 21–24, 32, 44–45, 73, 79,
 87–88, 90–92, 105, 134, 167; laborers, 30, 37, 40–41, 61, 73, 81, 84,
 86, 88, 92, 95–99, 100–4, 106–8,
 110–30, 132–37, 139, 142–44,
 146–49, 151–55, 157–64, 174; legal
 disputes, 89, 171–75, 216; mining
 technology, xiii, 37, 41–44, 57–58,
 76, 81–82, 84, 89–92, 94, 97,
 99–100, 102–8, 111–30, 132–33,
 135–37, 140–41, 143, 145, 147,
 151, 153, 157, 161–63, 173; quality
 of ore, xiii, 30, 37–38, 40, 59,
 63, 69–70, 79, 81–82, 84, 89–92,
 94–95, 99, 101, 103, 105–7,
 113–20, 127, 129, 132–33, 137,